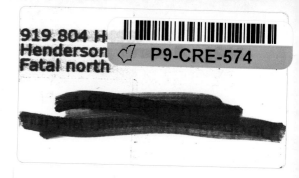

Fatal North

OTHER BOOKS BY BRUCE HENDERSON

LEAP OF FAITH:
An Astronaut's Journey into the Unknown (with Gordon Cooper)

TRACE EVIDENCE:
The Hunt For An Elusive Serial Killer

AND THE SEA WILL TELL:
Murder on a South Seas Island (with Vincent Bugliosi)

TAKING BACK OUR STREETS:
Fighting Crime in America (with Willie L. Williams)

ERNEST & JULIO: OUR STORY
(with Ernest and Julio Gallo)

EMPIRE OF DECEIT:
Inside the Biggest Sports and Bank Scandal in U.S. History
(with Dean Allison)

Fatal North

*Adventure and Survival Aboard
USS Polaris, the First U.S. Expedition
to the North Pole*

Bruce Henderson

NEW AMERICAN LIBRARY

New American Library
Published by New American Library, a division of
Penguin Putnam Inc., 375 Hudson Street, New York, New York 10014, U.S.A.
Penguin Books Ltd, 27 Wrights Lane, London W8 5TZ, England
Penguin Books Australia Ltd, Ringwood, Victoria, Australia
Penguin Books Canada Ltd, 10 Alcorn Avenue, Toronto, Ontario, Canada M4V 3B2
Penguin Books (N.Z.) Ltd, 182–190 Wairau Road, Auckland 10, New Zealand

Penguin Books Ltd, Registered Offices:
Harmondsworth, Middlesex, England

First published by New American Library, a division of Penguin Putnam Inc.

First Printing, February 2001
10 9 8 7 6 5 4 3 2 1

Copyright © Bruce Henderson, 2001

 REGISTERED TRADEMARK—MARCA REGISTRADA

LIBRARY OF CONGRESS CATALOGING-IN-PUBLICATION DATA
Henderson, Bruce B., 1946–
Fatal north : adventure and survival aboard USS Polaris, the first U.S. expedition
to the North Pole / by Bruce Henderson.
p. cm.
ISBN 0-451-40935-3 (alk. paper)
1. Hall, Charles Francis, 1821–1871—Journeys. 2. United States North Polar
Expedition (1871–1873) 3. Arctic regions—Discovery and exploration.
4. Explorers—United States—Biography. I. Title.

G635.H55 H46 2000
919.804—dc21   00-045568

Set in Galliard
Designed by Eve L. Kirch

Printed in the United States of America

BOOKS ARE AVAILABLE AT QUANTITY DISCOUNTS WHEN USED TO PROMOTE PRODUCTS OR
SERVICES. FOR INFORMATION PLEASE WRITE TO PREMIUM MARKETING DIVISION, PENGUIN
PUTNAM INC., 375 HUDSON STREET, NEW YORK, NEW YORK 10014.

For Laurel,
who showed me the way home from the Pole

CONTENTS

III. *Ice Hell*

IV. *Inquiry and the Search*

Break, break, break
  On these cold ice blocks, O sea!
And I would that my tongue could utter
  The thoughts that arise in me.

—Alfred, Lord Tennyson

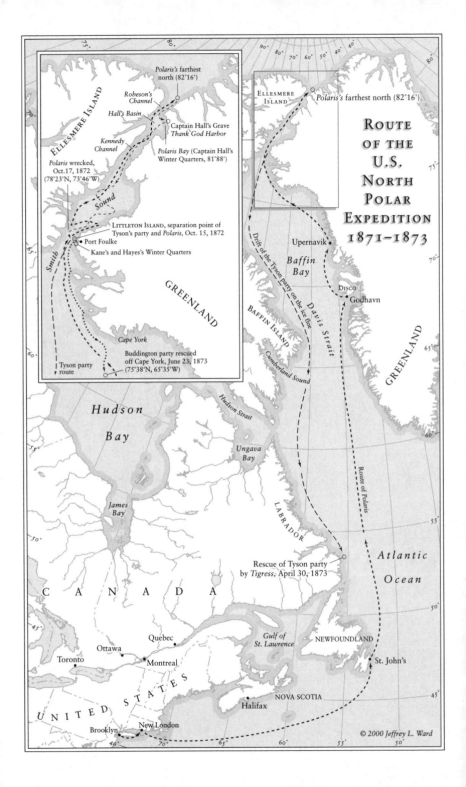

ROUTE
OF THE
U.S.
NORTH
POLAR
EXPEDITION
1871–1873

ELLESMERE
ISLAND

Polaris's farthest north (82°16')

Upernavik

*Baffin
Bay*

Disco

Godhavn

BAFFIN ISLAND

Davis Strait

Drift of the Tyson party on the ice floe

Cumberland Sound

GREENLAND

*Hudson
Bay*

Hudson Strait

Ungava
Bay

James
Bay

LABRADOR

Route of Polaris

Rescue of Tyson party
by *Tigress*, April 30, 1873

*Atlantic
Ocean*

C A N A D A

Quebec

Ottawa

Toronto

Montreal

Gulf of
St. Lawrence

NEWFOUNDLAND

St. John's

U N I T E D   S T A T E S

Brooklyn

New London

NOVA SCOTIA

Halifax

© 2000 Jeffrey L. Ward

Polaris's farthest
north (82°16')

Robeson's
Channel

Hall's Basin

Captain Hall's Grave
Thank God Harbor

*Kennedy
Channel*

Polaris Bay (Captain Hall's
Winter Quarters, 81°88')

Polaris wrecked,
Oct. 17, 1872
(78°23'N, 73°46'W)

Sound

LITTLETON ISLAND, separation point of
Tyson's party and *Polaris*, Oct. 15, 1872

Port Foulke

Kane's and Hayes's Winter Quarters

ELLESMERE ISLAND

Smith

GREENLAND

Cape York

Buddington party rescued
off Cape York, June 23, 1873
(75°38'N, 65°35'W)

Tyson party
route

The Members of the North Polar Expedition Aboard USS Polaris

THE AMERICANS

Charles Francis Hall Commander	Sidney O. Buddington Sailing-Master	George Tyson Assistant Navigator
Hubbard C. Chester First Mate	William Morton Second Mate	Richard W. D. Bryan Astronomer/Chaplain
Alvin Odell Assistant Engineer	Nathaniel Coffin Carpenter	Walter Campbell Fireman
William Jackson Cook		Noah Hayes Seaman

THE GERMANS

Dr. Emil Bessels Chief Scientist/Surgeon	Emil Schuman Chief Engineer	Frederick Meyer Meteorologist
Herman Sieman Seaman	Frederick Anthing Seaman	John W. C. Kruger Seaman
Henry Hobby Seaman	William Nindemann Seaman	Joseph Mauch Seaman
	Frederick Jamka Seaman	

OTHER IMMIGRANTS

John Herron, English Steward	John Booth, English Fireman	Peter Johnson, Danish Seaman
	Gustavus W. Lindquist, Swedish Seaman	

THE ESKIMOS

Ebierbing "Joe" Hunter/Dog Driver	Tookoolito "Hannah" Seamstress	Punny "Sylvia" age four
Hans Hendrik Hunter/Dog Driver	Merkut Hendrik Wife and Mother	Augustina Hendrik age twelve
Succi Hendrik age four		Tobias Hendrik age nine

PROLOGUE

Four men packing shovels, picks, and other digging tools walked across the Arctic tundra toward a lone grave.

The adventurers included a prominent internist from Massachusetts, an English professor from Dartmouth, a veteran outdoorsman, and an ex-Marine recently back from a combat tour in Vietnam. Flying in from Resolute Bay in Canada's Northern Territories the previous afternoon, they had been dropped off by a high-wing, seven-passenger Single Otter flown by an experienced bush pilot. In a hurry to fulfill other flying commitments, the pilot had taken off as soon as the men and their gear were unloaded, with the promise to be back in two weeks to return them to civilization.

The small party had been deposited on the vast, treeless plain known, since its discovery the previous century, as Polaris Promontory. It extended for some forty miles, and before the visitors left, they agreed that the expanse was disturbing in its lifelessness. Surrounded in the distance by a fringe of low hills—

1

some smooth, others jagged with cliffs, all equally barren—the terrain was empty and altogether inhospitable as far as the eye could see. There was no snow on the ground, and chunks of ice, some quite large, were floating in the nearby sound, christened Thank God Harbor long ago by its grateful discoverer. The passing icebergs helped maintain a perennial chill in the air.

Under the clear blue skies and surprising brightness of the unsetting Arctic summer sun, their first order of business was to establish camp. They knew the weather in this high latitude could turn suddenly, and they didn't want to be caught in the open without shelter. They set up their tents, secured the gear, prepared a spartan meal on a camp stove, and, with great excitement of what the next day might bring, settled down for the night in their thermal sleeping bags.

The morning after arriving at one of the most isolated spots on Earth, they crossed the stony flats toward the old grave and the grim task that had brought them here: to conduct an autopsy on the remains of its longtime occupant. The weather had changed during the night. The sky was covered with a low, dull overcast, suitably bleak, the men agreed, for the task at hand.

Spotting the grave was easy enough. The only manmade object in the desolate landscape, it was marked by a stone cairn in the shape of a burial mound, an old wooden headboard and, mounted atop two thick wooden beams, an impressive brass tablet, preserved by the dry air and burnished by the winds, with this inscription:

SACRED TO THE MEMORY OF
CAPTAIN C. F. HALL
OF THE U.S. SHIP POLARIS,
WHO SACRIFICED HIS LIFE IN THE ADVANCEMENT OF SCIENCE
ON NOVr 8th 1871

THIS TABLET HAS BEEN ERECTED
BY THE BRITISH POLAR EXPEDITION OF 1875
WHO FOLLOWING IN HIS FOOTSTEPS HAVE PROFITED BY HIS
EXPERIENCE

Dartmouth professor Chauncey Loomis, a lean six-footer in his late thirties with an unruly shock of black hair that fell over his forehead, knew that the British North Polar Expedition had brought the brass tablet from London in anticipation of passing the grave. From his research, Loomis had learned that not long after the ensuing ceremony at the grave—complete with the hoisting of an American flag—the British expedition came limping back, defeated by the most unwelcoming weather on the planet, having fallen short of its goal of reaching the North Pole and with two of its own, victims of scurvy, dead and buried in Arctic tundra.

The grave, which came to serve not as a warning beacon but as a beckoning signal to those who followed, had since been visited by other hardy souls. Those paying homage included, in 1881, the Greely Expedition; twenty-five American soldiers under the command of Augustus Greely, another failed Arctic effort, which cost the lives of nineteen and ended with the survivors telling tales of starvation, mutiny, shipwreck, execution, and cannibalism. American explorer Robert E. Peary passed several times aboard his support vessel, USS *Roosevelt*, between 1898 and 1909.

The final resting place of Charles Francis Hall, the commander of the U.S. expedition to discover the North Pole, had long been sacred ground to Arctic explorers of every nationality. It had to do with the remote location of the lone grave and the mysterious death of the man, as well as the nature of the mission itself. In a race against other nations—foremost among them England—America's first attempt to reach the North Pole had garnered the enthusiastic support of President Ulysses S. Grant and Congress, and captured the imagination of the press and public in the same way a future generation would follow the space race and man's efforts to reach the Moon.

The college professor came to understand just how sacred the old grave remained when he had sought permission from Denmark's Ministry for Greenland to travel to Polaris Promontory and disinter Hall's remains for an autopsy in the hope of solving the mystery that had long surrounded the captain's untimely demise. After months of official inquiry by the U.S. government, many troublesome questions had remained unanswered, including the biggest one of all. Had Captain Hall died a natural death, or had he been murdered most foully, poisoned to death by one or more members of the small, handpicked crew?

After a letter-writing campaign to officials brought no results, Loomis traveled to Copenhagen, where he met with Count Eigel Knuth, an adviser to the ministry on proposed projects in Greenland, a territory of Denmark. An archaeologist, anthropologist and experienced Arctic explorer in his own right, Knuth had been one of the last men to see Hall's final resting place a decade earlier—only the second visit to the Polaris Promontory since Peary had passed there fifty years before. Knuth, who had himself discovered the remains of an ancient civilization in northern Greenland, made it clear he was not disposed to approving a visit by a team of American grave diggers. In fact, the whole idea seemed repugnant to him. Loomis took the position that history deserved the truth.

"Given the high latitude of Hall's burial," the professor went on, "there is a good chance that the body will be well preserved."

"But, sir," Knuth replied, "this is *hallowed* ground."

Only when Loomis guaranteed that his team would leave the grave in the exact condition in which it was found did Knuth begin to relent. Finally, to the professor's surprise and delight, Knuth gave his approval.

Standing at the graveside, Loomis and his colleagues saw evidence that foxes had pawed at its surface. Also lemmings, a mouselike Arctic rodent, had at one time burrowed into the mound, no doubt for protection from the harsh elements.

The weather-beaten epitaph on the headboard, erected by one of Hall's crewmen within days of his death, was carved into a pine plank taken from USS *Polaris*. At the time, the ship was stuck in an impenetrable ice pack nearby. In addition to name, rank, age of the deceased, and date of his death were these words: "I am the resurrection and the life; he that believeth on me, though he were dead, yet shall he live."

Shovel in hand, the strapping ex-Marine, Tom Gignoux, who had been added to the expedition for his physical strength and youthful stamina, began to dig through the shaly surface, which resembled crushed rock more than earthen soil.

It was a shallow grave.

Less than two feet under, the shovel blade struck a solid object. After more digging and clearing, a pine coffin was revealed. The wood was surprisingly pale and fresh-looking, testament to the power of Arctic preservation.

During the spade work the men had cracked nervous, even morbid, jokes.

Looking down at the unusually long coffin, the internist, Frank Paddock, who had been the professor's longtime family doctor from his hometown of Pittsfield, Massachusetts, offered a bit too cheerfully: "They didn't build it for the short Hall, did they?"

All joking ceased when they caught the first whiff of human decay.

The plan had been to lift the coffin from its grave so that Paddock would have easier access to the remains. It soon became apparent that would not be practical, because the coffin was partly embedded in permafrost, a thick layer of ice a foot beneath the Arctic surface that never melts and radiates upward a constant bone-deep coldness, regardless of the ambient air temperature.

For ten minutes, as Gignoux carefully pried at the lid of the coffin with a crowbar, the three other men stood by silently. When a piece of the lid snapped off, they saw inside part of the field of blue stars of an American flag.

Once the nails were loosened, Loomis moved in to remove the lid.

The professor had already made several trips to the Far North. In his readings on the Arctic, he had encountered Hall's name and become fascinated by the questions surrounding his death. For three years Loomis had been digging through the records of the expedition, until he was convinced that it was "circumstantially possible," at least, that Hall had been murdered.

Loomis lifted the coffin lid and received help pulling it to one side.

The body was enshrouded by the flag except at the base of the coffin, where a pair of stockinged feet stuck out. From the waist down, the body was encased in a sheet of clear ice. The front of the upper torso was free of ice, but the corpse's back was frozen solid into the coffin.

Loomis stepped back, giving way to the physician, with whom he had done plenty of exploring, including digging for archaeological ruins high in the Peruvian Andes. What lay before them now was not clay pottery or gold statuary, and Loomis was well aware that he was far out of his field of expertise.

Frank Paddock, a compact, energetic man nearing sixty, was the kind of person, friends and colleagues agreed, who preferred running around the world on one of his "crazy adventures" to hanging around the local hospital tending to sick people. Leaning over the coffin, the doctor peeled the flag back from the corpse's face gingerly, as if uncovering a sleeping person without wishing to startle him.

The face had only partially decayed to a skull. Other than the nose, which was shrunken and nearly gone, the face was still well fleshed—a dark, leathery covering that stretched tautly over underlying bone. A carpet of stringy hair lay atop the head, and a full beard was so neat it appeared to have been recently combed. The eye sockets were empty holes of eternal darkness. The mouth was drawn into a kind of sly smile that would one day turn into a death's-head grin as the body continued its long journey from dust to dust.

Loomis was struck by the strange beauty of the slow decaying process at work on Hall's remains. The skin, tanned by time, was stained red and blue by the American flag that had pressed against it for a century, giving the corpse an abstract quality; not unlike an icon, Loomis thought.

Paddock had brought an autopsy kit, including scalpels, formalin, scissors, and glycerol. The only way he could reach the corpse was to stand in the grave and straddle the open coffin. As he did so, his companions handed him what he needed.

When he picked up by forceps a sample of head hairs, a piece of the attached scalp broke off with the hair roots. When Paddock took a fingernail, lifting a rather long nail, the whole fingertip broke off from the dried and shrunken hand.

On peeling back the jacket, vest, and underwear as far as possible, Paddock found the skin of the chest to be white except in the center, where it showed additional blue stains from the suit dye.

From a point above each breast, Paddock made the traditional Y-shaped incision, which met at the sternum and sliced downward into the lower abdomen. He found it difficult to remove the skin from the underlying rib cage. Where he succeeded in doing so, the muscle tissue underneath was found to be metamorphosed—doubtless by a combination of freezing and drying—to a slightly off-white, brittle material that he was able to shred off the bone.

Once he gained entry to the chest cavity, he observed that the area normally taken up by the lungs was empty. In fact, only the center part of the chest cavity contained any tissue, and this appeared to be of the same friable consistency as the chest muscle. The thoracic tissues were amorphous, offering only a suggestion of the whorls of heart muscle. Paddock found intact the structures of the trachea and the start of the bronchial tree—both were stained a moderate dark brown.

No other traces of organs or structures in the chest were identifiable.

Due to the rigid, folded arms of the corpse, Paddock could open only the upper portion of the abdomen. Like the chest cavity, this area was largely empty. The intestines presented themselves as a thin, yellowish, parchment-like ribbon. The spaces normally occupied by the liver and pancreas were filled by a small amount of the same whitish, structureless material present elsewhere.

Paddock stood for a minute to relieve his aching back and cramped arms from his awkward position working over the coffin. When he was ready, he turned to his friend and said dispassionately, "Chauncey. Handsaw."

With the razor-sharp tool in hand, the doctor positioned himself over the skull and began sawing. He found the bone to be of a normal, hard consistency, but extra difficult to cut through because the frozen pillow on which the head lay had curled up over the temporal areas, requiring him to cut through solid ice as well as bone.

Finally, Paddock removed a roughly triangular section of the forehead, giving him unimpeded access to the cranium. When he looked inside, he saw a dark void.

Loomis knew that with so many vital organs missing, pinning down the cause of death would not be easy. While certain parts of the corpse had been well preserved by the freezing temperatures, the decades had taken their toll. It would be a matter of turning over what they had found to a pathology laboratory and waiting for the results of a series of scientific and microscopic tests that might or might not prove a thing.

Samples of tissues were put into plastic bottles containing formalin, acetone, glycerol, and glyceraldehyde. The samples of hair, nail, and fingertip went into dry plastic bottles. The triangular skull section was encased in plastic wrapping. The entire collection was placed in a heavy metal toolbox for safekeeping.

Paddock, exhausted, was at last done. The autopsy had lasted three hours.

They did their best to redress the corpse, then put the lid back on the coffin.

The ex-Marine shoveled earth back into the grave, and re-created the mound exactly as they had found it, complete with some rocks that had been placed on top.

Charles Francis Hall was again at rest, less a few minor parts.

The men whiled away the rest of the two weeks by taking hikes along the beach, which they found more interesting and lively—with sanderlings, sandpipers, and plovers picking at the waterline and fulmars flying offshore—than the vast inland plain.

The sounds they would remember best were of water steadily dripping from thawing icebergs in the unending summer sun, and the occasional cracking and rumbles of mammoth ice breaking out in the bay. And this, they knew, was the Arctic in the summertime. What must it have been like here, ice-bound with no place to go, in the dead of winter?

When the plane returned for them, they loaded their gear and precious cargo and were off. As they circled Polaris Promontory one final time, all eyes looked down.

Chauncey Loomis believed he better understood now the man who lay in the shallow, frozen grave below, as well as the others like him, men who had been impelled to travel to the Arctic, yearning for its cold beauty and seeking Earth's most northern spot.

He realized now the truth of what he'd been told.

This *was* hallowed ground.

I

The Expedition

1

"North Star!"

A solitary figure had been pacing the corridors in the Capitol all day, the heels of his boots clicking on the marble floors and his black coat flapping behind him. He looked to anyone who didn't know him as if he had nothing to do and no place to go. Nothing was further from the truth.

Charles Francis Hall did have somewhere to go: back to the Far North, which he had come to consider more his true spiritual home than any place he had ever lived.

He stood about five feet eight inches tall and weighed close to two hundred pounds. His was a firmly knit, muscular frame that suggested power in the broad shoulders, and beyond—an inward strength. His head was large, with a profusion of coarse brown hair and heavy beard, both graying and inclining to curl at the ends. The effect was bearlike. His forehead was ample, and his small but expressive blue eyes often reflected the bemused twinkle of a dreamer. As he strode back and forth, the expression of his countenance was firm but not unpleasant. His

13

erect posture and robust movements suggested a man of boundless vigor who knew his course in life.

For the past ten years the Arctic had been his life. Back home in Cincinnati he had a wife, Mary, and a ten-year-old son, Charley, who hardly knew his father, since he had spent only a few months of the past decade at home. The rest of the time he was either on long trips to the north or traveling the country on speaking circuits, telling folks about his experiences and raising money for new expeditions. When he had first left for the Arctic ten years earlier, he had been ill-equipped and virtually alone. A small-time, only half-educated Midwest businessman who had been no farther north than New Hampshire, he had prepared himself for the Arctic by camping in a pup tent on Cincinnati's Mt. Adams and reading everything he could find on celestial navigation and astronomy. During his earlier Arctic trips— beginning with his first, in 1860, which he had undertaken in search of survivors of the ill-fated 1845 British expedition (two ships and 129 men lost) led by Sir John Franklin—Hall had learned the hardy ways of the Eskimos and adapted to the severe conditions found in the Arctic region. Partly, he had done so out of necessity, as his total budget for his first trip had been just $980. His second expedition—lasting five years—cost only about twice as much, and he embarked upon it during the middle of the Civil War when most of the country had more pressing matters at hand. His meager bankroll had served him well, however. During his stay on Baffin Island and, in the area of Repulse Bay, Isloolik, and King William Island on his second trip, he lived as few white men before him. He had traveled more than three thousand miles by dog sledge, hunted with Eskimos, learned to build an igloo, and developed a taste for seal blubber—believed by the Arctic natives to provide strength and recuperative powers in subzero temperatures. He came to genuinely like Eskimos as well, which could not be said of many Arctic explorers of his time; British, German, or American.

In promoting his latest and most ambitious expedition to the Arctic, Hall had solicited the support of the U.S. government at the highest levels. A consummate letter writer, he wrote acquaintances and strangers alike, and used introductions from well-connected friends in Washington, New York, and back home in Ohio to wangle meetings with members of Congress and the Administration so as to lobby his cause. Four days after arriving in Washington, he called on President Ulysses S. Grant, the popular Army general who, at the age of forty-six, had won the 1868 election in a landslide as the youngest president in history. Grant showed genuine interest in Hall's bold plan for reaching the North Pole, for he himself had an impressive knowledge of the history of Arctic exploration. A smaller man than Hall, Grant offered the explorer one of his custom-made cigars, and they had both lit up and had a grand talk about the best route for the expedition, the determination that would be needed to reach the Pole, and the physical deprivation that would be faced. These were engrossing topics to Grant, a born fighting general who never lost his tough edge. In Hall, Grant immediately saw someone of vision worth backing, and the President would never waver in his support, publicly or privately, for the man who regaled him that day with stories of the Arctic.

Hall's energetic one-man campaign generated sufficient interest that he was invited to lecture in the nation's capital on his Arctic experiences at Lincoln Hall. Numerous dignitaries were present that night, including President Grant and Vice President Schuyler Colfax. Both sat in the first row in front of the podium, smiling and nodding their approval throughout Hall's animated talk. Although at heart a modest man, Hall knew how to captivate an audience with Arctic facts and folklore. At a dramatic moment, he presented a married Eskimo couple, Ebierbing ("Joe") and Tookoolito ("Hannah"), whom he'd brought back with him from his last trip. Joe and Hannah, sweating profusely in their sealskin outfits, mesmerized the crowd simply by their appearance. The short-of-stature, chestnut-brown people of the Far North who called themselves *Inuits* were a great oddity at the time. For Hall's traveling show they had brought with them authentic bows and arrows, fish spears, dog harnesses, and other articles of Eskimo paraphernalia. When Hall announced that he was asking Congress for $100,000 to outfit a new expedition to discover the North Pole, the house erupted in applause, led by the President and Vice President.

What he did not tell the audience that night was that if his planned expedition failed to win government backing for a full-scale effort, then he was prepared to try for the North Pole on his own, by foot and by sledge with his trusted Eskimo couple, Joe and Hannah, as his guides. In the worst-case scenario, he told friends, he would ask the navy to transport him by ship and drop him, with whatever supplies he could manage, as far north as they possibly could. It was a plan based more on determination and stubbornness than good sense.

On March 8, 1870, the day after Hall's spellbinding appearance at Lincoln Hall, a joint resolution was introduced in the Senate and House to appropriate $100,000 for a "voyage of exploration and discovery under the authority and for the benefit of the United States." It authorized the President to provide "a naval or other steamer and, if necessary, a supply tender, for a voyage into the Arctic regions under the control of Captain C. F. Hall."

Hall, having never served in the Navy or commanded a vessel of any type, had no claim to the title "Captain." Though honorary at best, the title stuck, and overnight the former Cincinnati print shop owner became known as Captain Hall.

The resolution was assigned to committees in both chambers. In a long, impassioned letter to the Senate Committee on Foreign Relations, Hall struck a dual theme of patriotism cleverly combined with commercialism. "To whom are we indebted for all our Arctic whaling grounds, from which our country is getting millions of dollars worth of whalebone and oil every year? The answer is *to the English*!"

In truth, Hall didn't give a whit about the commercial whaling industry, except that it was expedient to his ultimate mission in life: being the discoverer of the North Pole and planting Old Glory at the top of the world. To that end, Hall, with the fiery righteousness and rhetoric of a Baptist missionary converting heathens, was convinced that he had been ordained by a "call from heaven" for the task by a higher authority than mortal man or mere politicians. Yet to succeed, he understood he needed the support of both.

"Neither glory nor money has caused me to devote my very life and soul to Arctic Exploration," his letter went on. "My desire is to promote the welfare of mankind in general under this glorious ensign—the stars and stripes." He bemoaned how few, ill-planned, and under-equipped the previous American ventures (privately financed projects seeking commercial opportunities) in the Arctic region had been, while "time and time again" the English and "other governments of the Old World" had sent out national "expeditions for discovery, for enriching science, and for the promotion of commerce."

Hall wanted nothing less than for the U.S. government, in a bid for international glory, to finance an expedition to discover the North Pole. This quest had already lured and killed scores of mariners and adventurers, and yet the goal seemed tantalizingly close. The feeling was that with the right ship, the right commander, enough money, and a little luck, man would finally set foot at the top of the Earth. As one newspaper claimed: "The solution of the Northern mystery would be the event of the nineteenth century." And in a heroic age, the discoverer would be the hero. Hall, of course, believed fervently that he should be that hero—the American who would put an end to more than two hundred years of British polar record setting. Who else, after all, had the vision, determination, and experience to lead such a historic mission?

Unexpectedly, another candidate stepped forward, a man with whom Hall had previously tangled over the Arctic. Dr. Isaac Hayes, a well-known scientist and author who had ten years earlier headed a well-publicized expedition in search of the open polar sea, appeared before the Foreign Relations committee to argue that an expedition he was planning deserved the government's backing more than Hall's.

It was blasphemy to Hall's ears. This same man, Dr. Hayes, had nearly cost Hall his first expedition to the Arctic region the same ten years earlier by *stealing* his ship's captain. Worse yet, in Hall's eyes, was that Hayes had sat with him and listened to his plans for that expedition, feigning support while conspiring behind his back. Hall had been forced at the last moment to find another ship's master. Not one to forget such "cowardice," "trickery," and "deviltry," Hall was aghast that Hayes would have the temerity to come forward now and try to ruin his hopes once again.

When Hall appeared before the committee, he defended himself as best he could against Hayes' main line of attack: his lack of formal scientific credentials. Hall had, on his earlier trips, made detailed maps and charts that were surprisingly accurate considering his lack of formal training in navigation and cartography. (Although he had found no Franklin survivors on his trips, he added much to the knowledge of what happened to the expedition through stories collected from Eskimos, and he returned with relics of the disastrous English voyage including silver spoons, a fork, a pair of scissors, and a mahogany barometer case.) Hall lacked even what could be called a liberal education. He was self-taught to a considerable extent, having finished with his formal education before graduating from high school. But he knew *Bowditch's Navigator* by heart and was perfectly competent to navigate a vessel. He excelled in the exactness and precision of his field work, in the determining of latitude and longitude, and in his careful, conscientious record of magnetic, astronomical, and geographical observations. For these accomplishments, as well as for his accurate and reliable charting of newly discovered coastlines, Hall had been complimented by the British Admiralty, and his work in the Arctic had stood the severest tests of both the U.S. Coast Survey Office and the Smithsonian Institution. He did not pretend to be a scientific naturalist, but he was thoroughly competent to make and record geographical discoveries, and that was the object of the proposed expedition.

"No, I am not a scientific man," Hall admitted before the Senate committee. "Discoverers seldom have been. Arctic discoverers—all except Dr. Hayes—have not been scientific men. Neither Sir John Franklin nor Sir Edward Parry were of this class, and yet they loved science and did much to enlarge her fruitful fields. Frobisher, Davis, Baffin, Bylot, Hudson, Fox, James, Kane, Back, McClintock, Osborn, Dease and Simpson, Rae, Ross and a host of other Arctic explorers were not scientific men."

Nevertheless, Dr. Hayes succeeded in convincing the legislators to strike Hall's name from the resolution, leaving the commander of the U.S. expedition nameless.

Even with such powerful senatorial champions as Charles Sumner of Massachusetts, John Sherman of Ohio (brother of William Tecumseh Sherman), and Reuben Fenton of New York, when the Senate—wrangling over larger issues such as reconstruction of the South—voted on the Arctic resolution it passed only when a tie was dramatically broken by the yea vote of Vice President Colfax.

Assured privately by legislative supporters that he was still the prime candidate for the command, Hall considered the vote a triumph. Then he waited for the bill to wend its way through the House of Representatives. Key to House approval, he was advised, was getting the bill through the influential House Appropriations Committee. Hall understood that even politicians who supported Arctic exploration might not always consider themselves at liberty to vote appropriations of public money for carrying it out. During the wait Hall looked, according to one of his supporters, Senator J. W. Patterson of New Hampshire, like a man "watching with a sick friend who hangs between life and death."

That was the man who had paced all day outside the Appropriations Committee.

Shortly before five o'clock, Hall spotted the clerk of the committee leaving the conference room. He pounced quickly, hoping for some word. The clerk said nothing, but handed him a folded piece of paper before heading through another doorway.

Hall unfolded the note. It read: "North Pole $50,000."

The sum was half as much as he had requested, but the $100,000 was to finance a two-ship expedition. He knew it could be done with one good ship, and the right crew.

Of course, there was still the matter of the unnamed commander, but Hall would not let that ruin the day. His fate, as he had been telling friends, was in God's hands.

Having powerful political allies also helped. The appropriation would be affirmed with dispatch by the Senate and House, and within days signed by President Grant, who a week later would send Hall his official appointment as commander of the expedition.

That day in the corridor of the Capitol, Charles Francis Hall trusted his fate.

He stretched to full height, raised an arm straight over his head, index finger pointed skyward, and dramatically announced to no one in particular and to everyone within earshot:

"*North Star!*"

2

A Ship and Her Crew

Charles Francis Hall was holding still another audience spellbound.

This time he wasn't raising money or seeking support, but bidding a fond farewell before the prestigious American Geographical Society at a reception in his honor. He had command of a fully outfitted steamer, moored at nearby Brooklyn Navy Yard, from where he and his crew would depart a few days hence for what was expected to be a nearly three-year expedition to the North Pole and back.

He had been ceremoniously presented with a folded American flag that had been carried not only to the highest northern latitude Old Glory had ever been, but also nearest to the South Pole. Hall cradled the colors in his arms as a minister might hold a cherished Bible or a grateful mother her firstborn. He was struck wordless by the honor as he stood before a capacity crowd that included not only members of the scientific community, but professors, judges, lawyers, Tammany Hall politicians, Wall

Street bankers, and newspaper reporters. Hall surveyed the faces before him. From the beginning of his Arctic journeys a decade earlier, he had received the support of this influential group, and he now considered many of its members, including its president, Judge Charles P. Daly, old friends.

In the silence of the moment, everyone waited expectantly.

"I believe," Hall's voice finally boomed, "that this flag in 1872 will float over a new world, in which the North Pole star is its crowning jewel!"

His optimism was greeted with loud applause.

Hall was not finished; he seldom was when his subject was the Arctic. Placing the flag on the lectern, he came out on the dais and apologized for not having the time to write a proper speech for the evening.

"Ladies and gentlemen, I would rather be making a sledge journey to the North Pole than talking about it," he said earnestly, bringing laughter from the audience.

Pointing out on a large Arctic map the route which he proposed to follow, he outlined his plan. He did not expect the first winter to reach above 80 degrees north—ten degrees in latitude and 800 miles short of the Pole. The ship would winter in the ice pack, and they would make exploratory sledge journeys, pushing as far north as possible. "I am not taking any sledges with me," he interjected. "I will have the Arctic natives make my sledges, since they can do it much better than white men."

In the spring, with the breakup of the ice, they would attempt to sail farther north, pushing as far as possible. When they were within striking distance of a few hundred miles—he hoped by next summer—they would make a dash by sledge for the Pole. "We will take five or six sledges with fifteen dogs pulling each one," he said. Each sled would be filled with provisions, he explained, and as fast as a load was exhausted, the empty sled would be sent back to the starting point to reload and bring back more provisions.

"And how will I know when I am at the Pole?" he asked rhetorically, giving voice to the criticism of some experts who had openly questioned whether such an accurate determination was possible, what with the magnetic disturbances that would render useless the readings of a compass. "On reaching that point called the North Pole, the North Star will be directly overhead. Without an instrument, with merely the eye, a man can define his position when there. It will be the easiest thing in the world.

"Suppose I arrive at the North Pole and the sun has descended?" continued Hall, Arctic dreamer extraordinaire. "Suppose there is an island at the North Pole; around it is the sea. I see a star upon the horizon. If I were to remain a thousand years at the Pole, that star will remain on the horizon without varying one iota in height. With the finest measuring instruments you have, you will not, from one day to the next, be able to determine one iota of change. It will be the easiest thing in the world to determine when you arrive at the North Pole. The phenomena displayed there will be deeply interesting, provided there is land there, and I am satisfied that I will find land there. From what I have heard from the Eskimos, I am satisfied that I will find people living there, too."

Hall said he and his crew expected to be gone from their families and country for approximately thirty months before their return home in the winter of 1873.

To that estimate, he added with emphasis: "God willing."

It had been a thrilling narration, and the crowd gave him another ovation.

"Many who have written to me," Hall went on, his voice with a softer edge, "or who have appeared to me personally, think that I am of an adventurous spirit and of bold heart to attempt to go to the North Pole. Not so. It does not require that heart which they suppose I have. For the Arctic region is my home. I love it dearly—its storms, its winds, its glaciers, its icebergs. When I am among them, it seems as if I were in an earthly heaven.

"Or perhaps," he added wistfully, eyes moistening, "a heavenly earth."

Before the evening came to a close, Hall acknowledged his gathered officers. He first introduced Sidney O. Buddington, who would serve as sailing master and ice pilot for the trip, and as such, operate the vessel and navigate her through the Arctic waters. In his late forties, he was a heavy, lumbering man who showed the world a cheerful face with a florid complexion. He had thinning gray hair and a full beard, generously dappled with salt and pepper. A native of Groton, Connecticut, he had worked on commercial whalers in northern waters for more than thirty years, and had been a shipmaster for two decades. He was familiar with the perils of ice navigation. Hall had known Buddington for ten years, and though he hadn't been his first choice for sailing master, Hall had confidence in him.

Next was Dr. Emil Bessels, chief of the expedition's scientific corps and ship's physician. He was twenty-seven years old, slight and somewhat delicately built, and of a quick and nervous temperament that suggested he was easily offended. With his jet black hair and beard and dark and bright eyes, he was a handsome man built on a rather small scale. A native of Germany, Bessels, who came from family wealth, was a graduate of the famous University of Heidelberg, where he had studied zoology and entomology.

Bessels had not been Hall's first choice, either. He had originally recruited an American Army doctor from San Francisco who had been on an Arctic voyage twelve years earlier but who lacked an extensive science background. Bessels had been recommended by a distinguished German geographer to the National Academy of Sciences, which was setting up the protocol for the expedition's scientific experiments, covering the fields of astronomy, meteorology, geology, glaciology, oceanography, botany, ornithology, and zoology. Bessels not only had a medical degree but was an expert in the natural sciences, and as such, came with more impressive qualifications for the expedition. Too, he had sailed on a Swedish sealing vessel in 1869, and made extensive observations in the seas between Nova Zembla and East Greenland. Understanding that he needed to appease the scientific community—especially given his own lack of scientific training—Hall went along with the change. Bessels, who had been serving as a volunteer surgeon in the Prussian Army in the Franco-German War, was released from his duties and caught a ship to the United States, arriving six weeks prior to the expedition's departure. For a time he had stayed at the Manhattan home of Professor Joseph Henry, president of the National Academy of Sciences. During his stay Mrs. Henry met with a severe fall and sustained injuries of a serious nature. She was attended to by the visiting doctor, who impressed her with his ability in the practice of medicine as much as he did in discussing the general sciences with professors Henry, Newcomb, Hilgard, and the other *savants* of the prestigious National Academy.

Hall was not about to be pushed around by those eminent men of science, however. When he first read their scientific instructions for the expedition, he found them so elaborate and detailed that he worried they might overshadow the main objective. Through correspondence with Professor Henry, Hall sparred with a worthy opponent; each was resolute, while not eager to offend the other. "From the fact that the National Academy was mentioned in the appropriations bill in connection with scientific instructions," wrote Henry to Hall, "it is evident Congress did not intend that scientific operations should be neglected." Hall immediately countered to Henry: "The primary objective of our expedition is geographical discovery, and to this, as the main end, our energies will be bent." In the face of Hall's intransigence, Henry finally granted that the main purpose of the expedition *was* to reach the North Pole. In his copy of the scientific instructions, Hall boldly underlined the last four words of this sentence: "Great difficulty was met with in obtaining men of the proper scientific acquirements to embark in an enterprise which must necessarily be attended with much privation, and in which, in a measure, *science must be subordinate.*"

Mindful of the audience's scientific bent, Hall asked Bessels to say a few words about the plans for scientific discoveries during the expedition. Bessels nodded curtly and walked stiffly to the lectern, which appeared oversized in front of his small frame.

Though not obvious to observers that Hall and Bessels had any personal dislike for each other, the foundation for future trouble over the scientific agenda had been laid. Professor Henry, by then a warm champion of Bessels, had addressed this concern in a final missive to Hall. "I doubt not that you will give every facility and render every assistance in your power to Dr. Bessels, who, though a sensitive man, is of a very kind heart." Later in the same letter, he repeated a similar phrase and issued an early storm warning: "As I have said, Dr. Bessels is a sensitive man; I beg, therefore, you will deal gently with him."

Beginning by apologizing to the audience for his unfamiliarity with English, Bessels briefly praised Hall's enthusiasm, then plunged into what he clearly considered the most important aspect of the journey: the science. "If anything could be a stimulus to us during our trip," he said in accented but educated English, "I think it will arise from the fact that such eminent men of science, such as compose this society, are watching with interest the actions of our expedition."

Hall next introduced George Tyson—the last officer to join the ship's complement. Tyson, forty-two, was a tall, lanky man with muscular arms and the big, callused hands of a sailor. He had a full beard like most of his shipmates, and thick brown hair brushed back. His most notable feature was his sensitive, brooding eyes, which suggested he had seen much and was little surprised by anything put before him.

Returning to the United States from his first Arctic journey, Hall had spent time aboard ship with Tyson, who had been shipwrecked in northern waters. From their many long discussions Hall came away impressed with Tyson's character as well as his knowledge of the Arctic region. Believing that a more able man could not be found, Hall had wanted Tyson on the expedition from the beginning. The previous year he had offered him the sailing-master position, but Tyson had already made a commitment to a whaler and had to decline. When that trip was canceled, Tyson contacted Hall, who by then had hired Buddington. By special arrangement with Secretary of Navy George Robeson, under whose jurisdiction the expedition was operating, Hall was able to create at the last minute the uncommon post of assistant navigator for Tyson. In fact, Tyson's appointment papers had not yet been delivered from the Navy Department. To his duties Hall had added "master of sledges." In no uncertain terms, Hall intended to have the capable Tyson with him on the final, historic dash to the Pole.

Tyson, a native of New Jersey whose family had moved to New York City early in his childhood, was a former iron-foundry laborer who as a boy had dreamed of a seagoing life. He first shipped out at age twenty-one, and did not see a Fourth of July within the United States for twenty years, having spent those summers whaling. While there was little he could not do on a ship, he was given to a natural reticence and modesty that made him popular with other quiet men of the sea.

Hall next introduced the first mate, Hubbard C. Chester. He was clean-shaven except for a wide, expansive brush mustache, which, together with a straight part that ran down the middle of his wavy hair, gave him a rakish appearance. He was in every way a man's man, with the big, broad, finely chiseled physique of a Roman gladiator, and a powerful baritone voice that commanded attention from the most lackluster crew. Thirty-four years old, Chester, a native of Noank, Connecticut, had been mate on a whaler that Hall had caught a ride on six years earlier. He had been impressed with Chester's marked force of character and shipboard abilities, and the veteran sailor was also gifted at handling small craft. Chester had spent the past ten years whaling, principally in the Bering Strait, but had also rounded Cape Horn, and taken a long voyage in the Pacific, as far as the Sandwich Islands and then to San Francisco. He had returned to New York by train in time to join the expedition.

When Hall came to his second mate, William Morton, he asked him to say a few words. A native of Ireland, Morton, nearing fifty, had spent most of his life at sea, including thirty years in the U.S. Navy—most of it aboard man-of-wars. He was grizzled and aged beyond his years, with a nearly white, full beard, reddish-gray hair, and dark bags under his eyes. He looked like a man ready for a rocker on a shady veranda, not another sea adventure. Indeed, he already had a considerable Arctic reputation—doubtless why Hall asked him to speak. Morton had made two memorable Arctic voyages with Dr. Elisha Kent Kane, an intrepid American Navy officer turned explorer, in search of survivors from the ill-fated Sir John Franklin expedition. On one occasion Morton crossed by sledge the great Humboldt Glacier with an Eskimo guide. Upon looking out on open waters, he announced that he had discovered the long-sought open Polar Sea, believed to be the route to the North Pole. It was, in fact, the route that Hall was planning to take; in Morton, he had along his own personal guide to the promised land. Morton had given long and faithful service to Kane, who had died in 1857 at age thirty-seven after a long illness.

Morton was a man of few words, but his simple eloquence greatly affected his receptive audience this evening. He told of his pleasure at serving under Dr. Kane, who months before his death had been awarded the coveted British Arctic medal for his efforts in the heroic but ultimately futile search for Franklin survivors. "It was my sad fortune to lose as brave a man as ever lived," Morton said of his former commander. "He has passed from among us into a world where martyrs receive their reward."

After the introductions, Hall had one additional comment.

"I have chosen my own men. Men who will stand by me through thick and thin. Though we may be surrounded by innumerable icebergs, and though our vessel may be crushed like an eggshell, I believe they will stand by me to the last."

The ship of destiny at her moorings in the Brooklyn Navy Yard was a two-masted, schooner-rigged, white-oak, 387-ton, 140-foot vessel with a war record.

Under orders from President Grant, the U.S. Navy had

given Charles Francis Hall the privilege of selecting any ship in its fleet for his expedition. After visiting several boatyards, he had chosen USS *Periwinkle*, a screw tug built at Philadelphia in 1864, christened *America*, then renamed when the Navy purchased her later that year.

Periwinkle had joined the wartime Potomac flotilla in early 1865 as a gunboat, operating primarily in the Rappahannock River. When a fleet of oyster schooners was threatened by a Confederate force, *Periwinkle* took part in blockading the mouths of the Rappahannock and Piankatank rivers to protect the fishing fleet. She also interrupted contraband business between lower Maryland and Virginia, cleared rivers of mines, and fought guerrillas ashore. After the war, she was based in Norfolk, where Hall had found her.

The ship was sent to Washington Navy Yard and hauled up on the ways. One of the navy's best ship constructors was assigned to the job, under orders from the Secretary of the Navy to spare neither pains nor expense in equipping the ship for Arctic service. The first time Hall visited the ship during the refitting, a hundred mechanics, carpenters, and other tradesmen were humming about the vessel like busy bees, much to his delight. Her wales, planking, clamps, and ceiling were removed and her decks taken out. She was rebuilt with thirteen extra tons of new timbers, making her four hundred tons. To strengthen her to withstand ice, new deck beams of increased size were put in, and she was newly planked inside and out. The bottom was thoroughly caulked, then double-planked, caulked, and coppered. New bulkheads and inboard works, new spars, rigging, and sails were added. She was rigged as a top-sail schooner, and her two masts were very long—dwarfing her pair of smoke stacks—giving her enough canvas to produce a good rate of speed independent of steam, if needed.

She had a round stern, with nothing about it that could catch the ice, and a well with a hoisting apparatus so that the propeller could be taken up at short notice; the rudder could also be unshipped in the event of submerged ice. The bowsprit, a spar running out from the stern to which cables that helped stabilize the main mast were attached, was rigged so that it could be run in immediately if there was danger of coming in contact with ice. Her bow was reinforced, made strong enough to resist any shock it was likely to receive. The stern had sheets of boiler iron bent around it and bolted through the solid wood. From these, similar plates were carried aft forty feet on each side, two feet above and below the waterline so that the ice would have no chance of cutting into the wood. In these respects, *Polaris* was better protected against ice than any vessel ever built; in a real sense, it was the world's first icebreaker.

Special cabin heating was installed, generated by small coal-burning stoves added to each compartment. The ship was not without amenities: a little cabin, handsomely carpeted, had been fitted up, and a cabinet organ, donated by the manufacturer, had been placed in it.

When the work was completed, all agreed that everything deemed necessary for safety and comfort had been done, and that no ship, even one especially built, could have been better adapted to Arctic service. Wrote Hall to a friend after visiting the ship: "I am very much in love with it." He was also elated when the government paid for the shipyard work without charging it to the $50,000 appropriation.

To Hall, there was just one thing wrong: the name. He could not fathom going Arctic exploring on a ship named after an evergreen herb of the dogbane family. The rebuilt *Periwinkle* was launched at the Washington Navy Yard in April 1871, renamed by her commander as *Polaris,* after a conspicuous bright star in the northern hemisphere which, until the year 1500, would mark the location of the north celestial pole. Hall's choice of name expressed his sanguine expectation of success.

A month later, a twenty-one-gun salute by a military honor guard echoed across the rows of piers and locks. On the deck of his ship, freshly scrubbed and full of snap, Hall awaited the presidential party that emerged from black horse-drawn carriages.

Warmly shaking hands with Hall at the top of the gangway, President Grant said he was pleased to hear how well preparations for the Arctic expedition were coming along and had come to see for himself. Hall took the President, the Secretary of the Navy, and other officials on an inspection of the ship. Then, on the main deck under a brilliant sky, the chaplain of the Congress led a brief service, blessing the ship, her crew, and commander on their long journey.

A month later in the Brooklyn Navy Yard, only twenty-four hours before the departure of *Polaris* for Arctic waters, another religious service was conducted aboard ship, the regular Sunday services for all hands, only with visiting members of a local Baptist congregation.

Standing close to Hall were his loyal Eskimos, Joe and Hannah, with their adopted daughter, Punny, age four, a beautiful child with porcelain skin and almond-shaped eyes. (Joe and Hannah had lost their own child, a young boy, to illness.) Joe, a Greenland Eskimo, was a swarthy fellow with a straight black mustache and coal-dark eyes. He was barely five feet tall, but pound for pound, when it came to hunting or driving a dog team on the ice, Hall would have taken Joe over any man alive. His English was limited, but Hall, from his years of living with the Eskimos, was conversational in Inuktitut.

They had met on Hall's first trip to the Arctic a decade earlier. One day he was in his cabin aboard ship, writing in his journal, when he heard a soft, sweet voice behind him murmur, "Good morning, sir," with a distinctive English accent. Hall turned, expecting to see a refined English lady before him. To his surprise, there stood a stout Eskimo woman, all of four feet ten, dressed not in skins or furs but in crinoline and wearing a large bonnet. He had heard of Joe and Hannah before meeting them, as they were well known throughout the Baffin Island region. In the early 1850s an English whaling captain had taken them home with him, and they had stayed several years in England, where they aroused so much curiosity that they were given an audience with Queen Victoria and dined with Prince Albert. At that first meeting, Hall couldn't resist asking the couple what they had thought of the Queen. "Very pretty," Joe said, smiling. Hannah was more impressed with where the Queen lived. "Fine place, I assure you, sir," she offered. The couple had subsequently accompanied Hall on his overland expedition, and without their assistance and knowledge in surviving the Arctic rigors, he would have surely died.

On the North Pole expedition, Joe would serve as hunter and dog driver, Hannah as seamstress.

The rest of the crew that stood on deck for Sunday services were a capable lot. At the time, the U.S. Navy and Merchant Marine both relied heavily on recruiting immigrants to run their ships, since the most adventurous Americans were going West rather than to sea.

Emil Schuman, a German national, had been appointed chief engineer of *Polaris.* A handsome, well-groomed man with a mustache, side whiskers, and slicked-back hair, Schuman was well educated in engineering principles and had spent years at sea, most recently as assistance engineer in the service of Lloyds Steamship Company. An excellent engineer and machinist, it would be his job to keep the ship, its boiler, engine, and mechanical gears running in the world's coldest, most adverse seas.

Alvin Odell, from Connecticut, was assistant engineer. A Civil War veteran who had fought for the Union, he was a good machinist and blacksmith, and a practical man. Rail-thin and stoic, he displayed an inborn Yankee shrewdness toward money and possessions.

Frederick Meyer, military academy graduate and former lieutenant in the Prussian army, would serve as meteorologist. Before he left Germany, he had held an appointment in Maximilian's army and had been destined for Mexico in support of the Austrian archduke's effort to rule that country. Upon reaching the United States, however, Meyer decided to stay and entered the U.S. Army. His was a fortunate decision, as within two years Maximilian was in disgrace in Mexico, court-martialed and executed. Detailed as a signal observer at St. Louis, Meyer had distinguished himself as a sergeant in the Signal Corps. The tallest member of the crew at well over six feet, Meyer was in his early forties, with a receding hairline and bushy mustache. He could be downright dapper in appearance, favoring a gold watch and chain in his vest pocket. Meyer was a natural at telling others what to do, and he had a disturbing tendency to believe that he was always right, even in the face of evidence to the contrary.

The ship's carpenter, Nathaniel Coffin, was the oldest member of the crew, a neat, natty little fellow of more than fifty summers. He was talented with saw and hammer, but at heart he was a poet and songwriter, and would often amuse his shipmates with his latest verses and renditions about life on the sea.

Of the ten common seamen who formed the deck crew, one was a Swede, one a Dane, and seven were German, several having fled their native country to escape nearly a decade of war in the name of German unification since Bismarck's rise to power in Prussia. Only one deckhand was American-born: Noah Hayes, twenty-six, a wide-eyed Indiana farm boy who had never been to sea. The remaining crew were two firemen—one American and one English—to work below deck in the boiler room, an English steward to help prepare and serve food, and a sad-eyed mulatto cook from New York named William Jackson. In all, the eleven Americans in the crew were outnumbered by fourteen immigrants, ten of them Germans.

After the services Hall, resplendent in his finest uniform, rose to speak. With sunlight dancing off his polished brass buttons, he introduced the ship's officers and thanked the Baptists for their presence. As he spoke, his preacher-like voice gathered strength and spread across the deck of the ship, carrying out over the harbor.

"I believe firmly that I was born to discover the North

Pole," he said. "That is my purpose. Once I have set my right foot on the Pole, I shall be perfectly willing to die."

Most of the men cheered, although a few officers exchanged glances. The ladies of the congregation smiled shyly under their bonnets, unsure what to make of such bold talk.

That day Charles Francis Hall heard only the cheers and saw only the smiles.

3

"Icebergs Dead Ahead!"

In the midst of a summer thunderstorm, with the U.S. flag he had been presented days earlier by the American Geographical Society hoisted at the fore, Charles Francis Hall stood on the bridge as the lines securing *Polaris* to the pier were released and she nudged away from the dock, where scattered onlookers stood under umbrellas waving good-bye.

At last the expedition was under way, sailing with a set of official orders addressed to Hall and signed by Navy Secretary George Robeson:

> *Having been appointed by the President of the United States, commander of the North Polar Expedition, and the steamer* Polaris *having been fitted, equipped, provisioned, and assigned for the purpose, you are placed in command of the said vessel, her officers, and crew, for the purposes of the said expedition ... the main objective attaining the position of the North Pole. All persons attached to the*

expedition are under your command, and shall, under every circumstance and condition, be subject to the rules, regulations, and laws governing the discipline of the Navy, to be modified, but not increased, by you as the circumstances may in your judgment require.

Near the end of the official orders, which seemed to provide for every possible contingency, was a paragraph addressing what would happen in the event of the death of the Expedition's commander:

In case of your death or disability—a contingency we sincerely trust may not arise—sailing master of the expedition, S. O. Buddington, and chief scientist, Dr. Emil Bessels, shall consult as to the propriety and manner of carrying into further effect the foregoing instructions, which I here urge must, if possible, be done. In any event, Mr. Buddington shall, in case of your death or disability, continue as the sailing master, and control and direct the movements of the vessel; Dr. Bessels shall continue as chief of the scientific department, directing all sledge-journeys and scientific operations.

It was a curiously worded clause that allowed for a kind of split command, unprecedented in U.S. Navy command structure, in which no loopholes were ever allowed for insubordination to creep, no way in which more than one person could assume authority at the same time. This tradition made good military sense, since divided authority led to unclear orders and weakened discipline. Most emphatically, the Navy had always followed the policy that command at sea, and all the life-and-death responsibilities that came with it, must fall to one individual.

With *Polaris*, however, the Navy could not make up its mind to trust anybody with full command of the expedition in the case of Hall's demise. It seemed as though the wintertime—when the ship would be stuck in the ice—was to be handed over to the physician-scientist, and the summer would belong to the sailing master.

Polaris pulled out of the Navy Yard and steamed past the bustling, vibrant waterfront of New York. As they headed south, where they would hook east around Long Island and head for the open sea, George Tyson felt strange having nothing to do with directing the ship. While serving as sailing master for his last five voyages, he had learned to withdraw, once the bow and stern lines were off, from any thoughts of shore and concentrate on the business of getting under way. Feeling the early morning sun in his face, putting everyone on deck to work, and taking charge as they headed for sea, more of a home to him than any he had ever known on dry land—he doubted there was anything better in the world.

But now he found himself sailing toward unknown seas without any duties on the bridge or even a clearly defined position. He still had not received his official commission papers. They were to be sent from Washington on a supply ship that was to rendezvous with them in Greenland. Tyson had no idea what an assistant navigator was supposed to do. Hall had simply wanted him along on the trip and said they would work out the details later. Tyson had agreed because the adventure would be high—of that he was certain—the pay was good, and he would be at sea, where he loved to be.

Tyson gave himself up to the novelty of observing others performing their tasks instead of commanding them, and enjoying the view as though a mere passenger. They passed down the East River with the great city of Brooklyn, fourth largest in the country with over 400,000 souls, on his left, and to their stern, the island of Manhattan, with nearly a million residents.

This was the Brooklyn of Walt Whitman—a city with a distinct seagoing and farming character to it, but one that was rapidly turning to manufacturing and becoming a bedroom community for people working in Manhattan. Numerous ferries plied the waters of the river, back and forth, an endless stream of cargo and humanity that even the future completion of the

Brooklyn Bridge and a network of elevated railways wouldn't put out of business. Off in the distance Tyson recognized the tallest building on the skyline, Trinity Church, which dominated Wall Street.

He wondered how many of these residents would concern themselves the next few years with reports of the expedition. The North Pole was a long way off, and meant nothing at all to their daily lives. He surmised that a good number of those who did think about the expedition considered the *Polaris* crew a wild and reckless bunch willfully going to their own destruction.

Some of his own friends thought that he was undertaking a wild goose chase, and he wasn't so sure if his wife, Emmaline, didn't silently agree. To anyone who asked, he had been saying that with "good leadership and management" he thought *Polaris* had a chance to get farther north than any ship before. He believed it was worth the try.

So many people in Washington, New York, and elsewhere had supported the expedition and bade them Godspeed. They had been able to look past the obvious danger to the honor of having an American be first at the Pole. They understood the mysterious attraction that had long drawn explorers to seek the unknown.

Tyson, as a youth, had been gripped by a longing to see the frozen north. His imagination had been stoked by published accounts of leading Arctic explorers of the day—Parry, Ross, Franklin—and he had wanted to follow in their tracks. Two decades of whaling had not diminished that flame—to gaze on unknown lands, enter mysterious, mist-shrouded channels, touch shorelines where no man had trod before, to witness novel scenes, and to share in the dangers of Arctic discovery.

On they steamed, until the blood-orange sunset was behind them. The bright summer night carried the cleansing scent of fresh rain and beckoned them toward open sea.

Off the coast of Newfoundland a week later, *Polaris* was enshrouded in fog, as it had been for three days and nights. The lookout in the crow's nest perched high up the forward mast-head could not see more than a hundred feet beyond the bow. Then, as if someone had drawn back a giant curtain, the veil lifted.

That evening a great change came over the sky. Dark clouds, turning every moment to a deeper blackness, massed above the horizon to the southwest. In an instant, the entire sky was blanketed. A sudden rain squall burst with violent, rolling thunder and brilliant lightning that seemed almost continuous, so incessant were the flashes. The very firmament was ablaze from horizon to zenith, while peal after peal of deep, reverberating thunder echoed and reechoed across the sky like the cannonading of contending armies.

Not just the weather had turned. Already, there were signs of crew unrest.

George Tyson noticed trouble brewing around the time of their arrival at St. Johns, Newfoundland, where the ship was coaled, and sledge dogs and skins for winter clothing were purchased. (Woolen clothing could keep out cold but was little protection against the subzero Arctic winds. Hall had hoped to procure highly sought deer skins, but none was available. He settled for seal and dog skins, which Hannah would sew together for winter clothing.) Although unaware of the dispute that had long simmered between Hall and the scientific advisers concerning the expedition's main priority, Tyson did recognize the strain. At this stage, he noticed little more than glances, gestures, and attitudes, but Dr. Emil Bessels and meteorologist Frederick Meyer were clearly acting as though they had a higher standing than anyone else aboard, including their commander. It was none of Tyson's business, for he had no official standing among the officers, but he was sorry to see early seeds of discontent.

Trouble was also fomenting on the bridge.

Two days out of St. Johns, Tyson was walking the deck alone one evening, admiring the stars and listening to the squeals of Newfoundland dogs in a makeshift kennel—a partially overturned lifeboat. Thus occupied, he nearly ran into Sidney Buddington as the sailing master burst forth from a hatchway, cursing a blue streak.

"Tyson, we are being led by a damned fool!"

Tyson glanced at some crewmen on deck nearby, and saw that they had heard the sailing master's complaint. He took Buddington's arm and guided him away.

"I will likely be going ashore at Disco," Buddington said, shaking his head.

Tyson knew that Disco, Greenland, would in all likelihood be their last stop before setting a straight course for the Arctic. He could not imagine what had happened to cause such vexation. He had known the sailing master for years. Buddington had been mate of the vessel on Tyson's very first voyage to sea twenty years earlier—which had ended in his first shipwreck, too. But they hadn't sailed together since, and only occasionally over the years had run into each other in one port or another.

"The worst part is," Buddington went on, "we're being led by a man not of the sea."

The sailing master spat it out as the worst form of insult.

Being in command was never easy, but Tyson saw what a precarious position Hall was in as expedition commander. The scientists looked down on him because he did not have their education, and so did an old salt like Buddington because Hall was not a sailor.

"That's why you're here, Bud," Tyson said, smiling, trying to defuse the charge.

"Not likely I'll be on this blasted ship much longer."

In the next few minutes it became clear what had happened, and Tyson had all he could do not to laugh. Buddington, it seemed, had been caught by Hall with his hand in the larder—helping himself to some extra sugar and chocolate. By nature a disciplined and parsimonious man, Hall had taken offense and severely upbraided Buddington.

An hour later, Tyson was summoned to Hall's cabin. The

commander explained the situation, and asked Tyson what he thought should be done with Buddington.

If Buddington was put off the ship, Tyson knew he would take over as sailing master. Yet that was not what Tyson wanted. He knew a last-minute switch could cause disruption among the crew, and he wanted no part of it.

"It was a careless trick, sir," Tyson said. "He'll probably do better in the future."

Privately, Tyson was more troubled by Buddington's conduct in front of the men. To maintain discipline, a sailing master should never lower himself to complain in front of the men, particularly about other officers, and also not consort with ordinary seamen but maintain an officer's distance. Foul-mouthed, ill-mannered Buddington had a disturbing tendency to do both, Tyson had observed, and *that* he found inexcusable. But of these concerns he said nothing; after all, Hall had known Buddington for ten years, sailed with him previously, and hired him as master of the ship. Also, Tyson continued to feel awkward about his status aboard *Polaris*. Still without his commission papers and lacking any official post, he remained more passenger than crew.

Not long after spotting the island of Greenland, they saw their first icebergs.

"Icebergs dead ahead!" cried the lookout aloft.

About fifteen came in sight at one time, great bergs flashing in the sunlight across the green and dappled sea. Many were from a hundred fifty to two hundred feet high, and those seeing the formations for the first time were most impressed by their sheer size. Their cold and mysterious beauty, suggesting they were the handiwork of a supreme sculptor, held the gaze of even the most experienced Arctic sailors, though to a man they knew well the danger icebergs posed to any vessel afloat.

They reached the island of Disco, halfway up the rugged western coast of Greenland, but did not find the Navy supply ship due to meet them in the small harbor of Godhavn, a Danish settlement nestled beneath two-thousand-foot treeless slopes.

Hall decided to await the anticipated rendezvous even though with each passing day of summer, the season for Arctic travel was shortening.

No sooner had the vessel been secured than Hall found himself faced with a blatant challenge to his authority. In his tiny cabin aft, he was confronted by Frederick Meyer, the Prussian-born meteorologist whom Hall had enlisted days earlier to help him keep his journal of the expedition. Meyer now told his commander that the clerical chore was interfering with his scientific duties.

At heart a fair-minded man, Hall considered the problem for a moment. In that case, he said, Meyer should stop making meteorological observations for the time being to concentrate entirely on the journal and to assist with other matters on the ship. Hall's reasoning was that meteorological records would not become critical until they were farther north. At that point, he would reevaluate Meyer's work schedule.

Journal writing was considered so vital to the record of the expedition that it had been spelled out in the orders from the Secretary of the Navy; every man aboard ship who could read and write was directed to keep a journal and turn it in at the end of the trip. That was in addition to the official ship's log. Virtually every movement of the ship and every finding of the expedition were to be documented. From Meyer, Hall had sought assistance in keeping up with some of this workload.

Although Meyer, as a sergeant in the United States Signal Corps, was accustomed to following orders, he refused, telling Hall that his scientific duties were more important than the captain's journal.

Hall was astonished. "Sergeant Meyer, this is not a request. This is an order."

"I have my orders from headquarters," Meyer retorted.

"You have your orders from headquarters?" Hall said. "Produce them, sir."

Meyer turned beet red. "My duty is taking meteorological observations. You are telling me to cease my observations to keep your journal. It is an order I cannot obey."

"Need I remind you," Hall sputtered, "that you and every member of this expedition are under my command and will follow my orders."

Meyer stood silent but defiant.

That evening, Dr. Emil Bessels asked to speak to Hall. He said that Meyer's scientific duties were so pressing that he could not be spared for other work.

Hall started at the audacious little German. Who did he think he was?

"If the sergeant is put off the ship," Bessels went on, "I will leave, too."

Word of the quarrel spread among the crew that night. The Germans were particularly alarmed, and after loudly discussing the situation with Bessels in their native tongue, they decided to a man that they would quit, too, should Bessels and Meyer leave the ship.

Hall was stunned by the depth of the plot Bessels was stirring up to defy his authority. This was no longer just one crewman's complaint about his duties. Hall understood it had turned into a test of his ability to command.

If the Germans left, Hall knew the expedition would be over before it started. He could not possibly go on, as there would be no way to replace at the last minute the chief engineer, two of the three scientists, and seven of the ten ordinary seamen. After all the support the expedition had received at home, and the ceremonious sendoffs, they would limp back in defeat with only a partial crew. They would be a laughingstock, his reputation as Arctic explorer surely ruined.

Hall spent the night brooding.

He knew the face of insubordination; he had seen it before. In the summer of 1868, after four long years in the Arctic, tempers had flared between him and some of the seamen who had accompanied him to Repulse Bay in search of the lost Franklin expedition. Tension in the camp had been rising for days, and at one point several of his men were in a mutinous state. Their leader, Patrick Coleman, an American, planted himself in front of Hall and delivered a rebellious ultimatum. Trying to reason with Coleman, Hall placed a hand on his shoulder, but Coleman, a powerful, muscular man, squared off against his commander. Hall ran to his tent, picked up his revolver, and returned, demanding that the men end their insolence. When Coleman became more threatening, Hall snapped and impulsively pulled the trigger. Coleman staggered and fell. Hall, realizing what he had done, handed an Eskimo his revolver and helped the wounded man to his tent. Coleman did not die immediately, but lived on for a horrifying fortnight before succumbing to his wounds. During that time a remorseful and shaken Hall stayed at the man's side, struggling vainly to save his life. Hall was never questioned by authorities about the shooting death; no one could determine under whose jurisdiction that remote region of the Arctic lay, and no one was much interested in finding out.

In the morning, Hall, bleary-eyed and exhausted from worry and lack of sleep, felt he had no choice but to capitulate to Meyer. Hall summoned the meteorologist and told him he could continue taking observations; he'd find someone else to keep his journal.

In a week, the Navy supply ship, USS *Congress*, arrived from New York with final provisions for *Polaris*, enough to restock her coal and food supplies before she continued her journey north. Arriving on *Congress* was the third and final member of the ship's scientific corps, Richard W. D. Bryan, who assumed his dual role aboard *Polaris* as astronomer and chaplain. Bryan had been employed as an astronomer at an observatory in Michigan since his recent graduation from Lafayette College in Easton, Pennsylvania. Recommended for the *Polaris* appointment by his alma mater, Byran had a freshly scrubbed look and youthful appeal, and his eagerness to do the right thing was irresistible even to the most hardened seaman. In addition, Byran was a young man of superior talent and intelligence who caught on very quickly.

When Captain H. K. Davenport, the skipper of the *Congress*, stepped aboard *Polaris* in full uniform, regal and patrician, he was shocked to find officers openly at odds with their angry and mortified commander, and to learn that the long-planned and well-outfitted polar expedition had nearly been scuttled by mass desertion.

Hall sought Davenport's advice. After reviewing the Navy Department's orders under which *Polaris* sailed, Davenport said that since the crew was subject to Navy discipline, he was prepared to arrest Meyer for insolence and return him to the U.S. in irons, adding that this example might go far to repairing Hall's authority.

Hall appreciated the offer but declined. He explained that the mission was more important than any one man. All he wanted to do was to get on his way to the Pole.

At Davenport's suggestion, Hall called Meyer into his cabin. The commander wrote out a paragraph from the navy's official orders: "As a member of the United States naval North Polar Expedition, I do hereby solemnly promise and agree to conform to all the instructions as herein set forth by the Secretary of the United States Navy to the commander." Hall asked Meyer to sign the statement, which the meteorologist did.

Davenport was not finished. Knowing how insubordination could sweep through a ship like a deadly plague, he had Hall call all hands together on the deck the day that *Polaris* was to leave Disco, and the *Congress* skipper delivered a brief but ringing lecture on naval discipline. He was thinking not only about Meyer and Emil Bessels, but also of Sidney Buddington. Hall had told Davenport of having caught the sailing master stealing food for his own consumption. Captain Davenport hoped his comments served to remind the crew of their responsibilities, and felt he had done everything in his power. Still, he worried.

The chaplain of *Congress*, the Reverend Doctor J. P. Newman, who had led a service aboard ship when President Grant's party visited in Washington Navy Yard and had come up on the supply ship for a final farewell to the *Polaris* crew, stepped forward to offer a parting prayer. The first part of his blessing was suitable for any naval journey, but at the end the minister seemed to address what was happening aboard *Polaris*. He prayed for the men to have "noble thoughts, pure emotions, and generous sympathies for each other while so far away from human habitations." From God he sought for them a charity that "suffereth long and is kind, that envieth not, that is not puffed up, not easily provoked, that thinketh no evil, but that endureth all things."

Then the visitors departed, *Polaris* weighed anchor, steamed from the Disco harbor, and turned north. The weather was fine and the seas calm, but many icebergs rode outside the harbor, and it required some skillful steering to avoid running afoul of them.

As the polar-bound ship passed *Congress*, Davenport's men cheered heartily.

Most, but not all, of the *Polaris* crew standing on deck returned the greeting.

In his benediction, the chaplain had offered a fitting prayer.

For *Polaris* and her divided crew, endurance and survival near the top of the world would soon become paramount.

4

Destination: The Pole

George Tyson had been prepared to quit the expedition in Greenland.

After what he had seen taking place aboard *Polaris* the week they were at Disco, he decided that if his commission papers failed to arrive on the supply ship, he would pack his bag and disembark. That would be a valid reason for returning home, even though he would be without a job, as it was too late in the whaling season to pick up a sailing assignment.

He surmised things would never work well between Hall and the scientific corps when they got north. Expressions were freely made by the two rebellious scientists that they, not their commander, would get credit for any discoveries of the expedition. My God, this is before they have discovered *anything*, Tyson thought bitterly. What will it be like when they really had something to fight over?

Hall's troubles with Emil Bessels did not surprise Tyson. Before the ship even left New York, he had noted a lack of mutual respect between the two. Bessels had been so outwardly discourteous to his superior officer that Tyson thought Hall would be justified in replacing the arrogant physician scientist before the

expedition started. The well-educated and wealthy Bessels practiced a kind of intellectual and social snobbery toward not only
lowly seamen but his own commander, whom he clearly considered ill-educated and well beneath his own station in life. Had
he been in Hall's place, Tyson would have had no qualms about
ridding his ship of the man that Hall had taken to calling "the
little German dance master."

Other members of the crew seemed bound to go contrary,
too. Whatever Hall wanted done was exactly what they would
not do. All the Germans were sticking together, and even some
of the officers had already decided how far north they would go.
"Queer sort of explorers these!" Tyson scribbled in his journal.

If this crew could not work together after only three weeks
at sea, Tyson knew that matters would only get worse during
the two long winters they were to be stuck in the ice pack. The
resulting deprivations and close quarters would test the loyalty
and stamina of even the most disciplined crew. With the *Polaris*
crew already so divided—explorers versus scientists, sailors versus landlubbers, Americans versus Germans—how in the world
would they survive?

When his commission papers showed up on *Congress*, Tyson
was somewhat disappointed, although not for long. Officially
appointed to an officer's billet, he felt obligated to Hall and to
the Navy Department to help the voyage succeed. He would
give it his very best, and gave no further thought to quitting.

In Hall, Tyson saw a commander who was energetic, perse-
vering, courageous, and, above all, unselfish. He was also beset
with problems and embarrassments from which, at times, there
seemed no way to free himself except by giving up all for which
he had worked so long and so hopefully. Instead, Hall subsumed
all distractions to the single ideal of pushing on to the Pole. He
was a man possessed, and he would not allow his bright hopes of
geographic conquest to be clouded by insubordination or other
human frailties. He dreaded nothing so much as being delayed,
or worse, compelled to return without setting foot at the top of

the world. He was willing to die in his quest, but not to abandon the expedition.

Three days out of Disco, the ship pulled into Upernavik, a small settlement on the upper western shore of Greenland, where Hall decided they would buy more dogs to fill out their complement of sixty needed to pull the sledges they had bought from native builders.

Also, they were looking for one final addition to the crew: hunter and dog driver Hans Hendrik, a Greenland Eskimo who had been a member of two earlier expeditions to the Arctic, one under the command of Hall's nemesis, Dr. Isaac Hayes, in 1860–61, and the other with the respected Dr. Elisha Kent Kane, in 1853–55. Although Hendrik had eventually deserted Kane to take a wife, Hall thought he would be good to have along to drive a dog team, and also to hunt for fresh meat on the tundra. Hall believed that Joe, Hannah, and Hans together would provide the expedition with an ample supply of Eskimo knowledge and skills, attributes he knew might one day be lifesaving.

After *Polaris* anchored in the Upernavik harbor, first mate Chester Hubbard took a small boat ashore to find Hendrik and present him with Hall's offer to join the expedition for a salary of $300 per annum. Hubbard's assignment turned into an overnight mission, since Hendrik had gone to another small settlement a short distance up the coast.

Hendrik accepted Hall's offer but insisted that his family and worldly goods come, too. This included his wife, Merkut, a short, stout woman who, like her husband, spoke no English, and their three children, Augustina, twelve, Tobias, nine, and Succi, four. Crammed into the small launch when Chester returned with the Eskimo family were bags, boxes, and skins, on top of which rode the children, dressed in ragged dogskin clothing. They also brought tents, cooking utensils, tools, implements of Arctic hunting, including a rifle, and four Newfoundland puppies whose eyes could scarcely bear to look at light.

Once they were deposited on deck, second mate William

Morton stepped forward to greet Hans. About the same size as Joe, with similar dark chestnut coloring, Hendrik was clean-shaven and had high cheekbones. The grey-bearded Morton remembered his Eskimo guide from the Kane expedition almost twenty years before, but Morton had aged so in the intervening years that Hans did not recognize him. When Morton pointed to the scars on the Eskimo's right hand and spoke of the gunpowder explosion on the shores of Smith Sound that had caused the burns, Hans finally placed him. Together, traveling by dog sledge, they had left the rest of the Kane expedition and reached Cape Constitution, where they were given their famous glimpse of the body of water they both were convinced was the open Polar Sea.

Hall, infatuated with the notion of the Polar Sea being nothing less than the glorious gateway to the North Pole, was pleased to have as members of the expedition two intrepid men who had seen it.

Reports reached them at Upernavik from a Swedish expedition conducting hydrographic surveys that the ice conditions in the north were still favorable to navigation. Upon hearing that very good news, Hall changed plans. Rather than proceeding westward through Jones Sound and taking a more circuitous route north, he decided to follow in Kane's wake: striking north through Smith Sound, the route Morton and Hans had taken on the way to their discovery.

It seemed like a good omen and outwardly invigorated the expedition commander.

After divine services the day before leaving Upernavik, Hall openly addressed, for the first time, the hostilities that had been simmering aboard ship since Disco.

"That man," he said, pointing at Bessels, "is trying to make a disturbance amongst the company of this ship, and I want it known that I shall not tolerate it. Any more such conduct, Doctor, and I assure you, the authorities back home shall be properly advised."

Bessels glared at the deck, eyes gone cold, lips pressed tightly together.

Typically, the *Polaris* crew was divided in their reactions. American seaman Noah Hayes thought that Hall was simply "asserting his determination to maintain order and obedience to all lawful commands," he wrote that day in his diary. German seaman Joseph Mauch, however, saw it as "insulting Dr. Bessels most severely."

Hall spun on his heel and marched off to his cabin.

In his last dispatch to the Navy Department, on August 24, 1871, Charles Francis Hall sounded like his usual buoyant and determined self:

> *The prospects of the expedition are fine; the weather beautiful, clear, and exceptionally warm. Every preparation has been made to bid farewell to civilization for several years, if need be, to accomplish our purpose. Our coal bunkers are not only full, but we have full ten tons yet on deck, besides wood, planks and rosin in considerable quantities, that can be used for steaming purposes in any emergency. Never was an Arctic expedition more completely fitted out than this. . . . The anchor of Polaris has just been weighed, and not again will it go down till, as I trust and pray, a higher, a far higher, latitude has been attained than ever before by civilized man. Polaris bids adieu to the civilized world. God be with us.*

The complement of *Polaris* was filled. Their final number was now thirty-three: seven officers, two mates, an assistant engineer, carpenter, cook, steward, two firemen to man the boilers, a deck force of ten ordinary seamen, and eight Eskimo men, women and children.

Three days out at sea, Tyson came upon Hall writing furiously. Tyson knew that Hall had brought along his journals from his second Arctic expedition and intended to fill the long, empty hours of the trip working on a new book. Hall had previously authored *Life with the Esquimaux*, published in London, in 1864, about his first expedition in search of the survivors of Sir John Franklin's expedition.

"Writing up your new book, sir?" Tyson asked.

"No, friend Tyson. I left those papers at Disco."

Tyson hesitated, not wanting to press his commander to explain.

The unspoken question registered with Hall, even though he didn't look up. A sort of gloom fell over him. Without lifting his head, he said ominously, "I left them there for safety."

Tyson would later learn that Hall had left his valuable papers with the inspector-general of North Greenland for safekeeping. That day Tyson made no further remark, but he could not help thinking about the incident. To the rest of the world, Hall remained upbeat, a man on a mission. But inside, the events that had transpired with the crew had obviously taken their toll. Tyson had to wonder, did the expedition commander have a premonition of a coming calamity?

Onward they went, north, as Hall was wont to do.

From the deck, the men could see ice gathering into packs in the channels—frighteningly huge packs that, pushed by high winds and seas, could easily collide with the ship. Beyond rose the stark coastal mountains of Greenland, inhospitable to all but the hardiest of God's creatures.

An occasional humpback whale surfaced, regarded them briefly, then flipped its big tail as if in dismissal and dived back down to the deep.

They passed a party of walruses basking on floes close by. While most of the large, ungainly creatures enjoyed their sleep, some of their number remained on watch to give the alarm in case of approaching danger. The vessel made little noise, and the lookouts of the walrus party evidently did not consider her dangerous, for their only sign of apprehension was a more frequent raising and rolling about of their heads. The rest of the company of walrus remained undisturbed except for the occasional one turning over lazily.

Meanwhile, all was excitement aboard *Polaris*. Many had never before seen the animals, and they were intrigued by their appearance and actions. Even those who had often captured them hurried to the side to get a nearer view of the sleepers. Joe, animated by the love of blood sport, readied himself in the bow with his rifle. It was proposed to Hall to man a boat and attempt the capture of at least one of the walruses, but he decided that this would delay the vessel too much.

Joe and several others took pot shots at the animals, who came suddenly awake. None were hurt, since it is almost impossible to kill a walrus from the front, unless one was lucky enough to hit an eye. Their skulls are very thick, except on the crown of the head, which is a difficult point to strike.

The sky was at times hypnotic. Crew members fixed their gaze upward as wide plumes of light, shaped like tornadoes, hung frozen overhead, turning into greenish, shivering bands of light strung out seemingly amid the stars, then exploding in great white clusters across the horizon.

Medieval scientists mistakenly believed the lights were reflections of sunlight and named the phenomenon for Aurora, Roman goddess of the dawn. It would not be known until the advent of high-powered, modern telescopes that the disturbances are caused by solar storms—solar flares that release bursts of energy into space. The term *aurora borealis* refers to lights in the northern hemisphere—or "northern lights."

Occasionally, amid the white and emerald slashes of light, the sky turned a blood red, leaving the crew of *Polaris* speechless, as it looked like an earthly event rather than a light show fifty miles high. Roman emperor Tiberius, upon seeing such an aurora, had been convinced a nearby port was burning and sent help to put out the blaze. To Eskimos, the dancing lights were spirits on their way to heaven.

Under sail and steam, in spite of floating ice and occasional fog, *Polaris* reached Cape Alexander and the mouth of Smith

Sound on August 27. Ahead lay three hundred miles of narrow waterway between Ellesmere Island and Greenland—waters often clogged with ice and whipped by violent gales that could send ice crushing into the hull of a ship, as both Kane and Hayes had learned. Both explorers, unable to navigate the rough waters, had been forced to drop back, leave their ships at anchor, and carry out the remainder of their expeditions to the north by sledge and small boat.

At this point Sidney Buddington began to outwardly display a skepticism toward their mission that would soon widen the breach between him and the expedition's commander.

To his wife and friends prior to departure, the sailing master had admitted he did not share Hall's confidence that the expedition could reach the Pole. Indeed, he had no intention of taking the kind of chances—with the ship, but especially with his own hide—that such an effort would require. He knew exactly how far he would go, and what he would do and not do. Why he hadn't shared these thoughts with Hall was obvious. Not only was the three-year sailing-master assignment well paying, but all were hoping they would receive lucrative congressional bonuses. Buddington wanted to make the highly publicized trip, but in relative comfort and safety, and at his own speed. Increasingly he ridiculed Hall behind his back. He was always most solicitous to his commander, while sneakily deriding Hall as a novice to the entire crew. It was a grave breach of naval ethics and discipline.

Buddington strongly recommended taking the ship into Port Foulke—Hayes' winter quarters a decade earlier—eight miles northeast of Cape Alexander, and having the expedition continue toward the Pole by sledge. That they were still hundreds of miles away didn't matter. He would stay with the ship, and the others who were so interested in exploring could forge ahead on foot.

To Tyson's relief, Hall refused. With clear water ahead, the commander decreed, *Polaris* would continue north as far as possible.

Just before midnight the following evening, the first mate

came down below deck and reported an "impassable barrier of ice" ahead. When Tyson came up a few minutes later to assume his watch, he found the vessel had slowed down. Buddington was in a fearful state of excitement at the prospect of going farther north.

Tyson climbed to the crow's nest and looked around. He saw a great deal of ice coming toward them, pushed by a light northerly wind. It looked bad ahead, but off to the west he saw a dark streak that appeared to be open water.

Tyson knew they would have plenty of light to navigate their way around the dangerous ice, since at this time of year the sun was setting around 11:00 P.M. and rising again at 1:00 A.M. He came down and reported to Hall that the ship could skirt around the ice by sailing a little to the south and then steer west-northwest. By then, Tyson said, they should be in the open water he had spotted from aloft. Over vehement objections from Buddington—"It's damn nonsense"—Hall gave Tyson permission to try.

In the next few hours, Tyson, selecting the weakest points in the ice to attack and taking advantage of the most favorable openings, managed to get the vessel over to the west side of the sound. There, as he had seen from aloft, he found a passage of open water varying from one to four miles in width. The obstructing ice they had avoided was thick—from ten to forty feet—revealing that it had been formed on shore before breaking free. As Tyson knew, ice that thick never formed in open water.

By the end of his watch at four o'clock, they had reached just above 80 degrees north. Hall was so gratified that he took Tyson's hand and shook it firmly. Rejuvenated by their progress, Hall said he hoped to get still farther north before having to stop for the winter.

Tyson ran into Buddington on deck. The sailing master looked chagrined and disappointed, and he was searching for Hall to have a talk with him. Tyson walked past without saying a word. Knowing the truth now, that Sidney Buddington was a coward, Tyson had resolved to avoid him as much as possible.

Polaris stopped briefly a half hour later. While Hall went ashore and coasted around in a small boat, Buddington summoned Tyson to the wheelhouse on the aft deck.

"Why is Captain Hall ashore?" Tyson asked before Buddington said anything.

"To look for a harbor," Buddington said smugly. "We cannot go any farther north. There is no open water."

"Yes, sir, there is plenty of open water," Tyson countered. "It is your duty to put this vessel as far north as possible before we undertake sledge journeys."

"Well, now, see here," stammered Buddington, perhaps tempted to dress down Tyson but then thinking better of it. "We must not go any farther north. We have gone far enough. We will never get back if we go any farther."

When Hall returned, he gave orders to move on, north. When they got to Cape George Back, the ice forced them to the northeast, and they crossed Kennedy Channel and then over to Cape Lieber, where fog descended on them about fifteen miles from land. Here they slowed, and a copper cylinder containing a record of their progress was thrown overboard, as mandated by their official orders and in the event things went badly.

Continuing north, they began having trouble forging through the ice. They had gained latitude 81 degrees, 35 minutes—farther north than any known ship. At this point, sailing in unknown waters, their charts were no longer of any help.

Meanwhile, Buddington was acting like a spoiled child. The sailing master was complaining to everyone—even the Eskimo hunters—and cursing behind their backs anyone he thought instrumental in convincing Hall to take the ship north.

They were now in the area where Morton and Hans had made their discovery.

Where is the open sea? Tyson thought as he searched the horizon from aloft.

All hands not working below were up on deck looking hard

for the same thing: the open Polar Sea, as reported by Morton and Hans, who were also on deck. So was Dr. Emil Bessels, who had announced that his wind and temperature readings in connection with the fog showed an indication of open sea farther north. Moist, foggy air from the north, the scientist contended, would not have passed over ice.

But it soon became sadly clear to everyone that there was no open sea, but only a stretch of water forty-five miles across. They were not deceived because they had sailed right across it. The surrounding land was plainly seen because it was quite high in elevation.

Aboard *Polaris* this day, everyone realized Morton and Hans had made a mistake. No one was surprised that their eyes had played tricks on them if it had been at all foggy when they were here. In reduced visibility they would not have been able to see across to the other side.

It was not the gateway to the promised land but a land-locked *bay*.

Hall, recovering from his disappointment, named it Polaris Bay.

Finding a channel not far from the mouth of the bay, they sailed on. The channel, some seventeen miles wide, was obstructed by heavy ice. Tyson thought they would get through, but from the long faces he saw on deck, it was apparent that some of the men would rather they not try.

Hall named Robeson Channel after the Secretary of the Navy. A good name, all agreed, for without Secretary Robeson's support and goodwill, they wouldn't be in these waters never before parted by the keel of any ship.

All night, surrounded by ice fields and fog, they slowly worked forward. The full force of the current was now felt, and the ship labored hard to make progress. To increase the difficulties of navigation, the fog again settled and shut out everything from view.

They fastened *Polaris* to an ice floe and waited all the next day for an opening in the weather and the ice. A second cylinder containing a dated dispatch giving their position was thrown overboard.

The crew grew perceptibly nervous, not unlike what ancient mariners must have felt as they ventured into unknown seas. "I believe," Tyson wrote in his journal, "some of them think we are going over the edge of the world."

Finally, at 7:30 P.M., the fog lifted. *Polaris* headed through broken ice toward the eastern coast, where they spotted a possible harbor. Anchoring out, Tyson joined Hall in a small boat and went ashore to see if it would be serviceable. Although suitable for a comfortable winter's home, the harbor proved too shallow for the ship.

Upon their return, with the ice pressing heavily upon the hull, Hall ordered a quantity of provisions to be taken out and put on the ice—in case something happened and they were forced to abandon ship. They waited out the night.

Under way again early the next morning, after bringing the supplies back aboard, they soon found the ice so compacted that it was impossible to force the vessel through. As far as the eye could see was impenetrable ice from one horizon to the other. At 6:00 A.M. on August 30, 1871, *Polaris* attained her highest northern latitude: 82 degrees, 16 minutes.

Although Charles Francis Hall did not know it, no land lay between him and his goal. The only obstacles were the constantly shifting pack, with its immense pressure ridges and hummocks, sculpted mounds formed by the aggregation of ice piled up by repeated pressure, and a solid sea of ice extending four hundred and seventy miles—all the way to the Pole.

II

Thank God Harbor

5

Providence Berg

Unable to maintain its northernmost position against a driving current and the pressure of the southward-drifting ice pack, *Polaris* steamed a few miles south before anchoring behind some icebergs for protection from a blowing gale.

Hall convened a council of his top officers. "Gentlemen, the turn of the season is close at hand," he said. "Do we seek a safe harbor at once and go into winter quarters, or do we attempt to proceed farther north?"

He gave no outward sign as to which option he favored.

Buddington weighed in first, strongly urging, not surprisingly, to take immediate refuge. On their way they had passed what appeared to be the entrance to a large bay some miles south of their present position. He pressed Hall to turn around and secure a winter anchorage there without delay.

Hall turned to Tyson, who was thinking that Buddington ought to have stayed home given his fears. The sailing master's highly praised seagoing experience—although he had never been farther north than 76 degrees—bore no relation to his courage and enthusiasm, both sadly lacking.

"Sir, we have not come all this way to seek refuge at first

opportunity," Tyson said, directing his comments to Hall and purposefully ignoring the sailing master. "Our mission is to get as far north as possible."

"That it is, Mr. Tyson," Hall agreed enthusiastically. "How might we do that?"

"I have just come from aloft," Tyson said.

From the deck of *Polaris*, the radius of sight was limited—no more than seven miles on a clear day. This morning it had not been possible to see any open water from the deck. Observing from a perch fifty feet up the main masthead, though, had provided Tyson a clear picture of what lay ahead for fifteen or twenty miles. He and first mate Hubbard Chester were the only ones who regularly climbed to the crow's nest.

"The channel is closed on the west side, where we are now, and up the middle," Tyson said. "But the wind has opened up the northeast. I saw an opening. We can go that direction."

North—the right direction.

"I urge you, sir, to return to the north," Tyson went on. "Add another two or three degrees to your record. Get us a hundred or two hundred miles closer to the Pole."

Hall's eyes lit up at the prospect, but he had obviously not yet made his decision.

The other assembled officers gave their opinions. Dr. Emil Bessels thought they should look for a harbor near their present location, on the west side of the channel. The two other scientists, Frederick Meyer and Richard Bryan, agreed.

Hall asked Hubbard Chester for his opinion. The experienced first mate, strong in spirit as in body, did not waver. "North, sir," Chester said without hesitation. "I agree with Mr. Tyson, there is an opening on the east side. I can't say we'll make it, but we should try to get over there and then as far north as we can."

Buddington turned his back, muttering between clenched teeth. "I'll be damned if we'll move from here." He stamped from the cabin.

Hall followed him and stood some time talking to him on deck.

When the commander returned, he told Tyson and Chester to see to the landing of some provisions ashore in case something happened during the night. That was all—nothing as to what decision, if any, had been reached concerning the ship's course.

Later that afternoon, Hall approached Tyson on deck and asked him more about going north. While every sign indicated he personally favored it, Hall seemed worried. Tyson could only guess he wished to avoid offending his sailing master.

"Sir, I should gain nothing by our going another two or three degrees," Tyson said, "but it will be a great credit to you to do so."

Since he had received his commission papers in Disco, Tyson had felt a stronger sense of responsibility for the expedition. At the same time, he wasn't entirely comfortable speaking his mind about Buddington, so soured had he become on the sailing master, who he knew had neither heart nor soul in the expedition. Tyson did not wish for Hall or anyone to misinterpret him in any way. He did not want to be seen as seeking a position to which he hadn't been rightfully appointed.

Tyson parted from his commander feeling they had gone as far north as they would that year, and his intuition proved correct. The next day *Polaris* was ordered to steam south, nearer inshore to find a safe harbor.

Tyson was disappointed and surprised that Hall had accepted Buddington's advice to turn tail. The extent to which Hall was able to overlook insolence and incompetence in those who owed him duty and allegiance was something Tyson had never before seen from a commander at sea. Was it a strength in this good man, he wondered, or a fatal flaw?

That night, they pushed over to the west shore and got beset by ice and drifted to the south. From the crow's nest, Tyson saw that the wind had opened up the east side, as he had predicted.

Had they headed over there they would have had clear steaming north.

Before they were clear of ice, they lowered a boat, and Tyson joined Hall in trying to get ashore to find an anchorage. They located a natural harbor but could not get into it, and they gave up after several tries. Hall named the place Repulse Harbor.

The ice suddenly set them free, and *Polaris* steamed through open waters, this time heading to the east side. From the crow's nest, Chester hollered excitedly that there was an open channel along the east coast as far north as he could see. But there was no more discussion about heading farther north. The first mate was convinced that had Tyson or someone else been sailing master, things would have been different.

On the east side, they came across an extensive bay and anchored out. As a winter home, it was by no means a snug anchorage. It was, however, inside the line of the main current, and was somewhat sheltered from sea conditions by a cape four miles to the northwest of the ship's position. Immediately before them lay a harbor formed by a large iceberg to the south and a little indentation on the coast to the north.

On September 7, *Polaris* steamed in nearer to shore. The officers held a brief conversation about whether to go over to the other side of the ten-mile-wide bay to look for a better anchorage, but Buddington declared that the ship should not move from where it was, and Hall relented.

Polaris was brought around behind the iceberg, aground in thirteen fathoms of water, and secured to it. Four hundred and fifty feet long, three hundred feet broad, and sixty feet high, the great iceberg lay about two hundred and fifty yards from shore and about one hundred yards inside the ebb current of the strong tide that would otherwise have tried to push them southward daily.

Their latitude was 81 degrees, 38 minutes. They had been, at one point, nearly fifty miles farther north.

As *Polaris* had approached shore, they almost had a potentially disastrous explosion on board. The fireman on duty had allowed the water in the steam boilers to get dangerously low. Low water was one of the most serious emergencies that could arise in a boiler room. Safe operation of a fire-tube boiler of the type that powered *Polaris* required that the tubes be submerged in water at all times. If the water level fell below the tops of any of the tubes, they could overheat and rupture. The result would be what old-time steam-plant operators called a "violent rearrangement of the boiler room." When boilers "blew up," nobody could say in which direction the red-hot boiler parts would go during an explosion. A vessel's hull could be ruptured as surely as if hit amidships by deadly cannon fire.

The problem caused by the inattentive water tender was discovered just in time. With that close call in mind, the crew worked through a blinding snowstorm, unloading stores on shore so that if the vessel were struck by a berg or suddenly lost in any other way, they would not be stranded if they had to quickly abandon ship. Also, a fire hole was cut in the ice near the *Polaris* for the ample supply of seawater in event of a shipboard fire.

That Sunday at divine services, Hall announced he had named their winter quarters Thank God Harbor, in recognition of "His kind providence" over them so far. He also named the iceberg to which *Polaris* was protectively fastened "Providence Berg."

Before long, Hall sought out Tyson and admitted he had erred in not pushing farther north. They were too far from the Pole to reach it by sledge that winter. "Next summer, we shall make desperate exertions to gain the ground we lost," he promised.

After a week, while one party was out surveying and another off hunting, Tyson went exploring to see what the country was like where they would be spending their long winter night. The landscape was of a dull neutral tint, a sort of cold gray. It would before long, he knew, be all of another color: white from snow and ice.

The coastal hills were from nine hundred to thirteen hundred feet high. They had great scars and cracks in them caused by wind, weather, frost, and ice. At the base of the hills were deposited large amounts of debris—stones, sand, and great scales from rocks that had been split off.

There had been no snow on the hills when they arrived, and what fell the first few days ran off and dried up fast. The mountain ranges, which could be seen in the interior, also appeared clear of snow. The land that surrounded them was bare of ice and snow except for the white ribbon of a distant glacier off to the south that swept around in a wide circuit and fell into the wide bay north of *Polaris*.

Tyson found the remains of an Eskimo summer camp, consisting of stones lying on the ground in a circle. While Eskimos lived in igloos in the winter, they used tents in the summer. Their tents were made of sealskin, and the stones were placed upon their outer edges to keep the skin taut over the ridge and to prevent the wind from entering or overturning them. Upon removing their temporary homes, Eskimos were accustomed to taking down the pole that supported a tent and dragging the skin from beneath the stones, while leaving the latter in position. There were several of these circles of stones near each other, proving to Tyson that quite a large party of Eskimos had passed part of a summer here. Nothing indicated the length of time since the camp had been occupied. Perhaps they used to come here for the summer, he speculated, and had since migrated permanently to the south. He found some spearheads made of walrus teeth, some pieces of bone with holes bored in them, and a small piece of copper once used as a needle. Among the ashes in the fire pit he found a piece of meteoric iron, their means of obtaining fire.

Nearby, the scientists had built a small structure out of scrap wood. Equipped with a coal-burning stove, the Observatory was a place where they could conduct weather, geological, and other observations. Its framework had already been reinforced once, as a stiff gale almost shook it down after only a couple of days. Inside the one-room shelter were various measuring instruments, including a standard thermometer, wet and dry bulb psychrometers, maximum and minimum thermometers, and an ozonometer. The first three were read hourly, the latter three once every twenty-four hours. An anemometer was fastened on an upright post, frozen into a barrel to keep it firm. Solar and dry radiation thermometers were also used, as was a barometer.

On his way back to the ship, Tyson spotted large flocks of brent geese sporting in the water, and occasionally a seal would raise its head in the vicinity of the ship to watch the intruders upon its feeding grounds.

Polaris, the North Star, was seen on September 21, for the first time since the establishment of winter quarters, and a large halo was observed encircling the sun.

Bessels and Chester, traveling in the company of Joe and Hans with a team of eight dogs, returned from a weeklong hunting excursion. They brought back on a sleigh the greater part of a musk ox that they had killed. The meat, when cut into steaks and fried, turned out to be very good, without the strong musk scent that male oxen emit when in rut. It tasted like fine beef.

Everyone was pleased by the fresh meat, no one more so than Hall, who understood from his time with the Eskimos its value in warding off scurvy, a disease caused by a prolonged deficiency of fresh fruits and vegetables in the diet, and a serious threat to the well-being of Arctic explorers. Often fatal, the disease is characterized by bodily weakness, inflamed gums, loose teeth, swollen and tender joints, hemorrhaging, and anemia.

Tyson continued to be amazed by his commander. For all his traits, both good and bad, Hall had a most pleasant way of getting along with the men. When it came to his attention that less food was being served in the enlisted men's mess than the officers' mess—on orders from Sidney Buddington—Hall immediately increased their rations, and instructed that henceforth everyone would eat the same food and in the same amount at both messes; two hot meals a day were to be served. "The American government is paying for this expedition," he explained. "We will all live as brothers, and eat and drink alike on this ship."

Highly pleased, the men prepared a letter of thanks, which they sent to the commander's cabin. Signed by the entire deck force and other enlisted crew, it read:

> *The men desire to publicly tender their thanks to Capt. C. F. Hall for his late kindness, not, however, that we were suffering want, but for the fact that it manifests a disposition to treat us as reasonable men, possessing intelligence to appreciate respect and yield it only where merited; and he need never fear but that it will be our greatest pleasure to so live that he can implicitly rely on our service in any duty or emergency.*

Hall was much pleased at receiving the letter from the men, and in response he wrote a letter of his own and had it posted below:

> *Sirs: The reception of your letter of thanks to me I acknowledge with a heart that deeply feels and fully appreciates the kindly feeling that has prompted you to this act. I need not assure you that your commander has, and ever will have, a lively interest in your welfare. You have left your homes, friends, and country; indeed you have bid a long farewell for a time to the whole civilized world, for the purpose of aiding me in discovering the mysterious, hidden parts of the earth. I therefore must and shall care for you as a prudent father cares for his faithful children.*
>
> *Your commander, C. F. Hall*
> *United States North Polar Expedition*
> *In winter-quarters, Thank God Harbor*
> *Sept. 24, 1871*

At the same time, Hall had a streak of piety. Not long after this exchange of letters, he overheard one of the men cursing another. Severely condemning the expressions, he issued an order forbidding all profane or vulgar language, probably a first aboard a naval vessel.

A violent snowstorm commenced on September 27 and continued for thirty-six hours. The ice began to pack around the ship. Due to the pressure on the hull, more provisions were taken ashore. They were quickly covered in snow, as were the provisions that had been offloaded earlier. The men were ordered to haul them across the flat ground and place them in the lee of a hill. When the storm abated, a house would be built to shelter them.

Ice piled up about the vessel in all manner of shapes. The giant iceberg, which had up until then steadfastly maintained its position, moved in toward the shore. The ice between it and the vessel was broken by long cracks and raised into hummocks. The pressure brought upon the ship was great, as was apparent from the strain upon her frame. Had *Polaris* not been strengthened and specially fitted for Arctic service, she would have been crushed. When the pressure ceased, it was found that the storm had forced the berg in toward the shore one hundred yards, and the ship fifty yards.

When the storm abated, a few seals were seen, and some of the men went out hunting them but got none. A white fox they saw also escaped them. Arctic foxes were the most cunning animals any of the men had ever seen, and proved difficult to shoot or trap.

The ice became so hardened, even where there had once been open water, that Hall began preparing a sledge party to go north. He intended to probe inland, preliminary to a more extended journey in the spring. Hall wanted to get an idea of the best route north, hoping to find better ways than over the icy floes and hummocks of the straits.

Tyson came across Hall ashore, not far from the ship. It was a rare opportunity to speak to him alone. Ever since Tyson had advised Hall to head farther north, Buddington always made a point to be alongside them so as to overhear any discussion.

"I would like to reach a higher latitude than Parry before I get back," Hall said.

More than forty years earlier British explorer Sir Edward Parry had set out by sledge for the North Pole. Before turning back, he reached latitude 82 degrees, 45 minutes north—a proximity to the Pole not attained since by white explorers.

"I would like to have you along, but—" Hall abruptly stopped. He pointed at the sailing master strutting on deck like a rooster. "I find he is a man I cannot place any trust in," he continued, a tinge of sadness in his voice. "I have been close to putting him off duty for his conduct—stealing food and drinking. I have decided to give him one last chance. If he does not conduct himself well in my absence, I will suspend him upon my return."

Tyson said nothing; he could see how the matter pained the commander. Tyson had suspected Buddington of drinking on several occasions since leaving Greenland. He had seen him wobbling on deck with unsteady steps—Hall certainly had, too—and knew that no good would come of it.

"I don't know how to leave him with the ship in my absence," Hall went on. "If something happens and the vessel should break out of the ice, it would be better for you to be aboard to assist with the ship."

Hall explained that if the ice broke up and the ship was forced from her position, steam should be gotten up as quickly as possible and no time lost in getting the vessel back to her former position, where the sledge party would return to.

"I understand, sir," Tyson said.

Hall presented another scenario: *Polaris* might end up stuck in the ice on a southward drift—as had happened to other Arctic expeditions—and be unable to return for the sledge party. In that case, Hall said evenly, he and the other men ashore would fend for themselves, and the *Polaris* crew should care for themselves and the ship.

Tyson knew that Buddington wasn't the only *Polaris* officer Hall didn't trust. The commander had confided in him that he didn't think Dr. Emil Bessels was qualified or equipped for the position he had been assigned. Tyson knew, as did everyone else on board, that the commander and the ship's doctor did not get along, and for the most part only barely tolerated one another in the course of their official duties. The rest of the time they were like two alpha wolves eyeing the other.

"I would like to go on the sledge trip, of course," said Tyson, intending not to reveal just how much he wanted to go. "I am willing to remain and take what care of the ship I can."

"Thank you, my friend," Hall said humbly. "I want you to know again that you were right. Had I listened to you we would right now be much farther north than we are."

The next day, Buddington surprised Tyson by asking him what he and Hall had discussed.

"I couldn't tell you," Tyson answered evasively.

"I'm in a helluva scrape, but something will turn up to get me out of this," Buddington said. "You'll see if it don't."

"What's going to turn up?" Tyson asked stiffly.

"Well, you'll see," Buddington said, slurring slightly. "I have been in a good many hard scrapes, and always something turned up to get me out."

Buddington had been drinking again.

"Considering where we are stuck for the indefinite future," Tyson said, "you might find this one harder to get out of."

"Oh, I'll get out of it. That old son of a bitch won't live long."

Following a week's worth of preparations, in which Hall had everything they were going to take weighed so as to not over-burden them, they seemed ready at last. They had outfitted with provisions and other supplies a single sledge—fitted with wagon wheels in the event they came to areas without enough snow—to be pulled by twelve dogs.

On the evening of October 10, Tyson and some of the men helped haul the heavy-laden sledge up the steep hill at the top of the promontory. They stood by as the sledge drove off across the plains, north by east, dogs baying woefully and the Eskimo driver cracking a whip overhead.

After the other men had returned to the ship, Tyson watched the sledge party become smaller against the white, frozen backdrop. He watched for as long as he could, then turned and went slowly back to the ship stuck in the ice pack.

6

"How Do You Spell Murder?"

Even after all the preparation and packing, Tyson had no doubt that his commander had forgotten something. Charles Francis Hall was, he knew, rather peculiar that way.

The day after the sledge party departed, Hans returned alone on foot with a missive from Hall. He was to bring a second sledge and more dogs so that they could divide up their heavy load. They had also forgotten not one item but several, and Hall and the rest of the party, consisting of first mate Chester Hubbard and Joe, were waiting five miles off for Hans to return with them.

Among other things, they needed more candles, dog lines, and coffee. Also, Hall wrote, "Do not forget my bear-skin mittens, which I left behind by mistake. While Hans is absent, we are to go on a hunt for musk-oxen. Hasten Hans back without the loss of a moment. May God be with you all."

The sun set behind the mountains on October 17 and would not be seen again that winter from the ship. For the next few days the only way to observe the slimmest patch of sun was to venture to the crest of a high hill. Then even those rays soon sank from view.

As the sun departed, the perpetual twilight deepened.

The crew began banking up snow around the ship to keep the frigid winds from slicing through the berthing compartments. They started by cutting blocks of snow from an icy bank and sledding them over to the vessel. When they were finished some weeks later, a wall up to eight feet thick and as high as the top of the ship's bulwarks would be in place, with a flight of snow steps leading up to the port-side deck. Blocks of freshwater ice from rain and snowfall were also cut from the nearby berg and transported to the icehouse aboard ship; from there, it would be melted on a stove, as needed, for drinking water. Other men worked on fixing up a canvas awning to cover the main deck. When it was completed, an opening was made in the awning at the top of the snow steps just over the forward gangway.

Stores of all types had been moved ashore—coal, clothing, guns, ammunition, and a portion of everything that would be most needed. They were packed in a ramshackle shed built mostly by Tyson. It could have been made stronger with more lumber, but Buddington refused Tyson's request for additional wood from onboard ship.

In Hall's absence, Buddington's behavior grew worse. Dr. Emil Bessels had a supply of high-proof alcohol, brought aboard for medicinal and specimen-preserving purposes, that was mysteriously declining. Bessels decided to set a trap and confront the culprit. One morning when everyone else was outside busy at chores, the doctor hid in the pantry near the locker where the alcohol was kept. In short order, he heard footsteps and the locker door swinging open. He sprang out of the pantry.

Before him stood Sidney Buddington, uncorked bottle in hand, ready for a morning eye-opener. Bessels grabbed for the bottle, but Buddington refused to let go.

"You are a drunk and a thief!" Bessels screamed. "You are unfit!"

Buddington grabbed the smaller man by his shirt. Pinning the doctor against the bulkhead with one arm, Buddington

The last message written by Captain Hall, while on his final sledge journey. It was addressed to Secretary of the Navy Robeson on October 20, 1871, four days before Hall took ill. (Smithsonian Institution)

"How Do You Spell Murder?" 75

tipped the bottle to his lips with the other. "I will have a drink whenever I want." He smacked his lips. "And *you* mind your own business!"

Bessels managed to free himself and darted off.

Hall's sledge party returned on October 24. They had been gone two weeks.

Tyson, who was helping bank snow around the ship, shook hands with Hall.

"How are you, Captain?" Tyson asked.

"Never better," an exuberant Hall replied.

The commander seemed invigorated rather than exhausted from his travels. Although they had hoped to go a hundred miles, Hall said they had made only fifty due to the configuration of the land. Nonetheless, he was encouraged.

"I think I can go to the Pole on this shore," an excited Hall told Tyson.

Hall went around to every man working on the ice and warmly shook his hand like a long-lost relative. He and his party then went aboard ship, and Tyson and the other men went back to shoveling snow.

Inside the fifteen-by-eight-foot upper cabin that Hall shared with five others since giving up his stateroom to serve as a winter galley, William Morton helped the commander remove his wet boots and outer fur clothing.

Hall said he was not hungry, but he took a cup of coffee brought to him by the steward, John Herron, a small, quiet Englishman.

Morton took away Hall's wet clothing and went to get a shift of fresh clothing from the commander's private storeroom. When he returned not more than twenty minutes later, the second mate found Hall looking pale and vomiting. Morton now noticed Dr. Emil Bessels in the cabin.

"What's the matter?" Morton asked.

"A foul stomach," replied Hall.

Morton helped Hall into fresh clothes and began washing his feet.

Hall had sent for Hannah, who now entered the cabin. She had earlier gone onto the ice to welcome back her husband and the commander, whom she lovingly referred to as "Father Hall." She had found both pleased with their journey. Hall told her he would "finish next spring," which Hannah construed to mean that he felt confident of reaching the Pole.

"I've been sick," Hall told her.

"What is it, Father?" she asked worriedly. "Did you get cold?"

"It's my stomach. I'll be better in the morning. Hannah, make things ready for my next journey. I will leave in two days. I will take Tyson and Chester, Joe and Hans."

Hannah and Morton helped Hall into his bunk.

An hour later, Tyson entered the cabin. Word had reached him on the ice that Hall had taken ill.

"What's wrong, Captain?" Tyson asked.

"Sick to my stomach. I think I'm bilious."

"Would an emetic would do you good?" It seemed logical to Tyson that if something was upsetting his stomach, it should come up.

"An emetic may be called for," Hall agreed. He had vomited already, he said, but felt the need to further empty his stomach.

"No, that will not do," Bessels said, striding importantly to Hall's bedside. "It will weaken you."

Hall, trying to get comfortable, winced and held his stomach in obvious pain. He weakly waved a hand at Tyson. "I believe we can take *Polaris* north to eighty-five degrees next summer. From there it will be a comparatively short distance to the Pole. Three hundred miles—we can do it by sledge. I wish to go back to explore further right away, and I want to take you with me this time. We will be going north in two days."

Tyson judged Hall's offer to join him a sincere one, and he felt gratified. But the commander did not look as if he would be going anywhere soon.

Before Tyson's eyes, Hall grew rapidly worse.

After complaining of the pain in his stomach and weakness in his legs, he dropped into unconsciousness. Bessels took Hall's pulse and announced it was irregular—from sixty to eighty beats per minute. The doctor described his patient's condition as "comatose."

Tyson had never seen anything like it in all his years going to sea. One moment this healthy, vital man had been returning from an expedition, excited, invigorated, and the next he was sick to his stomach and weak and now—*comatose?*

Bessels applied a mustard poultice to Hall's legs and chest.

In less than half an hour, Hall regained consciousness. In examining him, Bessels found that the commander's left arm and side were paralyzed. Hall complained of numbness on the left side of his face and tongue, too, and he had difficulty swallowing.

The doctor gave Hall a powerful cathartic; the laxative consisted of a dose of castor oil and three or four drops of croton oil.

Bessels motioned Morton and Tyson to follow him into the passageway. "I believe the captain has suffered an attack of apoplexy," the doctor said. "The attack is serious. I don't believe the captain will recover."

In his entry in the official journal of the expedition, Bessels would write in his neat, studious handwriting that he believed Hall had suffered "an apoplectical insult"—or stroke. He described the commander's paralysis as of both motion and sensation. He continued to prepare his fellow officers for the worst: the death of their commander.

About that the doctor would be correct: Charles Francis Hall was dying, although, not from an apoplectical insult or anything of the kind.

Hall slept for several hours that night.

The ship's two mates, William Morton and Hubbard Chester, took turns sitting up with their commander. Morton had the first shift; Chester relieved him at 2:00 A.M.

Chester had a difficult time believing that the sick man lying before him was the same individual with whom he had just spent two weeks exploring by sledge. He had enjoyed his time with Hall, whom he found to be an energetic and compassionate leader. The traveling had been bad, however. The snow was deep and soft in the beginning, and later, they came upon places with little snow over which they had struggled to pull the sledges. Their progress had also been blocked at times by mounds of ice and hampered by fog and freezing rain. Everyone, Hall included, had to assist with pulling the sledges. They had made six encampments on the way up, and stopped overnight at several of them on the way back. The Eskimos had built an igloo at each stop to provide protection from the adverse elements, and one night they all nearly suffocated inside their shelter. As was customary, after entering the snow hut for the night, they securely blocked up the entrance by a large wall of snow. But they had neglected to make a hole for ventilation, and the igloo, being very well built, was perfectly airtight. When, hours later, the kerosene lamp and candle went out, Hall attempted to relight them only to have the matches go out immediately upon being struck. While Hall was trying to account for this oddity, he began to feel the suffocating effects of the de-oxygenated air and called out, "Kick down the door," which Joe at once obeyed.

In six days they reached a point that Hall named Cape Brevoort after a longtime friend and Arctic supporter, J. Carson Brevoort of Brooklyn. It was located at the northern tip of a large bay that Hall christened Newman's Bay in honor of The Reverend Newman who had shown such kindness to *Polaris* and her crew. They could go no higher with the sledges due to thin ice, but they walked across the frozen bay. On the other side, near the beach where it could be seen by someone landing by ship, they built up a cairn and buried a cylinder containing a record of their journey. Joe and Hans shot at several seals, but were not successful in securing them. Traces of musk oxen had been seen, and also foxes, lemmings, an owl, and a few hawks. A large litter of Newfoundland pups had been devoured by the dog teams as soon as the pups were born. Leaving the Eskimos with the dogs and gear, Hall and Chester had walked north for eight hours in the deepening twilight. They reached the headlands of another bay, and then ascended to the high ground. From that vantage point, they could see the land heading off to the east, and the eastern shore of Robeson Channel, with a prominent cape, beyond which they could see nothing. On the west side they could see land stretching up for sixty miles. That, Hall said, was the direction he would go on his next trip. After spending that night at their encampment, they headed back in the morning. Hall's health, on the journey, had been first-rate. The lowest temperature they had endured was 25 degrees below zero, but they had adequate clothing and sleeping gear.

When they had arrived back at *Polaris*, Chester had gone below to the cabin he shared with Buddington, Tyson, Morton, engineer Alvin Odell, and Joe and Hannah. His first priority was to clean the party's sleeping bags and make sure they got properly dried so mold didn't set in. During the sledge trip, their bags, vestments, and virtually every article of clothing they wore had become saturated with moisture and frozen stiff, as they hadn't carried enough fuel with them to keep a fire going to dry them at each stop. They adopted a plan of taking their smaller articles, such as mittens and socks, to bed with them. By placing them inside their sleeping bags next to their bodies, the items became partially dry by morning. Whenever they unpacked their sleeping gear, the bags had to be worked a long time before they could be unrolled, so solidly frozen were they.

Below, Chester was pleased to find the interior of the ship at a comfortable sixty-five degrees; each compartment had its own small, coal-burning stove. Going about his chores to secure their equipment, Chester was surprised to hear, an hour later, that the commander was sick in bed.

When Hall awoke the next morning, his paralysis was mostly gone.

He ate some arrowroot for breakfast; and the smooth, starchy food went down well, although he complained of continued numbness of the tongue. Emil Bessels came in and administered another cathartic.

After the doctor left, Hall asked to see Joe. The Eskimo came into the cabin looking concerned for his old friend.

"Very sick last night," Hall told him.

"What is the matter?" asked Joe, who knew Hall had a good constitution. He had rarely seen him sick in the past ten years.

"Don't know. Drank a cup of coffee when we came back. In a little while I was very sick and vomiting."

Hall signaled Joe to come closer. When he did, Hall lowered his voice. "Now, Joe, did you drink bad coffee?"

"No. Cook gave me cup. No feel sick."

"There was bad stuff in my coffee. Felt it after a while. It burned my stomach."

A little later, when Hannah came to help with the commander, he also spoke of the cup of coffee that had been brought up from the galley for him.

"The coffee was too sweet," he told her. "It made me vomit."

Hannah regularly made coffee and tea for the commander. She knew he liked one lump of sugar to a cup. "Too much sugar in it, Father?" she asked.

"Not sugar. Never tasted anything in coffee like that before."

That evening, Hall again became very sick, and was in great pain from his constant efforts to vomit. He had a restless night, and hardly any appetite in the morning. He asked for some arrowroot, but when it was prepared for him he would not eat it. Instead, he had a few bites of preserved fruits—peaches and pineapple. He was also very thirsty.

When Bessels came in to see him, Hall complained of being chilled. The doctor checked and found Hall had a temperature.

Next to Hall's bunk, Bessels heated some little white crystals in a small glass bowl. He carefully mixed it in a clear solution that came from a bottle in his medicine bag, filled a hypodermic with the compound mixture, and gave Hall an injection in the leg. The doctor said it was quinine, a standard nineteenth-century treatment for fever.

Hall's temperature began to level off and returned to normal.

The following day, Hall's temperature remained normal and his appetite improved, but the numbness in his tongue returned. Bessels gave him another injection.

The next day, Hall's condition worsened. He had continued numbness of his tongue and mouth, difficulty speaking, and for the first time his mind began to wander. He accused people of trying to do him in. First, he pointed the finger at Buddington, saying the sailing master was after him with a gun. Then he saw "blue vapor" coming out of the mouths of several visitors to his cabin, and believed it was lethal.

His fears and suspicions soon focused on one man: Dr. Emil Bessels, whom he accused of poisoning him, and even of possessing "an infernal machine" that produced the mysterious vapor. From October 29 until November 4, Hall banned the German doctor from his bedside. During that time Hall, believing there was a conspiracy afoot to poison him, did not eat anything except canned food, and he wanted to open the cans himself. If he was unable to get a can open, he would call on Hannah or Joe to do so, or William Morton, in whom he confided: "They are poisoning me. You won't leave me, will you?" Hall would oftentimes ask those attending to him to taste his food before he would eat it.

On November 1, Hall seemed better, and was gaining strength. He was eating more and devoured with gusto a thigh and leg of a grilled hare. He was well enough one afternoon to dress and appear on deck—to the delight of the crew.

Seaman Noah Hayes wrote in his journal that day: "Captain Hall has grown rapidly better. He seemed to almost literally awake from his sickness, so sudden was the change."

Hall called four officers into his cabin—Buddington, Chester,

Morton, and Tyson. The commander had something important on his mind. He explained that he intended to resign command of the ship and turn it over to Buddington, while he would retain control over the expedition's movements. He said he was having the necessary papers drawn up.

"I think I could stand it better without day-to-day responsibility for the ship," Hall told the assembled officers. "The responsibilities of command have been great upon me, and I have had much worry on my mind. I think I will get well faster, and once I am fit I would have more time to devote to the exploring part of the expedition."

Tyson knew only three weeks had elapsed since Hall nearly suspended Buddington due to incompetence, and now he was considering giving the sailing master even more responsibility and control? Because of the measure of this man, Buddington, Tyson knew it would be a mistake. But Hall didn't ask any of the officers for their opinions that day. Granted, the situation had changed in those few weeks; they now had to consider Hall's deteriorating health. If this change would help him regain his strength, then by all means he should make it. Far worse would befall the expedition should Hall not recover. Tyson dreaded to think of it.

At times Hall seemed well on the way to recovery. When he was clearheaded, he talked eagerly to anyone who would listen about his plans for continued exploration of the Far North, and he worked diligently with a clerk to bring his journals up to date. A number of crewmen heard him in his cabin laughing and rejoicing at news that the Eskimo hunters had killed a five-hundred-pound seal, meaning fresh meat aplenty for weeks. Other times, he didn't act like himself—he would begin a sentence and not finish it, or he would start to talk about one subject and go off onto something else. His "disease" had been pronounced by the doctor as apoplexy, which Tyson thought strange. He had known only one person dying of apoplexy in the north, the engineer on an earlier expedition, and he had died very suddenly after suffering a stroke. He'd gone to bed well at 9:00 P.M. and was found dead in his cabin the next morning. Hall seemed to be afflicted with something more lingering, more chronic.

Nevertheless, since he was beginning to feel better, he shelved his plans to resign command of the ship. Tyson learned this indirectly from the steward, who had witnessed Buddington and Hall arguing loudly. At one point Buddington seized Hall and began choking him because he wouldn't sign some paper Buddington had put in front of him. Even in his weakened state, Hall had flung Buddington halfway across the cabin.

On November 4, after much persuasion by the doctor, Hall agreed to let Bessels treat him again. He received another injection and ate a large quantity of cooked seal meat for dinner.

For the next two nights Bessels dozed in a chair beside Hall's bunk, with one end of a string attached to his arm and the other to Hall's. If Hall needed anything, he could pull the string without awakening the other men in the cabin.

On the 6th, Hall looked and felt well, and strong hopes circulated among the crew for his recovery. Although counseled to remain quiet by Bessels, Hall got up and dressed after the doctor gave him an injection of quinine that afternoon. He remained up nearly all day, and was to all appearances getting stronger. A portion of the day he spent getting in order the handwritten records of his sledge journey. He dictated for several hours to Joseph Mauch, the German seaman serving as his clerk, and began to show interest in the ordinary duties of the ship.

Hall went to bed that night in apparent good spirits. Before turning in, he told his officers he would be joining him them in the morning for breakfast. He made a point of asking that Morton and Chester not sit up with him that night—he didn't like others losing sleep on his account—but Chester insisted anyway.

Around midnight, Chester noticed that Hall was having difficulty breathing.

Alarmed, the first mate awakened Bessels, who was asleep in his berth at the opposite end of the cabin. He told the doctor about Hall's troubling symptoms.

Bessels dressed hurriedly, passed Hall with barely a glance, pronounced he would be all right, and to Chester's amazement quickly departed for the Observatory.

Chester returned to his commander's bedside. Within a few minutes Hall rose in his berth and tried to say something, but it was incomprehensible. With horror Chester realized that Hall's tongue was swollen. He ran out on deck, spotted a crewman out on the ice taking tidal observations, and ordered the man to go the Observatory and bring back the doctor without delay.

On his way back to Hall's cabin, Chester stopped and awakened Buddington in the lower cabin. Buddington quickly joined the first mate in Hall's cabin.

To their surprise, they found Hall trying to write in his journal. He looked awful, sitting up in his berth, alternating between pale and flushed, feet dangling over the edge, head lolling one way and the other, eyes glassy. He had a frightful look, not unlike a living corpse.

"Tell me, how do you spell murder?" Hall asked.

When Bessels came into the cabin a few minutes later, Hall looked steely-eyed at the doctor. "Doctor, I know everything that's going on. You can't fool me."

Before Bessels could respond, Hall demanded some water. Presented with a glass, he undertook to swallow the water but couldn't get it down.

"I know you're all in it," Hall said, looking at Buddington. "You've all joined in with that little German dancing master to disgrace me. I don't care. I'm perfectly willing to leave this world."

Hall fell back on his bunk, breathing very hard.

When he had calmed down some, Bessels asked Hall how he felt.

"Worse," Hall groaned.

The doctor examined him and found his left eye was dilated and his right contracted—a sign, Bessels announced, of another attack of apoplexy.

Hall soon lapsed into unconsciousness, and remained co-matose most of the next day, lying flat on his stomach, breathing laboriously.

Staying beside Hall for the rest of the day, Chester heard a gurgle coming from Hall's throat that sounded like a death rattle. The first mate also noticed many sores around Hall's mouth and at the side of his nose.

Early that evening, the commander regained consciousness briefly.

Bessels appeared at his bedside. Hall looked up. "Doctor, you have been very kind to me, and I am obliged to you."

Hall turned over and went to sleep.

Those were the last words spoken by Charles Francis Hall.

Second mate William Morton sat quietly beside his commander's bunk. As the other men in the cabin slept peacefully, Hall's respiration became more shallow and labored. From hours spent at his commander's beside, Morton knew it was getting more difficult for the sick man to draw a breath.

Hubbard Chester came by and sat with Morton for a while.

"He's asleep," Chester said, "but I don't think he's any better."

"No," Morton agreed. "He's very bad."

Chester, exhausted from sitting up with Hall for twenty-four hours, turned in.

After a while Hall stirred, although he remained flat on his stomach. Morton spoke to him, mostly to assure him that he wasn't alone. Hall gave no indication he heard the soothing words.

The old sailor raised his commander's head in his hands as gently as he would an infant's. When he saw saliva about his mouth, he turned him partially on his back so that his head was a little more upright, and wiped his mouth. He tried to give Hall a teaspoon of water, but it oozed from his lips and Morton wiped his mouth again.

The hours ticked by on the brass chronometer hanging on

the bulkhead of the ship's bridge. At half past two in the morning on November 8, 1871, Hall took his final breath.

The sudden silence startled Morton. He placed one ear close to Hall's lips. He could detect no respiration. He placed his hand above Hall's heart; his chest was still.

Morton was struck by how peaceful Charles Francis Hall looked in those final moments. His face was placid and lifelike. There were no contortions or signs of pain, nor was his face red or flushed as it had been periodically during his illness. Morton understood now why they called it the sleep of the dead.

The second mate pulled himself away and went to the opposite side of the cabin, where he shook Bessels from a sound sleep.

"The captain is dead," Morton said.

Bessels blinked, seemingly awaiting further confirmation.

"He is dead, sir. Captain Hall is dead."

The doctor jumped from his bunk to go see for himself.

Morton next went to the lower cabin and awakened Buddington with the same news.

The upper cabin was soon filled with groggy but stunned men who, between the whispers and quiet prayers that mourners speak around the recently departed, looked sorrowfully and disbelievingly at their dead leader.

The Arctic explorer who had so trusted in his fate had been cheated of his destiny.

7

A Change of Command

O n deck outside the pilot house, Sidney Buddington leaned
against the icy railing.

A group of sailors huddled nearby, speaking in hushed tones.
Their commander had been dead less than two hours, and the
mood aboard ship was somber and depressed.

Seaman Henry Hobby, a German in his mid-thirties who
had been going to sea for seventeen years and in that time had
sailed much of the world on merchant ships, came topside for
some fresh air.

"We are all right now," Buddington said without looking at
the seaman.

"How do you mean that, Captain?" Hobby asked.

"You shan't be starved to death now, I can tell you that."

"I never believed I would," said Hobby, taken aback by
Buddington's comment.

It had been the sailing master, after all, who had shorted
the men on their rations and Captain Hall who had fixed the
problem. Hobby knew that Hall had also vigorously tried to
improve the quality of the food, although to no avail. As far as
the men were concerned, the cook, William Jackson, generally

spoiled the grub. He couldn't even bake bread that was edible and would usually end up tossing the half-baked dough over the side. Much of what he prepared was similarly wasted or ruined. Hobby had once overheard Hall angrily dressing down Jackson in the galley, telling the mulatto cook that if he didn't attend to his business and improve the chow, "you shall not have a cent of pay when you get home."

Buddington was clearly relieved that they would no longer be forced north by the zeal of a commander obsessed with discovering the Pole—a dangerous course that could mean uncertainty, even shipwreck and starvation like other Arctic expeditions. The cantankerous whaler who liked his drink had the helm now, and he intended to steer his own course. They would take it easy and get home safely, but not early, so as to draw their full pay.

"I'll tell you, Henry," Buddington went on, "there's a stone off my heart."

Meteorologist Frederick Meyer joined them. No one spoke for a while.

"Well," Meyer said, breaking the silence, "maybe now the officers will have something to say about this expedition."

Buddington went below, found the carpenter, and asked him to make a coffin. The work began immediately, and the carpenter's hammer echoed in the frozen stillness.

In the lower berthing compartment, Buddington came across a roomful of men. "Will anyone lay out the old man?" the sailing master asked.

George Tyson stepped forward. A few hours before Hall's death, Tyson had gone to his commander's bedside. Finding him unconscious and breathing laboriously, Tyson left knowing that Hall was not long for this world.

"I'll help," said William Morton, as genuinely bereaved as any crew member.

The two men went to the upper cabin, which had emptied out.

Charles Francis Hall still lay where he had expired, a light cover thrown over him.

Tyson pulled back the cover. As Morton had been earlier, Tyson was moved by the dead man's peaceful expression. Devoid of any suffering and angst, Hall's countenance looked more natural and fresh than any face of death Tyson had ever seen.

The two men found a plank and rolled the body onto it. Setting either end of the board on overturned crates, they stripped the corpse and washed it. Finding Hall's favorite blue uniform with shiny brass buttons, they dressed and groomed their late commander as if he were scheduled to stand a fleet admiral's inspection. They then lifted the plank onto the bunk, where they covered the body with a clean wool blanket.

Buddington entered the cabin and asked to speak to Tyson. They went into an alleyway between the cabin and the ship's rail. After checking to make sure they were alone, Buddington said, "Don't you say anything about it to anybody, but that bastard little German doctor poisoned the old man."

Tyson had visited Hall during his worst days and heard first-hand his wild talk about being poisoned. When the commander was most delirious, Tyson had himself been accused of breathing deadly "blue vapor" in the cabin. At one of his bedside visits, Hall had looked urgently in his eyes and said there was a traitor aboard—"a snake in the grass" that would have to be found and dealt with. Tyson knew from Joe and Hannah that a suspicious Hall had sometimes refused food and medicine. There had been a lot of talk aboard the ship about the commander's strange and sudden illness. If it had been brought on by the "heat of the cabin" coming in from a long sledge journey—as suggested by Bessels—why hadn't Hall stepped outside when he began to feel overheated? Besides, would heat exhaustion, not exactly a common ailment in the Arctic, present itself as an upset stomach? Tyson had not heard of Hall eating anything that could have sickened him; there was only that cup of coffee.

As for Buddington's accusation, Tyson well knew that Hall and Bessels had not gotten along, but had their animosity been terrible enough for the ship's doctor to poison the expedition's commander? What would Bessels be gaining from Hall's death? More leeway and authority to conduct his scientific agenda, without doubt. And added credit for anything that the expedition accomplished, perhaps even claiming himself as the discoverer of the North Pole. Tyson knew the seeds of jealousy had already been planted between the two men. Still, a murder plot struck him as unlikely. Although he didn't believe that the German doctor had done all he could for the grievously ill Hall, Tyson did not suspect foul play. He also did not want to consider the possibility of murder.

"I don't believe it," Tyson said softly.

"Yes, he did it," Buddington said emphatically. "I know, I tell you. But don't you say anything about it or it'll go badly for all of us when we get back home. Look out for Bessels. He poisoned the old man, and if you ain't careful he'll serve you the same way."

Of course, if Hall had been murdered, Buddington himself had to be considered. Tyson well remembered his words about Hall—"that old son of a bitch won't live long"—although at the time he had thought the sailing master was merely hoping for an accident to befall Hall on one of his sledge journeys. Still, Buddington had been looking for Hall's death, and his disturbing prophecy *had* come true.

And what of the possibility that Buddington and Bessels, each of whom had had serious disagreements with Hall, had entered into a conspiratorial pact to do away with their leader? That didn't seem plausible. Tyson could not see these two men working together on anything. The two had already had a nasty row over the liquor supply. Plus, long before that altercation, they had shown they despised each other. To Bessels, the sailing master was an uneducated, lazy slob, and to Buddington, Bessels was an arrogant elitist and a "damn Kraut" besides.

Tyson had more immediate matters to think about this day. Now that the body was prepared for burial, they had to dig a grave. He took Chester and some men ashore, and found a suitable spot about a half mile from the ship. The ground was frozen as hard as marble. By the light of lanterns, they hacked at it with picks, ice chisels, and axes for two days until they reached a depth of twenty-six inches—the depth of the permanent frost—considered sufficient to protect the coffin from hungry, marauding bears, the only Arctic creature capable of breaking into the wooden box. By the time the grave was dug, the simple pine coffin was ready.

The body, wrapped in an American flag with thirty-seven stars, was placed inside. Before the lid was nailed shut, all hands were called in to look, for the last time, upon the face of the man who had brought them to the Arctic. Most had appreciated his singleness of purpose and the force of his character. His zeal and forethought had animated and directed the smallest duties, and he had inspired enthusiasm and stimulated the efforts of the most indifferent. A sense of loneliness and loss filled the hearts of officers and crewmen alike.

Little was said as the sorrowful procession passed the open coffin. When the viewing was over, the coffin was closed and carried to the afterdeck.

Shortly before noon on November 11, 1871, the ship's company gathered on the ice. The ship's bell sounded as they departed, and the dogs howled a sad refrain. Under an overcast sky, the small cortege walked the short distance to the grave, the coffin sled-borne and covered by Old Glory. The men wore seal-skins to ward off the cold, and a few carried kerosene lanterns against the perpetual gloom of Arctic winter.

Tyson noticed that a storm was blowing up in the northeast, and he realized they might have to hurry the service. It was a day befitting of the event—the weather appropriately dismal, and the place rugged and desolate in the extreme.

As far as the dim light enabled the men to see, they were bound in by huge masses of slate rock, which stood like a barricade, guarding the barren land of the interior. Between these rugged hills lay the snow-covered plain; behind them were the ice-bound waters of Polaris Bay, shimmering in the clear light of the stars. The shore of the bay was strewn with great ice blocks. Not far off, the little hut they called the Observatory bore aloft, upon a tall flagstaff, the only cheering object in sight, and even that was sad enough today, for the colorful Stars and Stripes was dipped at half-mast.

Tyson led the way with his lantern, Buddington abreast of him. Two by two they proceeded: Bessels and Meyer, Chester and Morton, the other officers, then the crew. Several of them hauled the coffin by a rope attached to the sled across ground generally covered with snow, although blown bare in places by the wind. The Eskimos followed: including the heartbroken Joe and the weeping Hannah, inconsolable in her grief.

With Hall, Joe and Hannah had shared many trials and dangers. They had saved his life in the Arctic a number of times, and they were pained that they had been unable to do so this time. The couple felt very alone, on a ship now filled with strangers.

Even at noon it was almost dark, and Tyson had to hold up his lantern at the grave for Chaplain R. W. D. Bryan to read a short burial service.

As Hannah sobbed, the coffin was lowered into the ground.

Each mourner threw a handful of frozen dirt over it.

In twos and threes, they walked back to the ship, arriving just as the snow did.

Later that day, Tyson, by candlelight, wrote in his journal:

> *Thus end poor Hall's ambitious projects; thus is stilled the effervescing enthusiasm of as ardent a nature as I ever knew. Wise he might not always have been, but his soul was in this work, and had he lived till spring, I think he would have gone as far as mortal man could go to accomplish his mission. But with his death I fear that all hopes of further progress will have to be abandoned.*

Two weeks later, seaman Noah Hayes, the sole American among the deck force, was helping Dr. Emil Bessels in the observatory. Hayes, a particularly observant young man who would write one of the most literate and detailed journals of any in the *Polaris* crew, noticed that the doctor appeared uncharacteristically lighthearted.

The sailor casually asked him why.

"You know, Hayes," Bessels said, stopping to laugh before continuing, "Captain Hall's death was the best thing that could have happened for this expedition."

8

Stirring an Ice-Cold Grave

For more than a week after Charles Francis Hall went to his grave, a terrible storm raged: seven days of blinding snow blizzards and roaring winds, the likes of which members of the North Polar Expedition had not before experienced. Even the Eskimos, born and raised in the clime, were awestruck by the intensity of the celestial violence. During Hall's illness the weather had been unusually calm and clear for winter. Now, they agreed, it was as if the spirits were angry.

The night after Hall's burial, the ship's company were startled at midnight by a loud cry of distress. The carpenter, Nathaniel Coffin, was found crouching in horror in a corner of his bunk, believing that he had heard a voice calling to him from the adjacent storeroom. To pacify him, the storeroom was unlocked and searched. Despite proof that no one was lurking inside, the carpenter continued to believe that he had heard something. Because his bunk was so near the storeroom, he was offered an empty bunk in the upper berthing compartment. The carpenter was happy crawling into the bunk so recently occupied by Captain Hall, and he soon fell asleep.

Several men had close calls in the big storm.

Dr. Emil Bessels was trapped overnight in the Observatory by the howling snowstorm, a virtual prisoner. He went eight hours after running out of coal and having no heat in temperatures that dropped to 24 degrees below zero. Finally he was reached and brought back to the ship by the two Eskimo hunters and meteorologist Frederick Meyer, whose eyelids froze from battling the driving snow and icy winds up to sixty miles per hour. The storm was so violent it was impossible for Meyer and Bessels to stand against the wind on the way back to the ship, and even when creeping on their hands and knees they had difficulty making headway. The Eskimos had less difficulty with the trek, as they knew better how to battle the strong wind. All except Hans ended up frostbitten.

Herman Sieman, a thirty-one-year-old German seaman who had never before sailed in Arctic waters, went out to examine the tide gauge to make sure the vessel was not in danger of drifting from her anchorage. Solid and strong of build, Sieman was nonetheless lifted up by the storm and carried a hundred feet, whereupon he was thrown violently upon the ice, and covered by freezing water rushing up through huge cracks that opened. When he recovered from the shock, he found that he was lying on his back with hands and feet in the air. Fortunately, he still retained his lantern, which had not gone out. Getting up on his feet, he forced his way against the wind and reached the fire hole in the ice, which was where the tidal activity was read. The gale-force snowstorm was so furious that he could hardly keep his eyes open long enough to read the tide gauge.

The poor dogs suffered greatly on the ice. Their yelps of distress so affected the men that they were brought in off the ice and provided with shelter on deck under the awning.

The creaking of the masts and the howling of the wind through the rigging proved that the storm continued to rage without a lull. In the lower cabin, all felt the rocking of the vessel as well as the grinding of the ship's hull in her icy cradle upon the berg, causing everyone much anxiety. In the upper cabin, crewmen heard the heavy canvas awnings on the main deck repeatedly snapping like thunder in the wind.

The wind blew with such force against the broadside of the vessel that she was thrown over on one side, and the snow wall built around her gave way and sank several feet. The more than two-foot-thick ice encircling *Polaris* began cracking loudly, and the vessel was repeatedly driven against the ice with severe shocks.

The ice had broken all around the bay, and they were now surrounded by open waters within half a mile. Although still stuck in the ice floe, the vessel had begun to drift from the protection of Providence Berg. They quickly put out another anchor forward in eight fathoms of water, but *Polaris* still headed ominously toward the wind-whipped bay, filled with swirling icebergs.

Someone had to get a line attached to the berg, but Buddington hesitated to give the order, apparently unsure if it would be obeyed. The duty was made perilous by the extreme violence of the wind and the steep, slippery surface of the berg.

Seaman William Nindemann, a strong, quiet twenty-three-year-old German, stepped forward. "I'll try."

"Joe and Hans will give you a hand," said Buddington, volunteering the Eskimos.

To illuminate the work, a large pan containing tarred rope saturated with kerosene oil was set out onto the ice and lit.

Nindemann succeeded in getting across the cracking ice floe to the berg fifty feet away. Using a hatchet, he cut steps up the side of the berg and scaled its slippery banks. He carried with him an ice anchor and a line tied to a stanchion on deck. From the ship's supply he had taken the heaviest of the ice anchors, a seventy-five-pound iron hook that he strapped to his back. As line was fed to him by the natives from the ice floe, the seamen secured the hook into the berg and the line was pulled taut from the ship.

Once the ship was holding steadily to the berg, a cheer went up from the assembled officers and crew who had watched Nindemann perform his daredevil feat. For added security, two other anchors were made ready, and the Eskimos took these across the floe and up the side of the berg to the waiting Nindemann. With the three lines secured to the berg, the threat of the ship being carried away and colliding with fast-drifting bergs was eased. Nindemann and a native were frostbitten during their exposure but not seriously.

During a brief lull in the storm, the damage was assessed. Two sledges left outside had drifted away when the ice broke. Also missing were a handful of dogs, although they were soon found buried under a wall of fresh snow in a doghouse; cold but uninjured.

When the gale picked up again, the water crashing against the ship's side sounded ominous, and the shocks of the vessel against the ice were alarming. In spite of the heavy strain, the anchors and lines secured to the berg held fast.

When the storm finally passed, the vessel was found to be exposed to wildly drifting floes the wind had driven into the bay. It was decided to bring *Polaris* more under the protection of Providence Berg. Crewmen sawed a narrow opening through the youngest ice—already seven inches thick—in order to bring the ship around under better shelter. With all hands pulling on the hawsers and adjusting anchor lines as they went, they managed to move her through the gap in the ice floe eighty feet to the middle of the berg on its long side, but still a safe distance away.

Command of the ship had passed without challenge to Sidney Buddington, and his true nature was revealed early. As Hall's body still lay aboard ship awaiting burial, Buddington had summoned the officers to his cabin. They expected an important consultation or perhaps even an inspirational message, but to their surprise they found him already three sheets to the wind, waiting to play poker with them. Upon Hall's death, Buddington had inherited the captain's keys, including the one that opened the locked supply of wine, rum, and whiskey that had been boarded for special occasions. Also, Buddington took possession of Hall's personal effects, keeping some for himself and freely distributing the rest among members of the crew, sometimes selling or bartering them. The new skipper strolled the decks of the ship, sometimes sober and other times not, cursing and vilifying the memory of their tragically departed leader— often while wearing a favored article of the dead man's clothing.

Within days of Hall's death, Bessels prepared a document that he and Buddington signed. It read:

> *Consultation*
> *Thank-God Harbor*
> *November 13, 1871*
>
> *First consultation held between Messrs. S. O. Budding-ton and E. Bessels. Through the mournful death of our noble commander, we feel compelled to put into effect the orders given to us by the [Navy] Department, viz:*
>
> *"Mr. Buddington shall, in case of your death or disability, continue as the sailing master, and control and direct the movements of the vessel; and Dr. Bessels shall, in such case, continue as the chief of the scientific department, directing all sledge-journeys and scientific operations. In the possible contingency of their nonconcurrence as to the course to be pursued, then Mr. Buddington shall assume the sole charge and command, and return with the expedition to the United States with all possible dispatch."*
>
> *It is our honest intention to honor our dear flag, and to hoist her on the most northern part of the earth, to complete the enterprise upon which the eyes of the whole civilized world are raised, and to do all in our power to reach our proposed goal.*
>
> *S. O. Buddington*
> *Emil Bessels*

With that, the potentially divisive split-command clause had been invoked. Buddington could take the ship wherever he pleased, while Bessels was assured a free hand in carrying out his scientific chores, and for any discoveries that were accomplished by way of explorations north, the honor would redound to him as sledge-journey leader.

Whatever discipline had existed on *Polaris* died with Hall. Although now in command of the ship, Buddington exerted only minimal control over the crew. Unlike regular Navy officers, he did not appreciate the importance of finding work to keep idle men busy and out of mischief. Nor was any effort made to provide them with recreation, regular exercise, or religious expression. In one of his first official acts, Buddington put a stop to Hall's daily religious services, at which attendance had been mandatory. Then he also made Sunday services voluntary, saying that everyone was free to pray on his own. Personally, he said, he preferred a good walk on Sunday morning.

As for Bessels, he largely stayed to himself, spending much of his time in the Observatory and conducting various measurements and observations, although most of his scientific agenda would have to await better weather in spring and summer.

Late in the afternoon of November 28 the barometer started to fall, usually a sign of a pending storm. Early that evening a snowstorm with a stiff gale set in from the south. Huge pieces of ice were driven by the wind toward Providence Berg. The immense pressure was too great for the berg, and it broke into two parts, between which ice was blown until the two halves were separated by a distance of eight feet. This demonstration, providing undeniable proof as to what the shifting ice floe might do to the hull of a wooden ship, caused considerable anxiety. The dogs were taken aboard, and preparations made for an approaching crisis.

At eleven o'clock, the berg was found to be in motion, heading squarely for the vessel. The smaller part of the berg moved more rapidly than the other, pushing the cracking ice floe before it. In the interval before the berg reached the ship, even the bravest and most experienced Arctic hands held their breath, for it seemed that the vessel must be crushed in the onslaught.

Ice pushed against the ship, and she bore the great pressure without yielding, although groaning under the strain. Several times it was thought that the ice had been forced through her side. Though the ship was standing the pressure heroically, everyone knew that no vessel afloat could hold together for long in such a position. The wind at the time was blowing at forty-seven miles per hour, and the air was filled with swirling snow. The berg was moving in toward the shore, shoving the ship before it, until the tide turned and the berg ceased its threatening movement.

Soon a new danger presented itself. In the raging winds *Polaris* swung to her anchors, but she was soon forced upon the foot of the berg. At ebb tide, she keeled over, and lay nearly on her beam ends—careening so much that it was difficult for anyone to keep his footing on deck. The force of the ice floe had pushed the foot of the iceberg *under* the ship, raising the stern nearly four feet, shaking and straining the vessel badly.

With the ship in imminent danger of being torn apart by the berg, the Eskimo women and children were sent to the Observatory until the storm abated. Also sent ashore were additional stores in the event the ship had to be abandoned.

Evaluating the situation, Tyson thought there was a possibility that the vessel could be hauled off the berg. He urgently recommended to Buddington that they try. If she was left in her present position, there was a threat of the ship being pushed farther onto the spur of the berg. Such a strain could set her to leaking.

Buddington fretted about the situation but refused to give the order.

When the tide rose, the ship came to an even keel. There, on the berg, *Polaris,* having escaped two great dangers, remained ignobly stuck.

Thanksgiving arrived, and dinner was the highlight of the day. The cook and steward went to special lengths to prepare the fare: oyster soup, lobster, turkey, different kinds of meats, vegetables (the favorite being green peas), a fine plum sauce, apple and cherry pies, nuts, raisins, and wine punch. Dinner was set for all hands in the lower cabin, and much time was spent at the table. Chaplain R. W. D. Bryan said a few brief words.

Privately, Bryan was dismayed that daily religious services were not being held for the crew, and that attendance at the Sunday services had dwindled to only a handful of worshipers. But he said little about the situation. He was, by nature, a kind and true gentleman, and wished only to get along with everyone, including the new captain.

On the Saturday and Sunday following the holiday, there was a *paraselene*—an illusion of multiple moons showing beside the true one, arranged so as to form an eerie but beautiful cross. The true moon was surrounded by a halo, which also embraced two of the false ones, while the other mock moons had a separate halo, making a large circle concentric with the first. The two false moons nearest to the true moon showed the colors of the prism. It was a beautiful and curious sight—a strange phenomenon, sort of a double refraction—that brought the entire crew on deck to see for themselves.

The land to the east of Robeson Strait the men of *Polaris* now called "Hall's Land," and it would so appear on all future charts and maps. When the weather was calm and very cold, unbroken ice closed off Robeson Channel, but with every strong breeze that blew, the ice gave way, opening the channel for miles at a stretch. Spotting these changing conditions from high in the crow's nest, Tyson reported to Buddington that if they could get the ship off the berg and under way after one of the strong blows, they might succeed in making it into the channel; beyond, they could possibly find open water.

An early breakout might be possible, Tyson told Buddington. "We could head north." The word north in any discussion gave Buddington obvious discomfort.

Tyson could see his worst fear being realized—that without the heart, soul, and vision of Charles Francis Hall, the expedition's mission to reach the North Pole would be neglected or abandoned. Hall had been worried about this during his illness.

He had once held Tyson's forearm in a strong grip and beseeched him: "If I die, you *must* still go on to the Pole."

Tyson felt powerless to keep the promise he made to the dying explorer. For better or worse, it was now Buddington's ship to command, with Bessels in charge of sledges; there was little anyone else could do.

The perpetual darkness continued. Soon would arrive the shortest day of the year. In the everlasting twilight they were hardly able to tell day from night. If not for their timepieces, they would have been constantly confused—all the more with such scant regularity in schedule, duties, or gatherings observed. No longer was there even a stated time for lights out. The men were allowed to do as they pleased, and some of them often made nighttime hideous for others who wished to sleep; loud carousing and card-playing sessions, most often attended by Buddington, went on all night. The commander had, in fact, become one of the unruly mob rather than remaining apart as a strong, effective skipper to maintain discipline. Opening the armory, Buddington had distributed loaded revolvers and other firearms to the crew, although some of the officers, Tyson included, could not imagine what use, under the present circumstances when hunting was not possible, they were expected to make of them.

So far thirteen dogs had been lost—six large ones and seven puppies—from one cause or another. There still remained fifty-four—divided between Newfoundlands and Eskimo Huskies. These animals were exceedingly important to the expedition if there was to be any further advancement north by sledge.

The dogs were generally fed every three days. At first they were fed on dried fish bought for that purpose at the Danish settlements, and sometimes on old seal meat procured at the same time. When those provisions were exhausted, they were given pemmican, a powdery cakelike mix of dried meat, fat, and raisins that was a main staple for the crew, too, as it had long been for polar expeditions due to its ability to withstand spoilage. One forty-five-pound can of pemmican was given to the dogs at each feeding, an event that was also exciting sport for the crew.

When the dogs were to be fed, the whole pack was let in through the door in the awning over the gangway upon the deck. In the port gangway an Eskimo chopped up the pemmican and divided it in order to give each dog his portion. Several men were on hand to assist and control the dogs. When the food was ready, one dog at a time was allowed to go into the passage and remain there until he had eaten his portion; when he had finished he was put out on the ice again. Utmost vigilance was required to keep the dogs in order and prevent them, after being fed, from rejoining the others and getting a second share, thereby robbing another of his nourishment. At times their attack upon the door of the gangway was so violent that it was almost impossible to keep them back. Two men guarded the door, armed with clubs, which they were compelled to use occasionally upon the wildest and most determined of the creatures. For the men it was hard and dangerous work, but exhilarating, too—as well as a lively performance for those who came on deck to watch.

December arrived, and the ship remained perched on the berg, rising and falling with the tide. The creaking of her timbers as she moved up and down against the berg sounded like volleys of musketry. The berg, which continued to break into smaller pieces, pressed unrelentingly toward the vessel. The ice floe rested against *Polaris* on her seaward side, and to the right and left of this floe hummocks were piled to a height of thirty feet above sea level, some nearly as high as the berg itself. The effect of this constant pressure was to raise the vessel still higher, increasing her steep inclination at low tide. Thus, her condition became worse as the winter advanced.

With the ice piled up high about the stern from the constant pressure of the floe, it now appeared impossible to effect any change in the ship's position. During high tide she was very nearly on even keel, but at low tide the list was exceedingly disagreeable. As she listed to port, those who bunked on that side did not mind it as much, since they could stay inside their berths, but on the other side it was often difficult to keep in the bunks. A new fire hole was made in the ice and the tidal apparatus erected over it. The regular tidal observations were resumed, after a suspension of fourteen days.

On the second day of the new month, the weather was calm and the temperature rose to minus seven degrees, so many of the men took to outdoor sports. Some drove about the ice, having harnessed several of the dogs to sleds; others coasted on small push sleds near the Observatory. Those who stayed aboard ship whiled away the time in their cabins with cards, dominoes, checkers, and chess, with some games quite spirited.

Inside the compartments, ice formed on the bulkheads. This could not be otherwise, what with so much ice pressed against the hull of the ship, and with the frigid wind whipping against the ship unblocked now without a protective snow wall around them. The berths could not be kept warm enough by the heat from the small cabin stoves, and inside, temperatures dropped so much that outdoor clothing was kept on much of the day.

Tyson had not had a sound night's sleep since Hall's death. One evening, tired of the constant noise on board and longing for a moment's quiet, he wandered away from the ship. One had to be careful taking such casual excursions this time of year, not only because of the darkness and how quickly the ship could be lost from sight, but also the threat of strong, unexpected winds. There was no telltale whistling of the wind among trees, for none existed here. Once out on the open plain, the wind struck full force without notice. The wind was felt before it was heard, except in close proximity to a deeply cut gorge, down which it could come roaring like an out-of-control locomotive.

Once beyond the range of the men's voices, Tyson heard no other sound. It was entirely calm: no wind, no movement of any living creature—nothing but a leaden sky above, ice beneath his feet, and silence everywhere. It hung like a pall over everything. So painfully oppressive did it become that Tyson was tempted to shout aloud to break the spell. At last he did, but no response came, not even an echo.

The space was void; there I stood,
And the sole spectre was the solitude.

The twenty-first of December was not allowed to pass without that notice it always received from Arctic explorers. The twilight had daily grown less and less, until it was nothing but a light streak over the southern mountains for a few hours each day. It gave no light, and was just barely discernible. The long-continued darkness had become oppressive. The exclusive use of artificial light began to affect the eyes, and the trouble of carrying a lantern whenever one went out was trying. The absence of light produced the physical effect of languor, from which few in the crew were immune.

Christmas week, *Polaris*, her stem still resting on the foot of the berg and continuously rising and falling on her perch with the tide, sprang a leak. It would have been possible, the officers agreed, to begin repairing the leak—gradually, if not all at once—by working a few hours at a time as the tide permitted, but Buddington gave no orders to attempt the repairs. A regular watch kept up the pumping on an hourly basis.

On Christmas Eve, all hands gathered in the lower cabin to exchange gifts and trinkets, most drawn from the ship's stores. The object of the greatest admiration was a small Christmas tree that stood in the middle of a table, a regular pine in appearance that someone had found living a solitary life on the tundra. It was laden with golden fruit and toys; wax candles burning from every bough added to the effect.

Dr. Bessel sliced open a branch with a knife—not unlike bleeding a patient—and as the sap poured forth it was gathered in glasses, and pronounced by all as delicious.

The cook and steward set another bountiful table with very good steaks taken from a portion of the musk ox killed in the fall, and roast pork from a pig killed in Upernavik. The spare rib, notwithstanding its age of four months, was as fresh and sweet as though just taken from the animal, testifying to the preservation powers of Arctic cold. Among the desserts, mince pie appeared, made of fresh musk ox meat, dried apples, and raisins, and all declared it unquestionably good. A few bottles of wine were drunk.

The twenty-fifth was a beautiful, pleasant day, giving all indication that even Nature herself was joining in the celebration. The thermometer read 33 degrees below zero.

Three days later, Buddington finally decided to take action.

The vessel's position was so uncomfortable that life on board had become almost unendurable. At every low tide she lay over to port practically on her beam ends. It was desirable, for several reasons, to attempt to get her off the berg and enable her to remain upright. Not only were her constant movements a source of inconvenience to her occupants, but it was feared the vessel would sustain serious damage. Her rudder and propeller had not been unshipped in time and were frozen solid in place. They were so far under the ice that they could not be seen, and many thought that when the vessel lay over they were in danger of breaking off. It was also believed that the constant motion while the bow remained perched upon the tongue of the berg must necessarily result in wrenching the bow and breaking off the keel.

While Tyson and others now held little hope that much could be done until late in the spring, when human efforts would be aided by the warming of the sun, Buddington decided that they should try to break up the foot of the berg that had hold of the vessel by blasting with explosives.

Four large charges were exploded in different places not far from the ship's side, introduced under the ice by means of long poles that served to regulate the positions of the gunpowder-filled bottles. But beyond jarring the ice and the vessel, no effect was produced. The thick ice was not even cracked. However, it was considered imprudent to explode a larger quantity of powder.

To any who would listen, Buddington expressed anger that his advice in regard to winter quarters had not been followed. The vessel would have been safely anchored farther south he said, free from the dangers by which she was now beset. There would have been no drifting in the pack, no force upon the hull by the berg and ice floe, no daily gyrations in her icy bed, no need to break out and get closer to the musk-ox feeding grounds. For their current travails, he pointed a finger directly at one man: the man responsible for bringing them here, and the only one of those who had left America on *Polaris* who could no longer speak up to defend his decision.

At midnight on January 1, the ship's bell was rung merrily to welcome in the new year. The men forward fired a salute and sent a delegation to the cabin to congratulate the officers on the occasion. A bowl of hot spiked punch was brewed, and all were given an ample ration.

It was decided to launch a hot-air balloon, and nearly all the ship's company went out on the ice to watch the release. After stopping momentarily in the rigging, the balloon freed itself and moved off to the southwest, carried by a light wind from the east.

Silence filled the air. It was not lost on anyone that the balloon had effortlessly achieved something that they could not: freedom to go elsewhere.

When the balloon passed from sight, all were invited back to the cabin, where the remainder of the punch disappeared in a remarkably short space of time.

That first day of 1872 marked the eightieth day since they had seen the sun. It grew intensely cold in the early days of the new year, dropping to 48 degrees below zero.

An unusual atmospheric phenomenon became the subject of intense discussion among the members of the scientific corps. On January 10, at about 5:00 A.M., a bright arc was observed in the sky, extending from the western horizon toward the east and reaching up to the zenith. It appeared to be about twelve degrees from the Milky Way, and parallel with it. This continued only about an hour, but after it disappeared three cloud-like shapes of about the same brightness remained, resting near the zenith. Some narrow, bright stripes were visible coming from them. Whether this was an aurora or some unique electrical phenomenon was a question that remained unanswered.

As the month progressed, the twilight toward the southeast began increasing. Every eye naturally turned to that quarter many times a day, in anticipation of seeing the first splashes of direct sunlight.

To the north was open water, a clear sign that the ice was starting to drift freely in the strait. Bessels went out with two men and a sledge team to ascertain if the open water extended any great distance. He made only nine miles to the north and could get no farther because the headland was covered with smooth ice, over which the dogs could not go nor the men climb. They were unable to locate a route to get farther north, but as far as they could see it was open water.

When Bessels came back, the first mate thought he would give it a try. Chester took with him four men and a dozen dogs to draw two sledges. He thought they could get over the mountains or find a pass through them. They started at ten and returned about four o'clock that same day, as stymied in his efforts as Bessels had been.

Later in the month, a violent snowstorm hit, the wind blowing with hurricane force. It lasted two days, and during that time no one dared leave the ship, not even to take tidal observations.

When the storm ended, Tyson hiked alone to Cape Lupton, a bold headland two thousand feet high. He managed to get to the top, and from that elevation he saw that the ice was completely cleared out of the channel. In fact, there was free water everywhere except in the bay, where the ship was firmly encased in ice. For eighty miles to the north—as far as he could see—it was wide open. Tyson knew had *Polaris* been in the channel where he had recommended to Buddington they should try to get, they would now be sailing in free water instead of remaining locked in the icy embrace of Thank God Harbor.

Not long after, a thirsty Tyson got up in the middle of the night for a drink of water. As he passed Buddington cabin's—the ship's new commander had a small, private compartment for himself—Tyson saw him lying in his berth with the light on. Upon Tyson's return down the passageway to his own cabin, Buddington spoke up, asking him to come into his room.

Tyson went to the door of Buddington's room and stopped.

"Come in and shut the door," Buddington said.

Tyson did so, wondering why Buddington was being so secretive, since there was not another soul in sight. "Tell me, Tyson, what do you think of the talk going around some quarters that we should stay here another winter?" he asked.

Tyson knew that members of the scientific corps had expressed interest in conducting more observations and geographical surveys before heading home. Personally, he did not wish to spend another winter at Polaris Bay—it would be a waste of time and wouldn't accomplish anything meaningful—and he told Buddington so.

"Before going home we should either work the ship north," Tyson went on, "or do everything in our power to gain as high a latitude as possible by sledges and small boats."

"I don't want you to say anything about this," Buddington said. "We can keep our own counsel. It is my intention to go home come summer. I don't care a damn what the rest say. I want you to work with me, and the rest of 'em can go to hell."

Tyson said nothing.

"In the first place," Buddington continued, "we have no business being this far north. We ought to have spent the winter at Port Foulke. I came very near getting Hall to stop there. We would be a damned sight better off now if he had listened to me. I'll tell you what we are going to do, no matter what the rest say. I am going south this summer, and if we get out all right, we'll go down as far as Upernavik."

Upernavik was the northernmost of Greenland's Danish

settlements—450 miles south of their present position, about 73 degrees north.

"There are plenty of reefs along there, and we can easily, if it's a little foggy, pile her up on them without being blamed and do it without any danger to ourselves."

Tyson felt blood rushing to his head. The lawful commander of *Polaris* had suggested that they purposefully scuttle the ship? In all his years going to sea, Tyson had never heard such outlandish and cowardly talk from a ship's master. Was the man drunk?

"Then we can take the boats and go in to Upernavik," Buddington said as casually as if discussing plans for an extended holiday. "From there we can go down to Disco. We have everything there to make ourselves comfortable. From Disco we go to Denmark on a whaler, and then home on a steamer, with the government paying our expenses. We'll see something of the world, and our pay goes on as if we were still on the expedition. We'll make a damn good voyage of it."

Buddington waited for Tyson to comment.

Tyson decided that Buddington was sober, and that he was dead serious. "Why do you want to lose the vessel?" Tyson asked quietly.

"What the hell does the government want of the vessel?" Buddington said disgustedly. "What do they care for the vessel or the North Pole, either? This thing was started by a few damned fools in Washington to feather their own nest. Damn the North Pole! I came here for greenbacks. I never meant to pass Port Foulke. Old Hall got me in this scrape, damn him. He is dead and in hell, I hope."

"Captain, I can't go along with your plan," Tyson said firmly, eyes boring into the dishonorable man in whose hands nearly three dozen lives rested. "We ought to do what we can to carry out Captain Hall's wishes and the just expectations of the government and our country. If this season should prove as favorable as it was last year, there is no reason why we should not reach the Pole itself. It would be a lasting disgrace not to utilize to the utmost a ship fitted out with such care and expense. I want to go home—yes, sir, I do. We all do. And when that time comes, I think it will be more to your credit to carry the ship home with us."

At that, Tyson turned and left the room.

As Tyson lay on his bunk, sleep would not come. The astonishing proposition he had heard was enough, he knew, to make Hall stir in his ice-cold grave.

For hours he ruminated. Should he make a confidant of someone—perhaps the first mate—about Buddington's plan to wreck *Polaris* on a reef? The expedition had already been disgraced through the actions of the incompetent wretch now in command. Throughout the ship was such a state of distrust and suspicion that everybody looked on everyone else as possible enemies. He had never seen so much infighting among a ship's crew.

Tyson decided to say nothing for the time being. He would keep a sharp eye on Buddington and be prepared to act. In naval tradition, nothing was more serious than a mutiny, except a captain who would unnecessarily and incompetently lead ship and crew into harm's way. If that happened, it was the duty of another officer to step forward and assume command, even if it meant arresting and restraining the captain.

If I can get through this horrid winter, Tyson thought wearily, shortly before fitful sleep finally came, I think I shall be able to live through anything.

George Tyson had no idea just how severely he would be tested.

9

Land of Desolation

From the journal of George Tyson, assistant navigator, *Polaris:*

Feb. 22, 1872. Day is beginning to look like day, or rather dawn. We do not see the stars any more in the middle of the day, but neither do we see the sun yet. For over three months we have seen the stars in the day-time whenever the sky was unclouded, and the moon when it was not stormy. Much of that time the stars were very bright, and the moon also.

Sunday, Feb. 25. No service; walked over to Captain Hall's grave. Always seem to walk in that direction. It is now getting so much lighter that we shall be able to do something, I hope, soon. As yet, the hunting has amounted to nothing; where there is water one day, ice is found the next. Nothing to record; first a gale, then a snow-drift, then squalls, then fair weather, and repeat. This formula would do for the whole winter, with slight variations.

Feb. 28. A glorious day. The sun has showed himself. I happened to be the first to see him. If it had not been for the hills, we should have seen him yesterday, or day before.

Never was an expected guest more warmly welcomed. <u>It is one hundred and thirty-five days since we have seen his disk.</u> Poor Hall! how he would have rejoiced in the return of the sun. His enthusiasm would have broken loose today, had he been with us. And to think that there are those who are glad that he can not come back to control their movements!

The entire crew gathered on the ice eagerly to await the approaching spectacle. They waited expectantly, exchanging only hushed whispers as if not to scare off the solar god. A few small clouds over the tops of the mountains became brilliant with the light of the sun. Then, at 11:55 A.M., a small portion of the sun's upper half was seen through a gorge in the mountains. But before it was hardly recognized, it disappeared. Twenty-five minutes later, the entire orb suddenly appeared to all. It soon rolled in full glory over the southern fjord.

At that instant the floe seemed alive with young schoolboys out for a short recess; cheer after cheer went up from the joyful company. The crew leaped and jumped about, exclaiming their delight. "O! How warm it is!" "He has not forgotten us!"

As they watched, the sun continued rising above the horizon until two o'clock. At that time it appeared as an oversized red ball hanging over the straits to the southwest. Half a bottle of wine was given to each man along with a hundred cigarettes. It was the happiest day of the expedition.

With the reappearance of the sun, nights rapidly became lighter. By the middle of March, it could hardly be said nighttime was dark at all. Soon, as spring began to blossom in the land of extremes, there would be no perceptible difference between day and night; both would be equally sunlit.

The winter had not brought on any new cases of illness, and that special dread of Arctic travelers, scurvy, had not shown itself in the slightest form. As the sunlight increased so that the crew could look upon each other without the aid of artificial light, it was noticed that the long winter darkness and confinement had given everyone a peculiar pallor. There was nothing in this to cause real anxiety, however. After only a few days of sunlight, normal skin color returned.

Bessels decided in late March to undertake a two-week sledge trip south. He intended to get as far as Cape Constitution, and to make surveys and astronomical observations en route. It was the opposite direction that Tyson wanted to go, and he suggested to the head scientist that a trip north would be a more credible expenditure of energy and supplies. But Bessels had his mind set, and off he went with astronomer Bryan, both men in a single sledge driven by Joe and pulled by fourteen dogs.

Conditions had changed for the scientific corps since Hall's death. The scientists were now autonomous from the rest of the ship's complement, answering to no one but themselves, with Bessels serving as the final authority. The ship's most valuable books and charts, once kept by Hall, were now in the possession of the scientists. Importantly, so were all the best measuring instruments, compasses, and other devices necessary for travel in the Arctic. Because Bessels zealously guarded his domain and refused to loan out equipment to other officers, it was impossible for anyone else to mount an exploring party without his cooperation and involvement. The scientists spent most of their time ashore at the Observatory, and were supplied with all the coal they could burn.

Buddington, in fact, made sure *everyone* had plenty of coal, and encouraged the crew to burn all they wanted. "Burn away," he said upon reviewing a status report showing they had burned—for heating and cooking—five thousand pounds of coal for the month of November alone. "Damned if I care if we burn twice as much."

While Hall had instituted strict rationing to conserve fuel, food, and other supplies to last through the long expedition, the new commander encouraged gluttony. Although many in the crew appreciated Buddington's generosity, Tyson knew the real reason for the new captain's wasteful ways. He was intent on consuming provisions and exhausting the coal as fast as possible so that, come summer, there would be no opposition to heading south—a full year before Hall had intended for *Polaris* to return.

In his journal, which he no doubt knew would be read by others upon their return, Buddington laid the groundwork for the retreat. "If the consumption of fuel is continued at the same rate—stoppage of which [is not possible] without endangering our health—we will hardly have enough for two winters, to say nothing of using steam on our return. The idea of piloting the vessel with sails is an absurdity." He also added a dash of braggadocio: "The first opportunity, however, we get to leave this winter-harbor will be taken, and with the aid of steam or sails, as conditions permit us, we will attempt to reach a higher latitude, so as to enable us to carry out the objects we are sent for."

During this time Buddington made it clear that, once home, he expected to be recognized for taking *Polaris* farther north than any vessel had gone before, apparently believing that the record of his opposition to proceeding northward would be overlooked. He was, however, wary of Bessels trying to steal the show. "I believe that damned doctor wishes to take some honor away from me," Buddington complained to Tyson. "If he attempts it when we get home, I'll accuse him of poisoning the old man. Damn him if he thinks he has got me fooled."

As soon as Bessels left on the sledge journey south, Buddington headed for the locked cabinet where the doctor now kept his supply of alcohol. Buddington had managed to fit a key to the lock and was helping himself, albeit more carefully than before because with the regular supply of liquor gone he did not want the doctor to move the "medicinal alcohol" to a more secure location. Also, Bessels had put out the word that if he suspected his alcohol was being drained, he would poison some of the bottles and only he would know which ones—an odd threat given the suspicions still whispered among the crew. Believing he had gotten the best of the salty old sea captain, Bessels checked regularly to make sure the levels in the corked bottles were unchanged, blissfully unaware of Buddington's latest trick: when he emptied a bottle, he refilled it with water or urine, then marked the cork so he would not return to it.

Buddington led his sailors in a long binge. The revelers were shocked, four days after Bessels' departure, to see his sledge on the horizon. It turned out to be not the doctor interrupting the festivities, but Bryan and Hans returning to replace their damaged sledge while Bessels remained encamped on a little island in the mouth of a southern fjord. Hans was blunt about the cause of the damage. Bessels had been "too lazy" to get off the sledge when going over rough ice, and as a result one of the sledge's runners had broken.

Bryan was down below washing up when a fistfight broke out between a drunken John Herron and the cook, William Jackson. Bryan separated the two men, but not before the diminutive English steward was so badly injured that he would be confined to his bunk for the next two months.

Bryan and Hans departed the next morning in two replacement sledges pulled by fresh dogs to rejoin Bessels.

Aboard *Polaris*, the partying resumed, culminating in what Tyson described in his journal as a "bacchanalian feast."

One morning Buddington came to Tyson looking anguished. "I suppose the doctor will be back soon," Buddington said.

"He's been gone about a fortnight. He'll soon be here, I expect."

"Wonder what he will say about the bottles he left in his locker?"

Tyson saw many of them had been smashed to the deck or tossed over the side. "How many are left?" he asked.

"I put three back when I turned in last night, but they were gone this morning. I think that damned engineer, Schuman, got them. He has a key for every lock on board."

"Are they all gone?" asked Tyson, who knew there had been several dozen bottles.

Buddington, pacing up and down the compartment, nodded solemnly. Then he stopped and looked up with the start of a mischievous smile. "Won't the good doctor look comical when he opens up his precious locker and finds it empty?"

The first week of April, with the fair weather continuing, Tyson and Chester began fitting up two small boats for an exploring trip to the north they planned for May. Tyson would have preferred a journey by sledge, for although patches of open water could be seen outside the bay, there was still much floating ice that could damage a boat.

Tyson believed, as had Hall, that early April was the best time to head north by sledge. An expedition would have sixty or seventy days in which to travel without being interrupted by the fierce torrents that came pouring down the ravines from the melting inland snow during the summer. They would have until about mid-June to reach as far north as possible. They had forty excellent dogs, two good sledge drivers, and ample supplies. But his proposed sledge journey had been dismissed by Buddington as "not practicable." And what did Buddington know about Arctic exploration? The man hadn't stepped off the ship once during the entire winter, "not even to answer the call of nature," Tyson wrote scornfully in his journal. "He is lazy and fat, eats enormous amounts of food . . . [is] physically and mentally unqualified for any journey by sledge or by boat."

As far as Tyson was concerned, there was "no earthly excuse" for not exploring by sledge for a couple of months before the opportune time for boat travel. "One of the best opportunities ever known in Arctic experience," he wrote, "was about to be lost."

The first mate, a sailor and not an Arctic explorer by experience, preferred going by water, and Buddington, beginning to hear murmurs of discontent from some of the crew because of the expedition's continued idleness, agreed to give him the use of two boats. Chester would lead one boat crew, and Tyson, ready to participate in any push northward, volunteered to lead the other.

On April 8, Bessels and his companions returned, bringing with them the carcass of a large bear that Joe had shot, and also a plump seal. The fresh meat was welcomed by all hands. Even though they still had plenty of canned food and other stores aboard *Polaris*, a change of diet was always desirable.

One of the dogs had been injured in the bear hunt, and because he was a favorite of many, he was the object of great attention. He was a plucky Newfoundland ironically named "Bear" because, at one hundred and twenty pounds, he was among the largest of the sledge dogs. Like others of his breed, he had small, deeply set dark brown eyes, small ears that lay flat against his broad head, a massive chest, and a dense, water-resistant double coat, dull black in color. His feet were large, strong, and webbed for traversing marshland and shore. Powerful swimmers, Newfoundlands were known to have rescued humans from drowning and to carry lifelines from shore to ships in distress. "Bear" had taken several severe blows from Joe's eventual trophy, a nine-hundred-pound male polar bear, which had made a better fight than the creatures usually did, perhaps because mating season, when the males are more aggressive, was only a month away. The bear had thrown another dog with such violence against the ice that it was left for dead, but the next day it showed up at the party's encampment nearly recovered.

The Bessels party accomplished little in their two-week absence other than to discover inaccuracies in some of the earlier surveys of the area they had traveled. After crossing the southern fjord, which was twenty miles wide, they traveled along the coast for forty miles in search of Cape Constitution but did not find it at the location marked on the chart. Hans, who had seen the cape in person, decreed that it must be farther south. The party would have pushed on in their search but could not get their sledges over the steep, slippery hills along the coast, and the shore ice was so invaded by open water that they could not trust it for travel. As it was, they had to carry their sledges at several points.

Bryan and the two Eskimos returned from the journey with a very low estimation of Bessels' endurance, nor did they think much of his expertise or judgment as an explorer, the man having shown himself ignorant of Arctic navigation.

Upon their arrival at the ship, everyone was fatigued. Bessels had promised the Eskimos, who on the final stretch home had driven the sledges hard for thirty hours straight, shots of his long-hoarded spirits. When he opened his locker he found it empty.

He searched frantically about the cabin but found not a single bottle, empty or full. He let out an emphatic curse in English, then added incredulously, "Forty-eight bottles in two weeks!" He continued his diatribe in German for several minutes. It was the most anyone had heard him speak at one time, as he was a reticent man by nature.

Bessels slammed the locker shut and walked away, bewildered.

A couple of days later, Tyson was surprised to come across Buddington walking along the shore. He took the opportunity to speak to the captain about the urgency to launch a northward expedition by land. Buddington pointed out that Bessels was in charge of sledge journeys since Hall's death. The doctor was not up for a major land expedition into uncharted regions, Buddington explained with some satisfaction, and was against anyone else using them to try for the Pole.

Tyson persisted. "Go to the doctor and tell him how things stand," he said. "Tell him if we don't make our move by land now, it will be too late. If he is obstinate, take the responsibility in your own hands. If he rebels, I will assist you in putting him in irons."

Buddington considered that idea for a moment. "No, I've got him just where I want him. I don't mean that he shall do anything."

Tyson knew Buddington meant what he said. The last thing

the captain wanted was for anyone else to discover the Pole or do anything significant on the expedition.

"You know, Captain, we are not going to accomplish anything in the boats with all the floating ice. We'll not get far."

"I know," Buddington said smugly "I don't expect the boats to do anything. That damned Chester is always talking about the North Pole. I want to get that fool off in a boat and the doctor, that damned organ grinder, with him. Let them catch hell. I tell you, Tyson, we should never have come this far north. I mean to start south as soon as there's an opportunity to do so, and if those boats are not back, damned if I'll wait for them."

Tyson decided to appeal directly to Bessels the next morning. The doctor listened politely but refused use of the sledges, claiming that he had his own plans for them.

Feeling dispirited, Tyson took a long stroll. He thought about why he had come on the expedition, and realized that he had done so solely because of Hall's leadership and enthusiasm. That loss was incalculable.

When Tyson returned to *Polaris* that night, he ran into Meyer preparing for a sledge trip to Newman Bay—on Bessels' orders—to take observations and chart the different capes and prominent mountains along the way. "If you want to go musk-oxen hunting, come along," Meyer said, "I won't be gone longer than four or five days."

Tyson jumped at the chance to get off the ship for a few days.

Before he left, Tyson had a heart-to-heart talk with Chester, telling him his views about using the boats. The first mate was wrapped up in the prospects for his boat expedition, and Tyson could not make him see the folly of the venture.

Tyson still had not told anyone about Buddington's nefarious plan to wreck *Polaris* on the way home. He had kept silent because he didn't know if anyone would believe him, and also because he did not wish to be labeled as mutinous. He knew that Buddington, in his powerful position as captain, would have ample opportunity to make Tyson appear in such a light. Buddington could simply deny that he said it, and charge Tyson with conspiring to undermine his authority. Good men had sailed home in irons for far less.

Tyson now decided, however, to take a chance and tell Chester, whom he respected as a fellow man of the sea, of the captain's threat. The first mate was shocked, and agreed it was a monstrous plan that must be prevented at all costs. Chester promised to keep watch on Buddington and to report any dangerous or suspicious behavior.

On May 9, with the temperature warming to 16 degrees, Tyson left in the company of Meyer, Joe, and Hans, with two sledges. Each one was fourteen feet long, with two and a half feet between the centers of the two runners, which were two and a half inches thick and ten inches high. Fourteen crossbars, four by two inches each, were fastened by strong lashes of rawhide to the runners, which had a play of about six degrees. This flexibility of the runners, a feature common to all Eskimo sledges, was a great advantage when transporting a heavy load over rough ice.

They took an east-northeast direction inland and succeeded in reaching Newman Bay, which averaged seven miles wide and sixty miles long. Meyer surveyed the surrounding area, and from there they went farther until reaching a northernmost latitude of 82 degrees, 9 minutes.

Tyson reveled in the Arctic solitude. He remembered a passage in a book by an earlier explorer that referred to the Arctic plain as "the land of desolation." Tyson saw before him silent and mysterious works of nature on a colossal scale. Some of the ravines were at least a thousand feet deep—enormous slabs of limestone and slate cut out as if by a huge chisel in the hands of the Creator himself.

Concentrating on getting game, as the ship's company was always in want of fresh meat, Tyson noticed the tracks of musk oxen coming from the southeast, heading for the bay. The next morning they came across a large herd.

A long-haired, dark-brown ruminant related to goats and

sheep, musk oxen have a dense undercoat and an ankle-length outer coat for protection against the cold. Standing up to five feet tall at the shoulder on legs that are short in proportion to their size and weight, they travel in herds of ten to a hundred. When threatened, they form an outward-facing circle with the young in the middle, and so await attack. A heavy creature, weighing from five to six hundred pounds when fully grown, the musk ox is somehow able to develop on what looks like a slender diet. Its food is the moss and lichen growing on the rocks, and to obtain it the animal must first scrape away the accumulated snow with its hooves.

The Eskimos released the excited dogs, who were trained to keep oxen at bay, allowing the hunters to get off clear shots. One of the first dogs to reach the herd was immediately thrown by the curved horns of a bull ox.

Tyson and Joe fired and reloaded as fast as they could, and the animals made no rush at them. It was not very exciting sport, for there was no more chance of missing them than the side of a house. Once the oxen got themselves into a circle and had been checked by the dogs, the hunters merely had to walk up within range and shoot them. Tyson and Joe methodically killed eight before the rest of the herd panicked and scattered.

After securing the slain animals, they made several trips hauling them to the encampment. They had some heavy butchering to do to skin them and cut up the prime pieces to take back to the ship. The next day, following a trail, they came upon the same herd and bagged four more. Sledges loaded with fresh meat, they headed back.

As they came over the rise overlooking Polaris Bay, they stopped in their tracks.

For the first time in nine months, smoke was rising from the stack of *Polaris*.

10

Journeys North

Tyson could not imagine why *Polaris* had steam up.

He knew the engineering crew had made a thorough examination of the engine in early spring and found it in excellent order, surprisingly unaffected by its hibernation during the long, cold winter. And recently it had been overhauled and cleaned.

As they came down the sloping ground to the ship, Tyson could see that *Polaris* was still locked in the ice. So why, he wondered, was she burning precious coal?

When the hunting party boarded the ship, they found everyone asleep below deck except for chief engineer Emil Schuman and his gang of firemen.

The day before, Schuman explained to Tyson, the ship had been found to be leaking forward from a broken stem caused by her position on the iceberg. Her bilge had flooded and some pumps had become choked. Water had gotten into the lower hold, damaging a quantity of provisions. They had fired up the boilers in order to run the ship's donkey engines to drive the most powerful pumps, which were clearing out the water that had collected.

In late May, the temperature had reached a year's high of

26 degrees—the low, in January, had been minus 43 degrees—the two boats for the exploring parties were sent over the ice on sledges to Cape Lipton, seven miles northward, since that was the only place they could be launched. Provisions and stores were also ferried by sledge to the location. Between there and Polaris Bay, the channel was narrower and the ice still packed. It was anticipated that open water would first appear above Cape Lipton.

The weather continued to warm. The snow was disappearing from the mountains and the pack ice softening. While it was now too late for any extended journey by sledge, Tyson still did not like the look of the ice conditions for boat travel, even though outside the bay the ice had begun to move and the water to show. He was in an odd position: while expressing his opinion that he did not think much could be done with boats this time of the season, he stood ready to lead such an effort north.

Meanwhile, as the warm weather melted the snow and ice that surrounded the vessel, the icy grip on *Polaris* started to loosen. The ship began to rise in the water.

With the rising water came reports of more leaks. On June 3, four hours of continuous pumping with a small engine were needed to clear her of accumulated water below decks. Two days later, a new and dangerous leak was discovered on the starboard side of the stern at the six-foot mark; two planks were found to be split. It was little wonder, since the strain on the hull had been tremendous with her stem resting on the foot of the iceberg for months. *Polaris* was a strong ship, but her awkward position atop the berg was enough to ruin any ship. In the berthing compartment in the forepart, crewmen could hear water streaming in at floodtide—a sound no shipboard sailor wanted to hear. An attempt was made to stop the leak, but it was not successful.

On June 7, scouting parties reported openings in the ice above Cape Lipton, news of which caused the boat crews to make final preparations for their departure. They packed sleeping bags that Hannah had sewn from skins and covered with canvas.

Tyson spoke to Buddington a final time about the ill-advised nature of the expeditions, warning of the dangers of navigating the boats in the ice, reiterating that they would probably not accomplish anything, and that there was a good chance one or both crews would meet with "serious if not fatal disaster."

The captain shrugged. He hoped the boat crews would "catch hell and get a belly full," he admitted. "If the damned fools live to come back, they'll be ready to go south."

For the first time before Buddington, Tyson found it impossible to suppress his indignation. He was deeply offended that his captain was hoping for the boat crews to meet with trouble, and told him so. Tyson recognized that Buddington viewed the boat expeditions as a means of getting Bessels out of the way, while extinguishing any further talk among the rest of the crew of taking the ship farther north later in the summer. As Tyson marched away angrily, Bessels, who had overheard the conversation, came up and patted him on the back, telling him not to be discouraged.

Tyson decided the best thing he could do was take good care of his boat and crew.

Chester and Tyson were each assigned a twenty-foot launch equipped with oars, and which could raise a sail. Chester's crew consisted of meteorologist Frederick Meyer and four seamen; Tyson took along Emil Bessels and four seamen. On June 7, both parties headed north by sledge.

Chester launched his boat off the cape at noon on June 9, an act that Tyson considered foolish given the ice conditions. After climbing a hill, Tyson spotted Chester's boat—not a mile away—already in trouble and making an unplanned stop on a large ice floe.

Observing them through an eyeglass, Tyson muttered, "Damn fools."

Tyson went hunting in hopes of bagging fresh game. He

dared not go out of sight lest he miss a chance of the ice opening up to the north. He shot some gulls and dovekies, and saw
brent geese. When he returned, Tyson asked the men if they had
eaten their supper. When they said they had not, he suggested
they grill the game he'd shot and, if tired, turn in.

They looked at him in astonishment. "Sir, are we not going
to start out on our journey?" one asked.

"We will not start," Tyson said, "until we have a chance of
succeeding."

"They've gotten a start on us," seaman William Nindemann
complained. "We'll not see Mr. Chester and his men anytime
soon. They're on their way to the Pole."

"In twenty-four hours," Tyson said evenly, "Mr. Chester
will not have a boat."

The men walked away, murmuring in discontent.

Tyson believed it was better for them to think he was luke-
warm or even afraid to go north by boat than to proceed while it
was unsafe to navigate a small boat in the ice, and risk losing
lives.

The next day as the men were having morning coffee, a man
came hiking over a nearby hill. It was the first mate, his exhausted crew following single-file.

"What happened?" Tyson asked when Chester came within
earshot.

"Our expedition went to hell. We lost our boat and nearly all
that was in her."

While warming around a fire with hot coffee, Chester and
his men provided details. After stopping on the large floe and
drawing up their boat, they had discovered open water about a
quarter of a mile away. They hauled the boat over to the other
side of the floe and launched from there. But the ice quickly
closed in once again, and they went only a little more than a
mile before they were compelled to pull up again onto another
floe. This time they found themselves stuck between two icebergs
grounded on the shore—a very dangerous position, for at this
time of year during thawing weather, icebergs could explode at

any moment. They set up their tent and prepared to spend the night. One of the seamen had the first watch; Chester and Meyer had lain down to rest about twenty yards from the boat, and the other three men were lying in the tent close to the boat.

Suddenly the watch shouted out, "The ice is coming!"

All immediately sprang to their feet and sprinted for the shore. They had hardly cleared the ice when the heavy floe, full of hummocks, came on with such force that it shattered one of the bergs, which fell with a thundering crash, crushing the boat to pieces. At the same time the pack ice crowded in, countless blocks of ice overlapping each other. It seemed that they would lose all, but after a while the pressure ceased and they managed to get out on the ice and save some of their belongings, although Chester lost the journal he had been keeping since the expedition had started.

Tyson could imagine how pleased Buddington would be at the fiasco when he heard about the fate of Chester's boat expedition. He would go around to the remaining crew telling everyone, "I told you so. I knew they would make a mess of it. Let them get a belly full! Let them get all the North Pole they want!"

Two days later, after Chester and his men had left for *Polaris* with a sledge driven by Joe, clearings in the ice suddenly appeared. Surprising his men, Tyson announced that they would launch immediately.

Before Joe had left for *Polaris*, he had given Tyson advice on navigating the ice in a small boat. The Eskimo also said that if Buddington made good on his threat to leave for home without waiting for Tyson's boat party, he and Hans had agreed they would disembark from the ship and wait for the stranded men. They would winter together if need be, said Joe, and then strike south come spring. It was a very kind and thoughtful offer, and a brave promise. Tyson felt less vulnerable knowing that the experienced native hunters, whose Arctic expertise would be needed to get through a winter without the provisions and shelter the ship afforded, would not desert them—even if their captain and ship did.

As Tyson's boat skirted the ice and plowed through virgin waters, it was a humbling sight to see their little boat, powered by sail and oars, flying along under the dark shadows of the lofty and precipitous mountains above them.

They arrived at Newman Bay—twenty miles farther north—in two days without much trouble, as Tyson deftly worked the boat through openings in the ice until stopped by a solid ice pack. They hauled up the boat and camped, waiting for an opening to the north. Bessels became incapacitated almost immediately by snow blindness and could do nothing to help.

A week later, Chester followed them, arriving at Newman Bay with his party in a flimsy canvas boat fit more for children to paddle about on a placid lake than for service in Arctic seas. Determined to make another try by boat, they had brought the small boat by sledge to their original launching site. The canvas boat would have been easily crushed like an eggshell in the ice pack, and was dreadfully slow, making only three miles an hour and taking on water in the least wind. With one man having to bail constantly, they had labored for five days to get to Newman Bay.

Chester arrived with news of the ship: she was in the same leaky condition, pumping by steam and consuming coal fast. It was the first mate's dire opinion that when *Polaris* was finally released from the ice holding her, she might not even float.

The boat crews waited for open water to the north. Since the ice continued to move south, they hoped the channel northward would be cleared before long. The weather turned pleasant. Little willows that were more like vines than trees and rose only a few inches from the ground were found in the ravines. Mosses and wildflowers, made all the more colorful against the stark backdrop, were now to be seen everywhere.

A number of attempts were made during the next week to get farther north, but they were unable to force the boats through the pack. Stricken by sudden snow squalls carried by a stiff northerly breeze, the crews remained hunkered down for days.

When the ice in the channel began to thicken and it became apparent that nothing could be done with the boats, Tyson proposed to organize a pedestrian exploring party. His plan was to forge ahead—alone or with one or two companions—and divide the remainder of the company into two-man teams that would follow as far north as the lay of the land permitted. Tyson remembered, when he had gone musk-oxen hunting the previous month, standing at the highest latitude they had reached and observing land rolling away to the north as far as he could see. It gave him great hope of a landward route to the Pole. Each party would leave caches of food at marked intervals so that they would have something to eat on their return. They would also take their guns with them to assist in procuring food. Tyson believed they might be able to walk, during the Arctic summer when game of various kinds was abundant, all the way to the North Pole. But he could get none of the men interested in his plan. They either opposed walking hundreds of miles or, inexperienced in Arctic geography, feared getting lost.

The boat crews continued to wait for the channel to clear. Two men returned to *Polaris* for provisions, taking with them Bessels, still suffering from snow blindness. His desire to return to the ship had been voiced nonstop since their arrival.

Before Bessels left, he again counseled Tyson not to be discouraged. "We must persevere," Bessels said in a most serious tone.

Tyson looked at the little doctor who had been so useless on every journey he had undertaken in the Arctic. His large eyes, reddened and swollen, stuck out like a lobster's. *We must persevere?* Tyson couldn't help himself; he fairly roared with laughter. The doctor, not knowing the source of Tyson's amusement, dropped his eyes. Tyson followed his gaze downward only to find the doctor's two large feet—out of proportion to the rest of his undersized body—encased in Eskimo moccasins that made his feet look even larger.

Tyson could not control himself. He continued his outburst—the best laugh he'd had since leaving home—as he waved weakly to the doctor, who climbed into a sledge and carefully wrapped himself in blankets.

Looking up from the sledge, Bessels vowed to return as soon as his eyes improved. Tyson read it as an empty promise; the doctor, he could see, had had enough of ice exploration. In any case, his absence would be no great loss.

"Fear not, Doctor," Tyson said as the sledge got under way. "Persevere we shall."

Forty-eight hours later, the two men returned with a note from Buddington ordering everyone to come back to the ship immediately, and explaining that Tyson and Chester were needed to help keep the vessel afloat. The men reported that the captain had nearly detained them and blocked their return, and had relented only when they urgently requested to be allowed to round up their shipmates.

Tyson well remembered Buddington saying he intended to head south as soon as there was an opportunity even if it meant stranding men on the ice. Regrettably, he believed that the *Polaris* captain was capable of doing just that. They had no choice, Tyson told his crew, but to return to the ship right away. His men were in agreement, but Chester said he and his crew would remain in the hope that the ice might yet open up, although Tyson could not see them accomplishing anything in the canvas boat.

The state of the ice in the channel was now such that they were unable to proceed any direction by boat, not even back south. Tyson's crew carried the heavy wooden launch overland for two days of fatiguing labor before finding a secure place to leave it, and walked the rest of the way to the ship—some twenty miles—arriving July 8.

Buddington swore when he saw that Chester's crew had not followed orders. "With or without those men," he told Tyson, "I shall start south at first opportunity."

Tyson said nothing but resolved that he would have something to say about the matter should the captain give orders to leave any of the crew behind, although he could not be sure who, among the officers, would support him against Buddington.

Upon his return to the ship, Tyson found *Polaris* still leaking badly. No one had made another attempt at repairs. Determining that most of the water was coming from the forward leak where the stem was broken at the six-foot mark below the water line, Tyson proposed carrying all the ship's stores aft so as to put the stern down. Then they could try to lay her bow on shore at high water so that they could get to the leak and fix it.

Buddington said there was not tide enough to raise the bow and refused to try.

Tyson next recommended that the ship stop making steam for pumping. The crew could man the ship's four excellent hand pumps and thus conserve coal, which was rapidly disappearing. No such orders were given.

Several days passed, and everyone kept a lookout for Chester's crew. Finally, they came walking over the plateau. All were fit, except for Chester, who had come down with scurvy and was very discouraged. They had waited until the ice cleared, he explained, and tried to sail the little canvas boat south. In the roughness of the ice, they nearly capsized, and were forced to abandon the boat to save themselves.

"All is ruined," the first mate said darkly. "There's no earthly reason to stay here any longer. We should go home as soon as possible."

His voice had been among the most ardent for staying another year to try for the Pole. That Chester, after the useless and exhausting boat expeditions, now wanted to go home meant that Buddington had won, Tyson realized.

Tyson recognized they had little choice now. Coal and provisions had been wantonly wasted, the vessel was leaking, and the continued thumping on the ice was endangering the ship's superstructure. *Polaris* must return home.

But he did not have to go with her. Tyson went privately to Buddington and asked to be given four tons of coal. Tyson said he would endeavor to get four men besides himself and stay another winter. Since there were enough provisions in the Observatory to supply five men for one year, he asked only for the coal from the ship's stores, along with sledges and dogs for which *Polaris*, on her way home, would have no more use.

His vision was the land that he had seen rolling away endlessly to the north. "I do not like returning without ascertaining where the land leads," Tyson said. "With some coal, provisions, two sledges and dogs, a few men and I should be able to find out."

Buddington eyed him suspiciously. "I don't have coal to spare."

Tyson stared down his commander. "You have it to waste but not to spare?"

"That will be all, Tyson."

"The best chance ever known in Arctic exploration is lost," Tyson penned remorsefully in his journal that night. "Why? Because the wretch in command is too cowardly and too incompetent to do anything himself and determined that no one else on board should do anything either."

Two weeks later a gale from the north arrived, blowing ice out of Polaris Bay and partially opening a clear passage. More leaks were reported aboard ship, and several feet of water were found to have accumulated in the ship's hold. Tyson, again pointing out the diminishing fuel supply, recommended that the crew be divided into watches, with everyone taking a turn at manning the hand pumps. Chester supported the plan—to save coal that would be needed to get home, he told Buddington, who finally agreed.

Some of the men grumbled, thinking that pumping should continue to be facilitated by steam. Soon thereafter, there was a sudden increase of water in the hold. It was reliably reported that someone in the engine room had willfully opened the stop cocks and flooded her so that the power pump would have to be employed. Such was the lack of discipline and respect for authority onboard that when Buddington went down to the engine room to check on matters, he had the hatch slammed shut in his face.

Once the flood of water in the hold was gone, the ship was kept free of water with five minutes of hand pumping every hour. Aiding the effort, some of the timbers appeared to have swollen and closed the seams that had worked loose during the winter.

With their departure to the south imminent, Tyson went ashore to check on Hall's grave and put it in order for all time. When their commander had been buried eight months earlier, the ground was frozen too hard to do much except cover the grave with stones for security.

Tyson was assisted in the task by Chester and several crewmen. The men worked silently at shoveling soil, shaping the mound, securing the wooden headstone and cutting in it the simple epitaph that had been written on the plank in pencil previously:

> TO THE MEMORY OF C. F. HALL,
> LATE COMMANDER OF THE NORTH POLAR EXPEDITION.
> DIED NOV. 8, 1871
> AGED 50 YEARS.

When they finished, they stood and looked at their leader's grave one last time. It still looked lonely and dreary, but not as forgotten and neglected as it had.

From the journal of George Tyson:

> *Aug. 1. Still in Polaris Bay. What opportunities have been lost! and the expedition is to be carried back only to report a few geographical discoveries, and a few additional scientific facts. With patience we might have worked up beyond Newman Bay, and there is no telling how much far-*

ther. Some one will some day reach the Pole, and I envy not those who have prevented Polaris from having that chance.

Several of the men went back to Newman Bay to try to recover some valuable scientific instruments and other items that had been left behind. Bringing back all they could find, they reported the channel beyond the bay was still full of ice. In all, three boats had been lost on the ill-conceived boat explorations, leaving *Polaris* with but two launches—each built for no more than eight passengers—in the event of trouble at sea.

On August 12, Merkut Hendrik, Hans' wife, delivered a healthy baby boy that was named Charlie Polaris by acclamation of the crew, in honor of both their fallen leader and the ship on which they sailed. The birth came as a surprise to many in the crew, who had not realized the stout Eskimo woman was pregnant beneath all the loose fur clothing she regularly wore.

As centuries-old tradition dictated, Merkut had attended to the delivery herself, left alone to live or die in childbirth. Once recovered, she had severed the umbilical cord with her teeth. By custom, the clothes she had worn during the birth were never to be worn again, and were burned on the ice by her husband.

As if ordained by a master planner, within hours of the birth the ice magically opened, leaving a clear passage through the water to the south.

Reborn as a seagoing vessel, *Polaris* weighed anchor and steamed from the bay that had provided a safe anchorage for the past year and upon whose shores her commander had found his final resting place.

Turning her stern toward the Pole, she headed south, not for the safety of home, but toward impending disaster.

III

Ice Hell

11
Adrift in a Nightmare

As *Polaris* steamed southward through Kennedy Channel en route to Cape Frazier and the open sea of Smith Sound, she came in contact with shifting floes and chunks of ice broken off from massive bergs. Bumping, crushing, and grinding noises were heard throughout the ship—ominous sounds to even the most experienced sailors.

Tyson had the watch on the evening of August 14—her second day under way. He was keeping *Polaris* on course down the middle of the channel. He hoped that by early morning she would be out of the narrow, icy channel and into less dangerous waters on her homeward trek.

At nine o'clock, Buddington came topside to take the helm. He had obviously been drinking. With the ship's supply of liquor long gone, he had been rummaging about everywhere, including the personal belongings of the crew, looking for anything to drink. To Joe's dismay, the captain had even gotten into the camphor-based medicine that Hannah rubbed on the Eskimo's back to relieve muscular pain.

For an hour the ship reeled under Buddington's erratic orders, turning this way and that—virtually every point on the compass. Exhausted at last, he went below, leaving the ship a hundred yards off a floe she had passed an hour earlier. In the process a propeller blade had been badly bent, one of their small boats had nearly been wrecked when Buddington sent it out to check ice conditions, and they had burned five tons of coal.

Tyson put her back on course and remained on deck until relieved by another officer. By morning they had cleared the mouth of the channel and were moving into waters less concentrated with ice. They steamed southward at five knots, angling slightly toward the west shore because the center was choked with ice.

Tyson finally went below to get some rest. When he awoke several hours later, he stepped on deck as a brilliant, red-sky dawn was breaking over the horizon. He was astounded to see the ship stuck in ice in the middle of the sound.

During the night Buddington had returned to the helm drunk, Tyson learned, and allowed the ship to fall off course again. Before she could get headed right and regain her lost momentum, the ice had closed in, locking her in its powerful grip.

A thick fog rolling down from the north soon engulfed the ship.

Buddington stood there, arms akimbo, smiling blandly at Tyson before staggering below as if to be sick.

We've reaped the fruits of drunkenness and incompetence, Tyson thought bitterly.

Bessels came on deck, passing Buddington as he lurched down a ladder. Horrified, the doctor ran from one railing to the other. "We are stuck in ice! He is drunk again! Where does the fool get liquor?" Bessels followed after Buddington.

At the helm, Tyson was told by the exasperated chief engineer Emil Schuman that he would no longer make steam for the captain unless advised to do so by Tyson.

"Mr. Schuman, let's try to get out of here," Tyson said.

"Aye aye," Schuman said enthusiastically.

Under power, *Polaris* pushed her way clear and made some

progress, but she had little room to maneuver in the icy waters. Finally, thick fog compelled Tyson to stop next to a floe and order the ice anchors set in place.

The next day when the fog cleared, another attempt was made but to no avail. Open water could be seen from the deck, but it was rapidly disappearing, and the ship could not reach it. Heavy floes had closed on them and were holding the ship in a vise.

A quantity of stores, clothing, and bags of coal were placed on deck so that they could be readily slipped overboard if it became necessary to abandon ship in a hurry.

Tyson knew that the ice conditions in Smith Sound varied greatly from year to year. This sort of pack ice had baffled Kane in July and August but had been traversed those same months without difficulty by other explorers. There seemed to be no general rule. Tyson thought it might have something to do with the force and direction of the winds when the ice began to break up in the north and push southward.

All around them was ice, with large bergs in sight, some grounded and others like colossal floating sentinels watching the progress of the slowly drifting floe to which the ship was held fast. Young ice had formed over the open water, and was already strong enough to bear weight. Snow and rain and fog succeeded each other, and the ice, governing all, constantly groaned.

September came and went.

For six weeks they had done little except drift with the floe. Now and then they'd fired up the engines in a futile attempt to break free. On the last day of the month, open water could be seen to the south, but *Polaris* could not get to it. Water was also visible to the north, but still they were kept in the pack.

With the temperature dropping below zero, the crew knew that unless they could soon free themselves, they would be stuck on a leaky ship with a dwindling supply of coal to run the boilers, operate the pumps, and warm the berthing compartments.

October arrived fair and clear; with it came the realization by all that they would be spending a second winter in the Arctic. Tyson would not have minded wintering there, at approximately 78 degrees north, if they had been heading in the other direction with future northern explorations awaiting them come spring. Instead, without having done all they could in carrying out their mission of discovery, they had been waylaid not by the forces of nature but by the incompetence of a single man.

The captain had been increasingly surly and detached since they had been newly icebound. Wintering a second year on the ice had not been his plan but rather, a civilized Danish port on the coast of Greenland with ample food, liquor, women, warmth, and other comforts. He did not blame himself for the latest predicament, but while he still carried his mantle of authority, his leadership had been compromised and he knew it.

Tyson had had a confrontation with Buddington shortly before *Polaris* departed her winter anchorage. It had come to Tyson's attention that the captain and the ship's carpenter had been taking turns making "most foul use" of Hans' twelve-year-old daughter, Augustina.

"I am aware of this sordid affair," Tyson told his captain, "and it must stop."

"I am innocent," Buddington said indignantly.

Tyson did not back down. "She is but a child. I will not let it continue."

"I tell you I am innocent." Buddington looked about furtively to make sure no one else was listening. "But for God's sake, say nothing about it. Don't let the crew know."

In early October, a stiff northerly gale blew up, increasing their drift southward. More leaks were sprung; the power pumps now operated day and night, gobbling fuel at an alarming rate. As long as the ship remained supported in its cradle of ice, there was little chance of sinking. But should the ice crumble, causing *Polaris* to suddenly drift free, she could be smashed by the winds and currents against the nearest berg and sunk.

On October 14, Tyson had a nightmare in which the ship

was crushed against a mighty berg and the crew scrambled to save themselves. He awakened sweaty and shaking, with haunting images of being shipwrecked and stranded on the Arctic ice.

The next evening, pushed by a strong gale from the northwest, ice began to press in on *Polaris*. She did not lift to the unrelenting forces as much as she would have if she had been of a broader build—"flaring," as the whalers called it—which would have enabled her to rise more with the ice, reducing the pressure on her hull.

Tyson came out of his room on the starboard side, looked over the rail, then went to the port-side railing. He could see the ship struggling to rise to the pressure but unable to do so, then coming down hard on the ice, breaking it and riding it under her. The ice was heavy, and the ship creaked in every timber with her valiant effort.

Most of the crew came topside to see what was causing the unsettling noises.

At that moment the chief engineer sprang up from below. "She sprung a bad leak aft," Schuman cried. "Water is gaining on the pumps!"

Hurrying below, Tyson found Buddington in the galley and told him of the engineer's alarming report. Buddington threw up his arms and rushed on deck.

"Throw everything on the ice!" Buddington ordered.

Instantly, all was mass confusion. Startled crewmen began seizing things indiscriminately and throwing them overboard: barrels of flour and rice, forty-five-pound cans of pemmican, boxes of preserved meat, five or six tons of coal. Most were the supplies previously placed upon the deck in anticipation of such a catastrophe, but they were now being flung over the railing with no thought given as to how or where they were landing.

With her rising and falling motion, the vessel was constantly breaking ice around her and opening new cracks. Supplies were being thrown into these black holes and lost, while other supplies were crushed between the ice and the ship's hull.

To try to save provisions, Tyson and several men dropped

onto the ice; more followed in a new howling storm. The Eskimos, ordered off the ship by Buddington so they could be on the ice to help in the emergency, went over the side with all their belongings.

Tyson tried to get the crewmen still throwing stores overboard to stop until the supplies already endangered were out of the way, but was unsuccessful. Even as they worked on the ice, supplies were being tossed overboard, and most sank or ran under the ship and were lost.

The night was fearfully dark and stormy on the ice. It was impossible to see more than a few feet. The work was slow and hard going, and those working on the ice struggled until they could scarcely stand on their feet.

At ten o'clock Tyson went back aboard to check on the condition of the ship.

"How much water is she making?" he wearily asked Buddington.

"No more than usual," the captain replied nonchalantly.

It turned out there was no new leak, and the power pumps were holding their own. As the ice had lifted her up, the water in the hold had been thrown over to one side with such a rush that Schuman mistakenly thought a severe leak had been sprung.

While Tyson was disappointed with the chief engineer, an experienced and competent officer, he was utterly disgusted with the way Buddington had panicked and given life to such an emotionally charged and disorganized state. It was the worst example of naval leadership and shipboard discipline he had ever witnessed. What would have happened in a true emergency? he pondered. How many lives would have been needlessly lost?

As there were still supplies scattered about, Tyson went back on the ice. Unbelievably, some men were continuing to fling stores over the railing. From the ice, Tyson ordered them to stop.

Suddenly, there were loud cracking sounds, and Tyson felt the ice weakening under his feet. He yelled to Buddington of the new danger and insisted everyone on the floe be taken back on board as quickly as possible, along with the two boats.

Instead, Buddington ordered Tyson to move the boats farther from the ship, apparently still concerned about having to abandon ship during the night.

Tyson turned to obey—and at that instant the floe exploded.

The ice *Polaris* was tethered to burst into fragments, and the ship violently yanked free of her ice anchors. Some of the men tried in vain to reach the vessel, but the ice was breaking up too quickly. The drifting ship disappeared in the darkness.

It was snowing at the time, and the wind was blowing so hard that one could not look or even catch a breath to the windward. Tyson was not sure who was still on the ice and who had gone back to the ship.

Screams cut through the night; some men were floating away on small pieces of ice. Tyson hurried to launch one of the small boats, and noticed nearby a bundle of musk-ox skins stretched across a rapidly widening crack. He quickly pulled the bundle toward him, and to his astonishment he saw Hans' three youngest children rolled up in the skins, sound asleep. In another moment they would have been lost.

Shortly after Tyson launched to pick up stragglers, other crewmen took the second boat out. Soon everyone was together on firm ice.

They did not dare move about, for in the darkness they could not see the size of the floe they were riding. The men, women, and children—exhausted from the labor and excitement, sought whatever shelter they could from the storm by wrapping themselves in musk-ox skins and lying down.

Tyson alone stayed awake all night, listening and watching for any new ice breakage. All day he had been unable to shake his nightmare, and now, in the dark, in the midst of a ferocious storm, it had come terribly true.

When morning came at last, Tyson surveyed their surroundings. He could now see what had caused the immense pressure on the ship. Heavy icebergs had pressed upon and broken the floe to which the ship had been fastened. They were marooned on nearly a circular piece of ice a mile in diameter and about five miles in circumference. Their piece of ice was fast between heavy icebergs, which were grounded, and was therefore stationary for the time being. The floe was not level but full of hillocks, and also ponds or small lakes that had been formed by the melting of the snow during the short summer. The ice was of varying thickness; some of the mounds were probably thirty feet thick with the flat parts no more than ten or fifteen feet. The floe was covered with fresh snow.

By the light of day Tyson saw that his party consisted of eighteen persons besides himself: nine crewmen, all foreign nationals except for one; four adult Eskimos, and five children, ages twelve years to two months old.

The ice-floe party consisted of meteorologist Frederick Meyer, English steward John Herron, cook William Jackson, and German seamen John W. C. Kruger, Frederick Jamka, William Nindemann, and Frederick Anthing, Gustavus W. Lindquist, a Swede, and Peter Johnson, a Dane, both of whom were fluent in German. Also, the two Eskimo families: Joe, Hannah, and their child, Punny; Hans and Merkut and their children, Augustina, Tobias, Succi, and their infant.

Most of the stores thrown overboard and salvaged during the night were gone; they had sunk or floated away on pieces of broken ice. They were left with only a few sledge loads of goods that Joe and Hannah had managed to haul well back of the ship onto solid ice. A few saws, tools, and lanterns had been salvaged, and they were fortunate to find themselves with nine dogs, the rest having been taken aboard ship during the storm or lost when the ice split open.

The men had recovered guns, pistols, ammunition, and their bags of clothes and some personal possessions; most had brought their things with them before they went onto the ice. Tyson alone was without his belongings or even a change of clothes. He had on only the lightweight clothes he had been wearing when he stepped on deck prior to the ensuing panic: a three-year-old pair of tattered sealskin breeches, an undershirt, overshirt, cotton jumper, and a Russian cap. His heavy seal-skin outer garments were still on hooks in his cabin.

The gale blew itself out, and by midday it was almost calm. Every heart was filled with the same longing: when would *Polaris* come to their rescue?

Since that morning's first rays of light, Tyson had continually scanned the horizon but seen nothing of the vessel. The most logical explanation for the ship not coming for them was that she had been lost during the night. Because that was possible, he was determined that the group make their own way rather than wait around for a rescue that might not happen.

He surveyed the floe to find the best lead so that they could launch the two small boats and get to the western shore of Ellesmere Island ten or fifteen miles away. On its coast, he thought they might find what was left of the ship and any survivors. Failing that, they might meet up with local Eskimos who could assist them in procuring food and shelter during the winter. Before he went scouting, he had roused the men from their furs—many had been covered during the night by snow—and ordered them to make the boats ready for immediate departure.

When he returned, the men were still inert, and in no hurry to move. They were of the mind that *Polaris* would be back soon to pick them up, so why bother doing anything? They complained of being tired, hungry, and wet. Since they had had nothing to eat since three o'clock the day before, they decided they must eat first. Nothing could induce them to get going.

Tyson, impatient to get the boats off and reach shore, had to wait. Although he was the only officer in the group and therefore in command, discipline had been so lax aboard ship since Hall's death that the men were accustomed to doing largely as they pleased. He might have taken one of the boats himself, but he knew that if *Polaris* did not come and pick them up, they could not all fit into the remaining boat. Those left behind would certainly perish. So he waited.

Not satisfied to eat what was at hand, some men even set about cooking. They made a fire out of wood scraps from broken boxes. They had nothing to cook with but some flat tin pans, in which they fried slices of canned meat, and also tried to prepare coffee, although it proved undrinkable. Some men then insisted on changing clothes.

Tyson kept his eye on conditions in the sound. The wind had started blowing out of the northeast and was bringing loose ice down fast. Though he feared they were rapidly losing their opportunity to get ashore, he was determined to try anyway.

They at last got started at nine o'clock, carrying their supplies and nineteen lost souls.

When they were halfway to shore, the loose ice Tyson had seen coming south crowded on their bows so they could not get through, and they had to return to the floe.

Tyson was the first to spot *Polaris* rounding a point north of them, eight or ten miles away. Under steam and sail, she was making speed and appeared to be seaworthy.

There was great rejoicing, for all thought that rescue was at hand. Though the pieces of loose ice had stopped them that morning in the small boats, it was not thick enough to keep *Polaris* from coming and taking them aboard.

Determined to get her attention, Tyson ran the colors up the boat's mast, but he received no answering signal.

Polaris was keeping down by the land on the west shore. Then, instead of steering toward the middle, where the ice-floe party waited anxiously, she dropped behind a nearby finger of the land. Tyson wasn't sure what to make of this development; he did not feel right about the ship not coming for them. Clearly, she was not disabled.

Taking a spyglass, he ran to the top of a frozen hummock. From there he saw the vessel behind a low-lying island. Her sails were furled, there was no smoke from her stack, and she was lying head to the wind. To his dismay, she appeared to be tied up to the bay ice, planning to stay. He did not see anyone on deck or in the crow's nest.

Surely, Tyson reasoned, the dark signal flag and crowd of humans against the stark white backdrop could have been seen at twice the distance if someone aboard ship had only looked their way. Weren't they *looking* for their lost shipmates? What kind of orders, if any, did Buddington have the crew under? To the list of wrongheaded command acts committed by Captain Sidney Buddington, this surely was the most sinister of all.

George Tyson had a difficult time believing what he was seeing: *Polaris* was not actively searching for the nineteen people stranded during the night on the unstable ice.

They had been abandoned!

12

Encampment on the Ice

If *Polaris* would not come to them, they would try for her.
The ice floe upon which they had been stranded began to drift, breaking up some of the ice that just hours earlier had kept them from reaching shore.

Tyson decided to seize the opportunity. He knew how astonishingly quick young ice could form, and he had also seen how suddenly a gale could come up and close the ice, making it impassable. They could be frozen in at any moment.

"We must get to the far end of the floe and launch the boats," he said. Reaching *Polaris* was their best chance of survival, he told his companions. "If we can't make the ship, we'll head for shore. Work our way down to her."

For the second time that day, he directed the men to prepare the boats. This time he wanted to leave behind almost everything except a few days' worth of provisions. That would make the craft as light and maneuverable in the water as possible.

Tyson went to locate a place to launch the boats so they would not be hauling them about uselessly. He was very tired and had eaten nothing but hardtack and a cup of seal-blood soup Hannah had given him. But the opportunity to get off the floe and to shore renewed his strength.

After finding a site with suitable open water, he returned to the makeshift camp. "We start immediately," he announced.

There was a great deal of murmuring by the men. They milled about, speaking German, which Tyson did not understand. Then they methodically began to gather up all their things, obviously unwilling to leave anything behind.

Tyson was baffled. Did they not recognize the crisis at hand? From the disposition shown by the men, he knew it was going to be difficult to get them to do what was necessary, even for their own safety and survival.

As if still in a dream state, Tyson was able to see the whole of winter before them if they failed to reach *Polaris*. He did not like what he saw. How would they do it without ship or shelter or sufficient food to get them through the long, dark winter? At some point the ice they were standing on would break up into pieces too small to live upon. What then? And what about the women and children?

He feared if they failed to reach the ship, many if not all of them would perish before winter was done. Yet the men whose lives he was fighting to save stood their ground defiantly, wasting precious time.

Finally, a spokesman for the Germans announced that they would take their belongings with them and as many provisions as they could carry. Furthermore, they would haul only one boat across the floe because two boats would be difficult to take overland such a distance. Once again, it was apparent they felt no obligation to follow the orders of a ship's officer. A single overloaded boat in these waters trying to circumvent drifting ice was a recipe for disaster, but Tyson was outnumbered. All he could do was stand back as the men loaded the one boat.

Tyson led the way across the ice to the launch site he had found, followed by the Eskimo families and then the men bringing the boat with help from the dogs.

They had not gone more than two hundred yards before a

gale burst upon them, filling the air with flying snow and lowering visibility to only a few yards. Tyson got across the floe, but when he reached the water, he was surprised to see that the natives and seamen were not behind him. Only the cook, William Jackson, had followed, and when he saw the others were not behind him, he ran back for them.

When they finally arrived, the men complained about having to launch the boat after the exhausting trek across the ice. As they rested, Tyson set out to ready the boat. When he looked for the oars, he found only three when eight were called for; the sail was missing, and unbelievably, there was no rudder.

Tyson flung an oar angrily onto the ice. He had trusted the men to prepare the boat while he went to find a launch site, and this was the way they had done it! He could not imagine why the men were so lackadaisical about getting off the floe. For experienced sailors to start on a boat trip with three oars and no rudder and sail was inexcusable.

They launched anyway; by then the wind was blowing furiously in their faces. In the crippled condition of the overloaded boat, they were soon blown back and were compelled to haul the boat back on the ice. By this time the men were spent. No one had the energy to carry the boat back across the floe, so they left her where she lay.

Night was coming on. The day was lost, and their opportunity with it. They would be spending another night on the ice.

Back at camp, Tyson put up a small canvas tent. After chewing on a slice of frozen meat until it became edible, he was glad to creep into a tent he shared with several others, pull a heavy musk-ox skin over him, and get his first sleep in two days. The rest of the party slept under the boat, which was overturned to provide protection from snow and sleet.

Tyson was awakened in the morning by a cry of alarm. He quickly crawled from between the ox skins, now wet underneath because his body heat had melted the ice.

It had snowed during the night, but that was nothing.

Tyson saw the new threat: the ice had broken into several pieces. They were separated from the portion of the floe upon which they had left the other boat. He called the rest of the men awake, advising them to go for the second boat before it was too late. It could have been done safely with teamwork, for there was no sea running between the broken pieces as yet and they had not separated much. But the men, stupefied with fatigue and fear, were afraid. They refused to budge.

They had drifted southwest, Tyson reckoned, although he had neither compass nor chronometer with him. A compass had been left in the other boat, and he did not even have his watch, which was back aboard ship.

Their piece of ice, which had been the centermost and thickest part of the floe, was no more than a hundred and fifty yards across in any direction. A windswept sea was running, and before their eyes, piece after piece of their fragile island broke off into the frigid waters.

Standing with his frightened shipmates, Tyson offered a silent prayer.

God, grant us we may have enough left to stand upon.

Tyson beseeched Joe and Hans to catch seal. Hans had signed on with the expedition as hunter and dog driver, and he was capable in both regards. Joe was one of the best hunters to be found in all the Far North.

Tyson knew if Joe and Hans could hunt enough seal, they could all live through the long winter, even after their provisions were exhausted. Without seal, they would have no fresh meat and no warm food, for they would cook with blubber oil as the natives did.

Their first day hunting, Joe and Hans bagged three small seals, enough to feed a few people, but hardly more than a few morsels each for nineteen people. They could have caught more but for the irresponsibility of the men who frightened off many by taking long-range pot shots at the seals when they raised their heads in open waters.

For the next two days the weather was so bad they could do nothing on the ice. When it cleared, they saw their floe had been driven toward land—the eastern shore of Ellesmere Island was only six miles away. New ice had formed between their position and the land, however. It was too thick to get a small boat through but not yet strong enough to walk upon. They were stuck in a no-man's-land where, in ice closely packed and stationary, they were to remain for the next two weeks.

On the morning of October 21, Joe was hunting on the ice when he saw one end of their lost boat nearly buried in snow on a nearby chunk of ice floe, from which it seemed possible to recover the vessel.

Tyson and Joe set out to do so right away. They knew they might not have such a good a chance again. They took the dogs and, when they reached the boat, harnessed them to it. In this way they were able to drag it back, and managed to do so without damaging the hull. They also recovered one large can of pemmican, twenty-seven two-pound cans of preserved meat, and six large bags of bread.

Everyone now agreed that their best chance was to wait for the ice to get strong enough for them to walk to shore. Tyson rued the fact that they had no sledges. If they used the boats to haul their provisions over rough ice, there was the danger of damaging them and rendering them unseaworthy should they be needed to escape by water. Still, as bad as their situation was, having the boats with them was a piece of luck. The vessels were their salvation, for in an emergency they could use them for both water and overland travel.

Tyson saw that a large floe had shifted during the night and lay halfway between them and shore. Since their piece of ice was shrinking constantly, he convinced the others that they should move to the bigger floe while it was so close. They did so on October 23, dragging the loaded boats over the ice by dog and manpower, then launching them for the short trip. In the process they expended every ounce of their energy and used all of the few hours of diminishing daylight the Arctic afforded them in mid-fall.

The only things left behind on the dwindling piece of ice were the kayaks belonging to Joe and Hans. None of the white men knew how to use the unballasted sealskin shells, but they were indispensable to the natives for open-water hunting in spring and summer. When Tyson asked for volunteers to help save them, no one stepped forward. After Joe and Hans started off alone, the cook, William Jackson, and William Nindemann, the brave seaman who had climbed an iceberg to secure *Polaris* by ice anchors, ventured over to help. Unfortunately, only Hans's kayak was saved.

The next step was making shelters. They built igloos, with Joe doing most of the work because he knew how and was energetic, but with all hands assisting and carrying out his directions. First, the ground was leveled off, and then the half of the floor farther from the entrance was slightly raised above the other half. The raised part at the back was the parlor and bedroom; the front part was the workshop and kitchen. The walls and arched roof were composed of square blocks of hard snow, packed solid by the force of the wind. A block was about eighteen cubic inches of compressed snow or ice. A piece of animal membrane, if one was to be had, could be fitted in for a window. The entrance was very low, and because it was reached through an alleyway of similar construction, one had to almost crawl inside. At night or whenever it stormed or was very cold, the entrance was closed up—after the residents were inside—by a block of snow. There was hardly room to turn around in the huts, and an ordinary-sized man could stand up straight only in the center of the dome. From that point the walls sloped gradually until they met the ground.

Their form allowed igloos to withstand the harsh Arctic weather well. Often snowed under so that they could not be distinguished from natural hillocks, these ice huts could not be blown over in the fiercest wind. Eskimos used igloos in winter only; the summer sun was fatal to them, as was rain. When the igloos began to thaw, Eskimos took to their sealskin tents for shelter.

Quite an encampment was built: a large igloo for the men, a smaller one for Tyson and Meyer to share since they were the two senior ranking members of the party, a storage hut for the provisions, a cookhouse, and a residence for Joe and Hannah and their daughter. These structures were united by arched alleyways built of snow, with one main entrance and smaller ones branching off to individual huts. An igloo for Hans and his family was built separately but nearby.

With an oil-burning lamp, an igloo could be kept sufficiently warm. The lamp traditionally used was made out of a soft sandstone indigenous to the land. It was hollowed out, like a shallow dish, with an inverted edge on which was placed a little moss for wicking. When lit, the moss sucked up the oil from seal or whale blubber. This was all the fire Eskimos had in the cold country for heating their huts or for cooking.

They had no proper lamp with them on the ice, however. One was contrived out of an old pemmican can, and having no moss, Hannah cut up a piece of canvas for wicks. It worked so well she made more for the other huts, although somehow the seamen could not understand how to use the makeshift lamp. They either got the blubber all in a blaze, or else they got it smoking so badly that they were driven out of their igloo.

The men, frustrated, soon began breaking up one of the boats for firewood.

This was bad business, Tyson knew, for the boats were not designed to carry more than eight men. That had been obvious when they loaded the entire party into one and found it impossible to make progress. If they had to travel in a single boat again to save their lives in treacherous waters, it could be disastrous. But he could not stop them, situated as he was without any authority other than what they chose to concede to him.

What's more, the men were armed, while Tyson was not.

While he had been on the ice trying to look after the ship's stores as they were being flung overboard, the crew had been gathering their guns and other possessions in the event the ship was abandoned. If for no other reason than the guns they all carried, Tyson knew to choose his battles with the men carefully.

He took account of their provisions. By successive trips across the ice, they had gathered all together nearly everything that had been on the floe when they first drifted away from *Polaris*. He found they had twelve bags of bread—each containing a dozen loaves—fourteen cans of pemmican, fourteen hams, ten dozen cans of meats and soups, one can of dried apples, and twenty pounds of chocolate and sugar. While the pemmican cans were large, each weighing forty-five pounds, the meats and soups were only one- and two-pound cans; the hams were small and the dried-apple can was a twenty-two pounder.

When the food was divided into portions for nineteen people, it was obvious—unless they reached land or could catch seals to live on—that they would not survive. If they had to remain on the floe, it would be April or May before they would drift far enough south where they could expect to be discovered and picked up by a commercial whaling ship.

Tyson instituted a daily allowance of eleven ounces for each adult, and half rations for the children—just enough, he reckoned, to keep body and soul together. A pair of scales, using shot as weights, was fashioned to measure out portions so there could be no complaints of favoritism. He established this system and insisted on its observance or else their supplies would soon run out altogether.

This caused a good deal of discontent, particularly from those who had regularly been eating more than others. It was hard for some of them to reduce their intake, and a number of men became weakened. Tyson, built on a large frame, became so weak as his body struggled to adapt that he staggered from sheer want of strength, but he understood and accepted—as some of the men did not—the sheer necessity of rationing.

Tyson saw that this was a new concept to the Eskimos, who

traditionally preferred to eat while they had food and let tomorrow take care of itself, even if they knew that they might have nothing for many days. As a result, Eskimos sometimes had abundance and other times were reduced to famine. They would on occasion store away provisions and build caches on their traveling routes, but this was done only when they had more than they could possibly consume at the time—as when they had been fortunate enough to kill a whale or walrus.

Tyson gave the Eskimos the same amount as everyone else. He secretly hoped the rationing would encourage continued determination in their seal-hunting efforts. However, there was one consequence he did not foresee: Before anyone noticed, Hans had taken away two of the dogs, and killed and skinned them. His wife cooked the meat over the blubber-oil lamp in their igloo, and it was served to the hungry family at one sitting.

They were now down to seven dogs, and soon those too would go from companion to entree. There was nothing for the dogs to eat, since the canned meat was in too limited supply for the humans to share with animals. The dogs would eat only in the event of surplus seal meat. In the meantime, they were down to nothing and almost dead.

Joe and Hans went out daily in search of seals. The blubber was nearly gone, and if they did not bring in some seals, the igloos would soon be in complete darkness and the party would be eating frozen food, with no means to cook or even thaw it. They also needed to keep melting freshwater ice for drinking. Fortunately, enough of this type of ice had gathered in crevasses from the snowstorms, but they still had to have a means of melting it.

On a cold and dark night Tyson, weak and hungry, wrote by flickering light in the igloo he shared with the Eskimos:

Oct. 26. We lost sight of the sun's disk three days ago. May the great and good God have mercy on us, and send us seals, or I fear we must perish. We are all very weak from having to live on such small allowance, and the entire loss of the sun makes all more or less despondent. There now seems no chance of reaching the land—we have drifted so far to the west. We are about eight or ten miles off shore.

> *"Miserable we,*
> *Who here entangled in the gathering ice,*
> *Take our last look of the descending sun;*
> *While full of death, and fierce with tenfold frost,*
> *The long, long night, incumbent o'er our heads,*
> *Falls horrible."*

13

Cry with Hunger

L ike a wandering tribe of the Far North in the dead of winter, the lives of the ice-floe party now depended on their native hunters finding seal.

The seal had long been the Eskimo's staple winter food and most valuable resource. It provided them with not only their own diet but also food for their sledge dogs, as well as clothing, material for making boats, tents, harpoon lines, and fuel for light, heat, and cooking. But finding seal in winter is not easy since they live principally under the ice and can be seen only when the ice cracked. An inexperienced person would never catch one.

Being warm-blooded, seals cannot remain long under water or ice without breathing, and in winter they are forced to make air holes through the ice and snow through which to breathe. At the surface these holes are small—not more than two and a half inches across—and are not easily distinguished, especially in the dim and uncertain light of wintertime.

Seals are very shy, too, and seem to know when they are being watched. A native hunter sometimes remains sitting over a seal hole—bundled up in skins and not moving or making a sound—for as long as forty-eight hours before getting a chance to strike. And if the first stroke is not accurate, the game is lost.

At that time barbed spears were used. Because the skull of the seal is exceedingly thin, if the blow was well aimed it was sure to penetrate. The seal could then be held securely until the breathing hole was sufficiently enlarged to pull the body through. Although Joe and Hans sometimes shot seals, they had to spear their prey before it sank or floated away.

On most days the two Eskimos went out hunting, and nine times out of ten they returned empty-handed. The long hours of traversing across the ice through blustering winds and near-zero visibility and waiting patiently over seal holes did not demoralize them, nor did their repeated failure to find game. Each understood his role and was prepared to do it again the next day, and the day after.

Following a brief storm, thick with new snow, the weather cleared up on November 4. Tyson could see that the floe was entirely surrounded by water and drifting swiftly in the current.

Two days later, Joe killed a seal, for which everyone was grateful. Its carcass provided a few bites of fresh meat for every man, woman, and child, blood for a strong fat-laced broth made by Hannah, and enough blubber to keep the lamps going.

The weather turned bad the next day, and all were confined to their igloos, with the exception of Joe and Hans, who went hunting in a driving blizzard. After they had been out for some time, they became separated. Joe, after trying his luck hunting alone, made it back to the camp, fully expecting to find Hans had preceded him. Joe was much alarmed when he learned Hans had not arrived. He persuaded one of the seamen to go back with him to find Hans. As they were going along, peering through the fast-coming darkness, they saw what they took to be a polar bear approaching them. They cocked their pistols and made ready to open fire as soon as he came into range. When the creature came a few steps closer, they saw that it was not a bear but poor, lost Hans. In the heavy weather they had been completely deceived. The fur clothing Hans wore was covered with snow, and he had been crouched over nearly on all fours, scrambling up a snow-covered hummock.

Frederick Meyer, with whom Tyson had increasingly been at odds as the meteorologist assumed leadership over his fellow Germans, decided he would rather reside with his countrymen, and moved to the large igloo housing the men. Tyson found Meyer to be a strange, arrogant man. He had recently come up with a story that he was somehow related to Prussian royalty. Believing him, the Germans showed "the Count" new deference.

With Tyson facing a winter alone in his igloo, Joe and Hannah graciously invited him to move into their quarters, which he did.

When the daily allowances were handed out at the supply igloo they were taken back and prepared at three different messes. The men cooked their own food over a fire, burning the remains of the wood stripped from the boat. Hans' wife, Merkut, cooked for their family over an oil lamp, and Hannah did the same for her husband, daughter, and Tyson, who found that the Eskimo woman could make a meal out of almost anything. Granted, he preferred not thinking about the contents of some of her dishes before eating them.

On November 15, five dogs were shot after suffering much from hunger. They were skinned and eaten. Only two remained.

We are all prisoners, Tyson, sick with rheumatism and hardly able to hold a pencil, wrote in his journal on November 19. *By the movement of the ice, I judge we are drifting to the southward. The natives tell me that they saw two bear tracks and five seal holes, but they brought home nothing. I wish they had better fortune, for we need the fresh meat very much. The children often cry with hunger. We give them all we can.*

That day Joe saw three seals, but was unable to secure any of them.

Living on such short rations meant the subject of food was constantly on one's mind, a particularly cruel effect of starvation. While the stomach is gnawing with hunger, it is almost impossible to think clearly, for any length of time, upon anything else but the matter of eating. As body weight declines, a starving person becomes sluggish and lethargic. The skin thins, becoming cold, pale, dry, and stiff, and the body's natural defenses against disease deteriorate.

How long they could bear it, Tyson did not know. If they could make do on what little they had left and get through until early April, they could rely on their guns to hunt. If game failed them then and rescue was not imminent, they would perish.

On November 21, Joe and Hans saw two bear tracks and five seal holes. They each staked out a breathing hole, and soon had bagged two seals. The seals brought in were received with much gratitude. So keen were the appetites of the party that the seal meat and skin was eaten uncooked, with the hair still on. Scalding water would remove hair, but they did not have sufficient heat to boil such quantities of water.

From the effects of exposure and want of food, some of the men trembled as they walked, and were unable to do much around camp. Mostly, they stayed in their huts, wrapped in skins and furs. It was now too dark to walk about, and even if there had been a reason to, it was too cold. The chill was made more pervasive because they had so little heat in their systems from lack of food. Exercise, which creates hunger, was avoided as a matter of economy. Remaining still and keeping as warm as possible was found to be the most agreeable mode of passing the time, and best suited for the circumstances.

Still, Joe and Hans ventured out in search of food. Without their courage, fortitude, and invaluable services, the party's chances of surviving the ordeal would have been much diminished. While the winter darkness lasted, few seals were to be found, but those that were became life-sustaining. When the period of daylight became longer, the Eskimos expected to hunt not only seal but bear and fox as well.

When Tyson learned that the men were hatching plans to

break up the last boat for firewood, he ventured uninvited into their domain to speak his mind.

"It will not do to touch the other boat, even if it means no fire or warm food," he said sternly. "The time must come, if we live to see it, when the boat will be our only means of safety."

Things were said in German that he did not wait to hear translated. Tyson wondered again why the men who could speak English and had done so freely aboard *Polaris* were unwilling to do so now. In any case, he did not intend to discuss this issue. Nineteen lives depended on the one remaining boat.

Tyson turned abruptly and departed.

> *Nov. 22. My situation is very unpleasant. I can only advise the men, and have no means of enforcing my authority. But if we live to get to Disco they will have to submit, or I shall leave them to shift for themselves. I will not live as I have lived here. But here I am forced to live for the present: there is no escape. It is not altogether their fault either; they were good men, but have been spoiled on board Polaris. For the last year nearly they have been allowed to say, do, and take what they pleased. Such as they were, had they been under good discipline, and left on the ice like we are, I could have saved them; but I don't know how it will be now. And then, too, there appears to be some influence at work upon them now. It is natural, no doubt, that they should put confidence in one of their own blood, but they will probably find out that all is not gold that glitters before they get through this adventure.*

Tyson lay sick for several days and ate scarcely a thing for a week. He was so weak upon getting up that he could hardly stand. He knew he must eat for strength alone, and partook of his daily allowance, leftovers from Joe's last kill: seal, eaten raw.

Everyone was suffering greatly. The cold seemed to penetrate to the very marrow. The Eskimos had long believed that man could not repel cold well without a certain quantity of fresh meat, and that no better meat served the purpose than seal. But now there were days when Joe and Hans couldn't go onto the ice to hunt given the total want of light and heavy winds that piled snowdrifts high around the encampment.

In contrast to the increasing alienation he felt from the men, Tyson enjoyed living with Joe and Hannah. In the long days and nights they spent together in close quarters, he came to appreciate their loyalty and intelligence. He could see why Captain Hall had grown so fond of them.

He was able to communicate his plans and wishes intelligibly to them, and they to express their ideas to him. He played checkers with them on their makeshift board, using buttons on squares marked out with pencil on a ragged piece of canvas. They could also play a respectable game of chess, and they understood card games as well as any sailor. Decks of cards went wherever sailors ventured; the first "civilized" instruction that natives of any land got were usually card games from sailors.

He also became close to their little girl, Punny. She sat wrapped in musk-ox skins, every few minutes saying to her mother, "I am *so* hungry." Hearing her and the other children cry with hunger made Tyson's heart ache, knowing that they were obliged to bear such privation with the rest. At such times he tried occupying her by playing games or drawing pictures together. Both wished to be elsewhere: his were mostly of ships under sail, hers of birds in flight.

He witnessed how, in Eskimo society, marriage was a partnership forged from a necessity for physical survival, based on strict divisions of labor. The husband and wife retained their own tools, household goods, and other personal possessions. Men built shelter, hunted, and fished, and women cooked, prepared animal skins, and made clothing. Drying and mending clothing was a crucial job, for in subzero temperatures dampness or the smallest tear in outerwear could bring sickness and death. Tyson understood better why Eskimo hunters made a habit of traveling with their women at their side.

Cry with Hunger   **165**

For Tyson, the worst part of the long, dark days was not the cold and hunger, but the sheer boredom of sitting all day with nothing to do but keep from freezing. It nearly drove him mad. There were few people to talk to and nothing to read—no books, Bible, magazines, or newspapers. He hadn't seen printed words, other than his own, in more than a hundred days.

They saved the tin of dried apples for Thanksgiving. That day Tyson ate a few dried apples as they came out of the can, a small portion of chocolate, and two biscuits, the size of which made ten to a pound. That was the "thanksgiving" part of the meal. To satisfy his fierce hunger, he was compelled to finish with strips of frozen seal entrails, sealskin—hair and all—just warmed over the lamp, and frozen blubber, which tasted sweet to a starving man. He was thankful that there was food of any kind to put in his stomach.

> No doubt many of my friends who may one day read this will exclaim, "I would rather die than eat such stuff!" You think so, no doubt; but people can't die when they want to, and when one is in full life and vigor, and only suffering from hunger, he doesn't want to die. Neither would you.

Tyson thought of home and family all day long. He had been away at sea on many Thanksgivings before but always with a sound keel under his feet, clean and dry clothes, and no thought of what he would have for dinner, for it would doubtless be turkey with all the trimmings aplenty and delicious. Never did he expect to spend a Thanksgiving without even a plank between him and the waters of Baffin Bay, making his home in an igloo with Eskimos on an ice floe. But he had this to cheer him: his loved ones were together in safety and comfort, and they knew nothing about his perilous situation.

> I wonder what they had for dinner today. It is not so hard to guess: a fifteen or sixteen pound turkey, boiled ham,

and chicken-pie, with all sorts of fresh and canned vegeta-
bles; and celery, with nice white bread; and tea, coffee, and
chocolate; then there will be plum pudding, and three or
four kinds of pies, and cheese, and perhaps some good sweet
cider—perhaps some currant or raspberry wine; and then
there will be plenty of apples, and oranges, and nuts and
raisins. And if the children have been to Sunday school in
the morning, they will have their little treasures, besides all
their home presents spread out too. How I wish I could look
in upon them! I would not let them know I was here, if I
could. How it would spoil their day!

With the arrival of December, complete darkness descended
upon them.

There was little change in their way of living. Mostly, they
lay still in their bunks; the more quiet they lay, the warmer they
stayed and the less food they could live on. The daily allowance
was now six ounces of bread and five ounces of canned meat.
These ingredients were mixed with brackish water for seasoning
and warmed over lamp or fire. Even this inadequate ration was
more than they could spare from their depleting stores.

While the darkness lasted, they had little hope of getting
seals. Bears only come where seals are to be caught, and foxes
usually followed in the trail of bears. However, the first week of
December a poor, thin fox wandered into camp in search of
food and was shot and killed. It had hardly a pound of flesh on
its bones—"all hair and tail," as one of the men said—but they
ate what there was of it, and picked its bones clean.

In the constant darkness, a serious disagreement arose as to
which way they were drifting. Frederick Meyer announced his
opinion that they were drifting eastward across Baffin Bay and
nearing Cape York, on the western shore of Greenland.

Tyson was certain they were not heading east at all. He
knew heavy ice such as the floe they were riding did not obey
the winds—not as loose, floating surface ice often did. Assuming the currents had not changed their natural course—and

he had seen nothing to indicate that they had—he knew from sailing these waters the past decade that they must be drifting south-southwest, which would put them closer to the eastern shore of Ellesmere Island and perhaps *a hundred fifty miles from Greenland.*

Normally, it would not have mattered what opinions were entertained as to the course of the floe, except that the German seamen wanted to believe Meyer, their tacit leader, that they were nearing the coast of Greenland. There was much discussion about taking the boat and heading to land, which they would then follow down to the Danish settlement of Disco, where they knew a large store of provisions had been left for the expedition.

Tyson realized if they started off in the hope of reaching Greenland, the result would be the death of all of them. Too late they would recognize that they were nowhere near Greenland but had the whole of ice-clogged Baffin Bay before them.

Would the men set out for Greenland, leaving Tyson and the Eskimo families to fend for themselves on the floe? If they were left behind without a boat, they could never get off, and would be doomed—awaiting the inevitable breakup of the ice floe underneath their feet, from which there could be no escape.

Tyson would not voice such thoughts without proof of their intentions, but he was concerned about what some of the men might be capable of doing. They openly complained about their miserable circumstances, as if those conditions weren't shared by everyone. In Tyson's view, they did not possess much self-control, courage, or endurance.

Had they moved more quickly to reach shore that first morning they had been separated from *Polaris*, the outcome would have been very different, Tyson knew. They could well have made it back aboard ship. He had since understood that the men that fateful morning had discussed the drift of the *Hansa* crew, and the gratuity of one thousand thalers donated by the Danish government to each man of that party. There had been talk that if they should drift likewise, they would get double pay from Congress! But Tyson appreciated the difference in the circumstances, even if they did not. The *Hansa* party had had ample time to get all they wanted from the vessel—provisions, clothing, fuel, and even a house frame—because there had been firm leadership aboard ship and no panic. And they had drifted along the east coast of Greenland, where the weather is moderate compared to that of the west coast. If this incident had influenced them in any way, they must have by now—after months of suffering—realized the sad mistake they had made. Why did they think Congress would handsomely reward them for coming back without their ship, and with their popular commander in his grave?

Everyone's weaknesses were most felt in the flesh, on attempting to do any kind of work. Tyson could not imagine where Joe and Hans found the reserves to go forth and hunt. While the crewmen were evidently uneasy, and their talk and plans at times bold, whenever they ventured outside and faced the cold, they were glad to creep back again to their shelter and such safety and certainty that they found there.

However, the Germans are organized now, Tyson wrote, *and appear determined to control their destiny. They want to be masters here. They go swaggering about with their pistols and rifles, presented to each of them after the death of Captain Hall. I see the necessity of being very careful; any disorder would be ruinous. They think the natives a burden, particularly Hans and his family, and they would gladly rid themselves of them. Then they think there would be fewer to consume the provisions, and if they moved toward the shore, there would not be the children to lug. With the return of light and game, I hope things will be better, if I can manage to keep all smooth till then. But I must say I never was so tired in my life.*

One day in their igloo Joe, who had all along kept his rifle and pistol and had not been willing to lend them to Tyson even for hunting, gave him the handgun and ammunition. Hannah sat next to him, their daughter wrapped in furs and asleep in her arms.

"Why are you giving me your pistol?" Tyson asked.

"Not like look in men's eyes," Joe said solemnly.

Tyson had never seen the Eskimo hunter afraid of anything, but he was now.

"They are very hungry, sir," Hannah said. "Joe and Hans not get enough seal."

"You're doing your best," Tyson protested. "Without you they'd be dead men."

"Afraid for family," Joe said. "Help protect?"

With horror Tyson realized the couple's worst fear was not abandonment on the ice by the rest of the party. It was far more evil: Joe and Hans would be killed first, then their wives and children would be killed—and they all would be *eaten*.

"With my life if they should try to harm any of you," Tyson promised.

It was a dark moment for them, facing the unthinkable.

Tyson brooded for days. Aside from the obvious crime against humanity, it would be the worst possible decision for the men to kill the natives. They were the party's best hunters; in winter or spring, no white man could catch seal like an Eskimo, who had practiced it all his life. It would be killing the goose which lay the golden egg.

Yet, Tyson sadly agreed with Joe and Hannah; he could not trust what that group of desperate, frightened, and hungry men were capable of doing—they who stayed to themselves so much and spoke only their language and did only what they wanted to do.

Keeping the pistol at his side whenever he ventured out, he kept a close watch. He was armed for the first time, and it would go hard with anyone who tried to harm his friends Joe, Hannah, young Punny, and the other Eskimos—the very people who had been doing the most to see that everyone survived on this God-made raft.

Dec. 7. Joe and Hannah are much alarmed. Cannibalism! God forbid that any of this company should be tempted to such a crime! If it is God's will that we should die by starvation, let us die like men, not like brutes, tearing each other to pieces.

Dec. 16. The fear of death has long ago been starved and frozen out of me; but if I perish, I hope that some of this company will be saved to tell the truth of the doings on Polaris. Those who have baffled and spoiled this expedition ought not to escape.

14

The Sun Rises

For Christmas dinner they divided up their last ham, which they had been saving for the occasion. That day they also saw land for the first time in months. It showed itself to the west—at a distance of forty to fifty miles. In all likelihood it was desolate Baffin Island, the largest island in Canada and 950 miles long. If the Germans were relieved they had not followed their leader's advice and set off to the east to find Greenland across treacherous miles of icy seas, they kept it to themselves.

The shortest and darkest day of the year was now behind them, and their southward drift was helping them to gain fast on the light. Bright streaks of twilight were beginning to show in the sky.

Tyson considered how different his feelings would be if they were drifting northward, into the Arctic night, instead of away from it. That would have been cheerless, if not altogether hopeless. Heading south, there was still hope they could make it if they had adequate daylight to hunt productively. He hoped yet to land safely on the coast of Labrador come spring or, better yet, to drift to the whaling grounds and have the good fortune to be picked up.

Two days after Christmas, Joe and Hans went hunting. They found the ice broken in many places and saw two seals but could not get them. The sun had not been seen in the sky since October, and they could see plainly in a kind of twilight for only about two hours in the middle of the day—an hour before and an hour after noon—and only then if the weather was clear.

That night Hannah tried to make a meal from a few pieces of dried sealskin she had saved for repairing clothing. Even after cooking, the remnants remained very tough. The natives had extremely strong teeth that could rip through almost anything, but when Tyson tried, his jaws ached as he chewed the old skin. They also ate all the refuse of the oil lamp: dried-out, burnt blubber. They were now willing to eat anything that would aid in sustaining life.

Hans shot a seal the next day but lost him. If they had been catching plenty of seal, such an accident would have gone unnoticed. But to the men, it seemed very stupid. Later that day Joe shot and killed a seal in a stretch of open water. As it floated away from him he shouted as loud as he could for his kayak, and some of the men carried it over to him. After getting in, he paddled off and was fortunate enough to bag his game.

It was a Greenland seal, a pretty creature when observed in its natural habitat. Its fur is a shiny white and beautifully spotted on the back and sides. It ordinarily weighs fifty to sixty pounds, and appears singly or in families.

To divide a seal properly, Eskimo-style, first the "blanket"— the skin, which includes the blubber—is taken off. It is inseparable as it comes from the creature, and is opened carefully in such a way as to prevent the blood from being lost. With the seal placed in such a position that the blood will run into the internal cavity, the blood is then scooped out and either saved for future use or passed around for each participant to drink a portion. The liver and heart, which the Eskimos consider delicacies, are divided equally so that all in the family get a piece. The brain is a tidbit, too, and is either reserved or divided. The eyes are given to the youngest child to eat. Then the flesh is cut up into equal portions, according to the size of the company. The entrails were usually scraped and allowed to freeze, and later eaten. The skins were usually saved by the natives for clothing, and also for many other domestic purposes, such as kayaks, the reins and harnesses for dog sleds, and tents. In fact, almost everything an Eskimo wore or used was furnished by the seal. Even the membranous tissues of the body were stretched and dried for the purpose of making semitransparent windows to their huts.

In their present circumstances of near starvation, they had but two uses for the seal: to eat it and reserve portions of the blubber for the lamps. The seal that Joe shot and recovered was but a small one, and when eighteen hungry people (the nineteenth, baby Charlie Polaris, was breast-feeding) were finished, there was nothing left but the skin and entrails. They would eat those, too, but not that night. The meal gave everybody new strength. The blubber derived from the little seal was almost invaluable to them for their lamps, and would last three weeks—warming their food and igloos, and providing light.

New Year's Day, January 1, 1873, was the coldest day they had yet experienced on the floe: minus 29 degrees. If they had been well fed and better clothed, they would have thought less about it, but as it was, the bitter wind flayed one through and through, letting each person know every weak and sore spot in his abused body.

"We cannot join in the glad shout at the birth of another year," Tyson wrote. *"I have dined today on about two feet of frozen seal's entrails and a small piece of congealed blubber. I only wish we had plenty of even that, but we have not."*

The natives went hunting every day as the light slowly increased, but were still thwarted by so little open water. On January 3, Joe found three seal holes in the ice, but it was so intensely cold that he could not stay to watch them. It stayed very cold for four days, making the ice firm and compact.

They were drifting in the widest part of Baffin Bay. Land to the west was still visible in the distance, now about eighty miles off, and solid ice extended in all directions as far as one could see. While there was more chance of open water on the Greenland or eastern side of the bay, Tyson knew there was little or no chance of the southward current taking them to it.

Provisions were disappearing faster than they should. Because Tyson distributed the rations, he knew there must be pilferage among the men, and as they were under no control, it did not surprise him. He would have set a round-the-clock watch to guard the stores if it was possible to stand the cold nights, but in their weakened condition it would have been fatal. Certainly, his own clothing—the same he had been wearing when he took to the ice that fateful night—was too thin to consider standing guard. He had been wintering without coat or pants, wearing only short breeches that went as far as the tops of his boots. None of the men had been willing to share with him any extra clothing they had, preferring to wear multiple layers for their own comfort.

Tyson was shocked to learn that the men were still planning to strike out for Greenland—next month, when they thought Disco would be due east and within reach, as they were told by their chosen adviser. They would not listen to reason or to anyone else. If they were risking only their own lives, the decision would have been bad enough, but the safety of the whole was imperiled, especially since they were determined to take the only boat. Having burned up one in their fires, they would not hesitate to appropriate the other.

On January 13, the thermometer stood at 40 degrees below zero. A gale came on for the next two days, bringing hope that it would open the ice for the hunters. When the wind abated three days later, the two Eskimos set off early for seals, which everyone prayed they would find.

Tyson recognized just how desperate their plight had become:

Jan. 16. I hear a pleasant sound, because it is a promising one for water; the ice is pushing and grinding, which

will surely open cracks. It seems strange to think of watch-
ing and waiting with pleasure for your foundations to
break beneath you; but such is the case. In our circumstances,
food is what we most want; with enough seal meat we can
face all other sorts of danger, but with empty stomachs we
are ill prepared to meet additional disaster.

At eleven-thirty that morning, he heard a glorious sound—a life-inspiring shout. The natives were calling for the kayak. That meant they had found water, and water meant seals.

Tyson called to the men to get the kayak. They had not yet turned out from their igloo to begin the day, and a long time passed before there was any response to his call. Eventually, help came, and they carried the little boat about a mile, where they found Joe and Hans and, nearby, a dead seal floating in the water. Joe quickly paddled out and retrieved it, and the small party returned to camp in triumph.

Upon their arrival, Tyson directed the seal be taken into Joe and Hannah's igloo to be divided up. However, the Germans, led by John Kruger, one of the worst of the malcontents among the crew and a man whom Tyson had come to suspect was pilfering at least some of the stores, snatched the carcass and took it toward their own hut.

Tyson reached for his pistol—only to discover he had left it in the igloo. At that moment he realized he would have gladly killed Kruger where he stood, no doubt triggering a fatal gunfight.

With such evil intentions being openly displayed by the men, and short fuses possessed by all, Tyson realized it might be impossible to save the party—worthy and worthless alike—from disobedience and lawlessness.

The men divided the seal to suit themselves, and the division went hard on the Eskimos and their families, the very men who had hunted day after day, in cold and storm, while these men lay idle on their backs or sat playing cards in the shelter of their igloos, mainly built by these same natives whom they wronged.

That night, Joe and Hans told Tyson that they had very

often suffered before for the want of food in the North, but they had never before endured anything like the present circumstances. The daily allowance was not enough to furnish heat or enable their bodies to resist the cold. Considering that they were outside battling the elements so much more than the rest, walking around and hunting, they really ought to be given a larger allowance of food. Tyson gladly would have, but he knew it would cause open mutiny among the armed men, destroying any semblance of harmony.

> *Jan. 17. The natives are out as usual, hunting for seal. They only got a small portion of the meat and a little blubber of the one last caught, the men keeping an undue proportion for themselves. This way of managing discourages the hunters very much; they labor, and see others consuming the fruits of it. But they dare not say much, for they are afraid for their lives.*

How the last two dogs continued to live Tyson did not know. Attempting to hunt for their own food, on January 16 they had a skirmish with a bear and came limping into camp somewhat disabled. Two days later, Joe found signs on the floe that one of the dogs had encountered two bears earlier that morning, and evidently had held them at bay for some time. One of the bears must have struck the dog, because he came bleeding into camp with a superficial wound that needed treatment. That bears were rising from the water and wandering on the floe was a good sign: seal must be close by. And if a big bear could be shot, it would provide a bountiful addition to their impoverished larder, but alas, the hunting was equally bad for man and beast.

On January 19, Joe saw a number of seals, but the wind was blowing heavily and it was very cold at the time. He tried to shoot the closest one, but he was shaking so with the cold that he could not hold his gun steady, and his fingers were so numb that he could not feel the trigger of the gun. The seal escaped.

Later that day, a great and unexpected event occurred: the sun reappeared after an absence of eighty-three days. The previous year, when they were on board *Polaris*, it had been absent for one hundred and thirty-five days, but they were far south of the previous year's winter quarters, so the sun had shown itself that much earlier.

Tyson happened to be the first to salute the rising orb. He had not been expecting it for several more days, and was therefore surprised as well as delighted. It was a blessed sight, giving happiness and renewed hope. The sun meant more than light to them, it meant better hunting, better health, relief from despondency—hope in every sense now that their path to rescue would be lit.

When the English steward, John Herron, came out of his hut and saw the sun shining for the first time, he broke into an impromptu jig. Tyson realized that it was the first display of merriment on the ice floe, so destitute had been their situation.

After the sun dipped down about one o'clock that afternoon, Tyson thought he could again see, in the gathering darkness, land to the west.

An hour later, Meyer, a fount of all knowledge for his German brethren, announced that they had drifted within a few miles of the land—that being the western coast of Greenland! And furthermore, they were exactly due west of Disco.

Meyer had a few navigational instruments; he had forbade anyone else from using them, and had even turned down Tyson's request to take his own readings. Nevertheless, Tyson was certain that the meteorologist was mistaken as to their position, whether due to his inexperience in these waters, inexactness of the instruments, or his mishandling of them.

The men became anxious again to try for Greenland.

"We should not pass Disco," Meyer said. "No other place will suit us as well. There's food, tobacco, and rum there, left for us by *Congress* and already paid for."

"We can take what we please!" added one of the men excitedly.

"Yes, indeed," Meyer promised, as if the provisions left for the expedition by the U.S. Navy supply ship belonged personally to him.

"Listen to me," Tyson said urgently. "Your lives depend on what I am to say. I have sailed these seas too often to be deceived about our course. As long as we are able to see land to the west, we cannot possibly be close to Greenland."

Baffin Bay, he pointed out, was three hundred miles wide.

"Disco is a very high, rocky island," Tyson went on. "You must recall that from our stop there. I have been there many times, and know all of the coast north and south of it well. Disco can easily be seen on a clear day at sea eighty miles distant."

Tyson locked eyes with Meyer.

This arrogant self-professed "German count"—this man of such questionable wisdom—had caused Hall considerable trouble and been put down for it. Hall had had the power and authority to do so; Tyson did not. Since their commander's untimely death, the German element, including the doctor, had assumed more control over the expedition. Tyson did not know whether Meyer intentionally wished to make trouble for him or not, but his illusions and misinformation had that effect on the men, and everyone else on the floe whose lives depended on calm and rational judgment.

Had Meyer by whatever quirk of fate been left on *Polaris*, Tyson was certain that the German seamen would have behaved better, for they would not have had anyone to mislead them. His influence over them was considerable because they thought of him as educated, as a scientist, and because he was also their countryman, they fancied he took more interest in their welfare.

Tyson went on to tell the men that he wanted to get off the ice as badly as they, but that their chance of making landfall would be much improved if they waited until next month, then tried for Holsteinborg, the next Danish settlement down the coast, two hundred miles south of Disco. "Not only will the drift probably take us closer to Holsteinborg, but the weather and ice conditions will be better for travel by small boat."

The men listened, then filed silently back to their hut.

Tyson had no idea what they would decide. But he knew if they opted for killing themselves through stubbornness and stupidity, they would in all likelihood doom the rest of the party—men, women, and children—who had fought so hard to stay alive.

Charles Francis Hall, engraving based on the only known photograph of him, taken during the winter of 1870. (*From the collection of Chauncey Loomis*)

USS *Polaris* being fitted for her voyage to the Arctic at the Washington, D.C., Navy Yard. This is the only known photograph of the ship. (*Smithsonian Institution*)

George Tyson
(*ARCTIC EXPERIENCES,*
Harper & Brothers,
New York, 1874)

Hannah, "Tookoolito"
(*NARRATIVE OF THE*
SECOND ARCTIC
EXPEDITION COMMANDED
BY CHARLES F. HALL,
U.S. Government Printing
Office, Washington, D.C.,
1879. From the collection of
Chauncey Loomis.)

Joe, "Eiberbing" (*NARRATIVE OF THE SECOND ARCTIC EXPEDITION COMMANDED BY CHARLES F. HALL, U.S. Government Printing Office, Washington, D.C., 1879. From the collection of Chauncey Loomis.*)

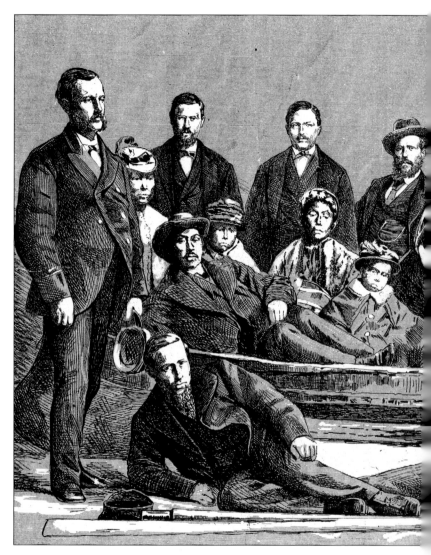

**Captain Tyson and the Party Who Spent a Half Year
on an Ice Floe** (from left to right)
Front row: Peter Johnson, Frederick Anthing
In the boat: The Eskimos—Hannah, Joe, Punny, Merkut Hendrik,
Succi Hendrik, Augustina Hendrik, Tobias Hendrik, Hans Hendrik,
and William Jackson, the cook (seated on the boat)

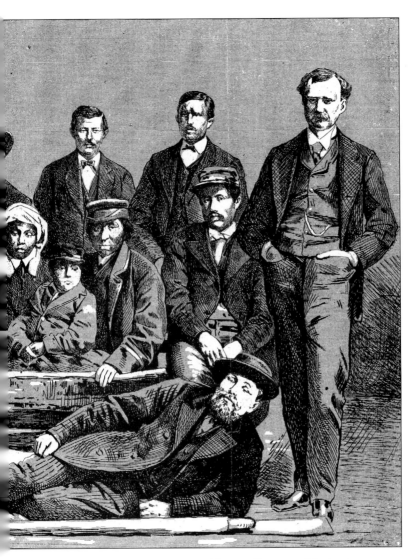

Standing: Captain George Tyson, Gustavus Lindquist,
William Nindemann, John Herron, John W.C. Kruger,
Frederick Jamka, Sergeant Frederick Meyer
(*The Tyson Collection, National Archives*)

Sidney O. Buddington
(*ARCTIC EXPERIENCES,*
Harper & Brothers,
New York, 1874)

Dr. Emil Bessels
(*Photograph by Julius Ulke.*
National Portrait Gallery,
Smithsonian Institution)

Grave site of Charles Francis Hall.
(*Photograph by Chauncey Loomis*)

Charles Francis Hall in his grave, 1968.
(*Photograph by Chauncey Loomis*)

15

Terror and Beauty

Alone in the igloo he shared with Joe and Hannah, Tyson was startled when German seaman John Kruger barged in uninvited.

Wearing a long-barreled pistol at his side, Kruger angrily accused Tyson of "spreading lies" about his stealing food and committing other improprieties. The seaman berated Tyson in the most foul and hateful language, even threatening him with personal violence.

Tyson did not have far to be pushed. Fed up with the likes of this troublemaker, whom he had been ready to shoot a few days earlier for seizing Joe's seal catch, he coolly told Kruger that he was willing to let him try his "skill or luck" in any contest.

Tyson placed his hand on the butt of his loaded pistol.

Kruger, twenty-nine, seemed surprised by the overt challenge. He had apparently expected Tyson, older by more than a decade, to back down. When he left shortly thereafter, the seaman seemed to have shrunk a size or two. Perhaps, Tyson thought, he had been boasting to his cohorts about what he could do to the American officer and had been dared by them to act imprudently.

I know not how this business will end; but unless there is some change, I fear in a disastrous manner, Tyson wrote in his journal. *They are like so many willful children—all wanting to do as they please, and none of them knowing what to do.*

The next day, Tyson received word that the Germans had decided against trying for Greenland, at least for the time being. He found himself thinking the decision had less to do with their collective wisdom than the fact that they had been housed all winter, safely out of the worst elements and not having to fend for themselves. While in their igloo the men might talk bravely about their plans, but let them get out in the cold for a short time and all their pluck was frozen out of them.

For two days in a row Joe brought home game, a small seal on January 23 and a considerably larger one the next day. He had been obligated to go about six miles, hopping dangerously from one floe to another, until finding seal. Joe had staked out blow holes, and the moment a seal put up his snout to breathe, he was quickly speared.

Both seals were taken into Joe's hut to be cleaned and divided. The men had learned that skinning a seal was not pleasant work, and they were now willing to have it done for them. As a precaution against accusations of unfairness, Tyson invited two of the men to watch, but they declined. He instructed that half the meat, blubber, and skin go to the men's igloo, and the other half was divided amongst the two Eskimos huts.

The larger seal in particular furnished a fine meal for all. Tyson hoped that with full stomachs, everyone would find themselves in an improved frame of mind. As for himself, he dined on a small piece of raw liver, warmed seal meat, and pemmican tea with a little fresh seal blood. He now wholeheartedly agreed with the Eskimos about the recuperative benefits of seal blood.

Hannah prepared "tea" by pounding a slice of bread very fine, then for flavor melting a few chunks of saltwater ice in a tin can over the lamp. She then mixed in the pounded bread and pemmican, and warmed up the mixture. It reminded Tyson of greasy dishwater, but when a man was near starvation, he could ingest many things that his stomach would otherwise find revolting. *The offal of better days is not despised by us now.* For dessert he had sliced blubber seared over the lamp.

As they dined, they were permeated with dirt not seen at a civilized table. They could scarcely get enough water melted to serve for drink, and could spare no hot water for bathing. The "carpet" spread out over their floor of ice was a bit of old canvas. When Hannah had taken it into the sunshine to pound out for the first time, it was a sight to behold: clinging black icicles hanging on a cloth encrusted with the accumulated drippings of grease, blood, saliva, ice, and their dirt for four wearying months, not all of which could be removed with their limited means of cleaning. Tyson was glad the interior of the hut was not well lit, for some things were best left unseen.

Settling back for a smoke of his pipe—he still had a little tobacco left for that daily comfort—he kicked his heels together, trying to get some warmth back in his feet. Finally, as satisfied as one could be trapped on an Arctic ice floe in subzero temperatures, he slipped beneath thick musk-oxen skins and turned in for the night. He awakened in the morning—their one hundred and third on the ice—to the coldest temperature they had yet experienced on the floe: minus 42 degrees.

As a ship's captain, Tyson had relieved parties stranded on ice. They had not drifted so long, to be sure, nor come so far, nor had there been so many of them, and they were always men, not women and children. But they had been far away from their ships, hungry and destitute. He had rescued some runaways from the *Ansel Gibbs*, and another party separated by accident from the brig *Alert*. He had also relieved Captain Hall twice on his earlier land expeditions, at times when Hall was most pleased to see a relief ship.

Tyson prayed that Providence might send his party a rescue before it was too late.

*   *   *

The hunters each took a dog in the hope of tracking a bear. Hans lost his dog when he removed its harness and they became separated from each other in a gale; the dog was never seen again. Joe returned with "Bear" loyally at his side, but upon their arrival, the large dog lay down, closed his eyes, took a few shallow breaths, and died.

Without a surviving dog, it would be a difficult matter to hold a bear at bay for a hunter to get off a shot. The dogs would be missed, too, for their usefulness in pulling loads over the ice.

The loss of the party's last and favorite dog was a sad event. Tyson had fed Bear the night before, sharing what he was eating: seal skin and some well-picked bones. It may, he thought, have been the bones that caused the dog's death, as Bear had hungrily swallowed large pieces.

Bear's passing was the first and only natural death—animal or human—to occur on the ice floe in three months; surely a wonder considering the conditions they all had endured. Tyson wondered if hope played a role in survival. Hope could help keep humans alive but not a poor beast like Bear. The Newfoundland had felt all their present miseries, no doubt, but could not anticipate relief. Had Bear given up? Had he died from lack of hope?

Even now, with a new storm raging without, and while fierce hunger raged within, and though sometimes overcome with great sadness and despair, Tyson could think of family, children, and friends at home; he was not without hope.

> *Feb. 1. God, in creating man, gave him hope. What a blessing! Without that we should long since have ceased to make any effort to sustain life. If our life was to be always like these last months, it would not be worth struggling for; but I seem to have a premonition, though it looks dark just now, that we shall weather it yet. Hope whispers, "You will see your home again. The life-spark is not going to be extinguished yet. You shall yet tell the story of God's deliverance, and of this long trial."*

When the Eskimos returned from their hunt the next day, they reported to Tyson that cracks in the ice where they had been sealing were not limited to the "young ice," but were cut clear through the old—an indication that their floe might split open at any time. Already heavy pieces from the edge of the floe had dropped off, they said, and icebergs that had accompanied them on their long journey were moving rapidly before the wind.

As yet, they had not been threatened, although if any of the massive bergs surrounding them were driven upon their floe, it would be crushed instantly. This caused some reflection among the crew. The ice, they knew, must break up sometime, and whether they would survive that upcoming catastrophe they could not know. They were at the mercy of the elements.

Early the next morning, Tyson, fighting a freezing wind the entire way, ventured to the edge of the floe to check the ice conditions. He was shocked at the loss of strength he felt with the effort, the first serious exercise he had done in weeks. It was poor encouragement for attempting a fatiguing journey over the ice with an enfeebled company. Before they started out, it would be absolutely necessary to increase the rations. They could not move forward and drag the boat on their present allowance, yet if they had larger rations, how soon all provisions would be gone! One bad storm would likely be death to them all, since they would receive its brutal force in the open with no shelter.

He looked for land in every direction, but all was ice and icebergs, dreary yet enchanting. The sun lit up the massive forms, its rays shooting through the projecting peaks, showing all the colors of the rainbow. Each berg presented, in contour, the effects of its battles with wind and water, rain and storm, and the rough jostling with other bergs it had experienced.

Icebergs do not grow in the water, as many people imagine, but originate at the foot or outlet of glaciers. A sea of ice throws off a large number of rivers of ice, or glaciers, and these slowly make their way to the coast, often reaching the shore over high rocks. No matter what is in their way, they push on to the sea. Everywhere on the northwestern coast of Greenland these project into Baffin Bay. The foot of the glacier, which can often be measured in miles, projects under the water as well as above it, and when it grows beyond a certain height and depth, the tides force a way under it. This erosion, combined with its own weight hanging over the precipice, finally separates a piece from the parent glacier. From this great breakage, an iceberg is born.

Bergs vary greatly in appearance; some being solid, wall-like ramparts with square, almost perpendicular faces, miles long and half as broad. Others might, at a distance, be mistaken for a splendid palace, a Turkish mosque, or a Gothic church. There is no limitation to form and size, and the most beautiful and most grotesque might sail side by side. One may be a mile square, and the other only forty or fifty feet. Whether large or small, only a small portion of a berg is visible; the greatest mass is always below the water. The proportion varies according to the amount of salt in the water, but a berg never shows more than a seventh or an eighth of itself.

Upon its birth, a new berg sails off to fulfill its destiny. Some are grounded not far from their birthplace; others travel on, get shored up on a floe, and keep it company for hundreds of miles. Some pursue a solitary course toward the open sea and melt in the deep swell of the Atlantic. Others make straight for a ship and send her foundering to the bottom with her precious freight of human souls.

A great berg, Tyson marveled, was terror and beauty combined—not unlike the Arctic itself.

The powerful winds had surely carried them past Disco, Tyson thought, and the Germans sensed it, too. They appeared downcast at the thought of their promised land gone forever, and scarcely showed their heads out of their igloo for more than a week. They had dreamed of an abundance of eating and drinking, taking what they pleased—clothing, liquor, cigars. Each was to buy a gold watch, and then they were to go home by steamer, as passengers—each an Arctic hero in his own estimation. Yet the elements had not favored them, and here they still sat huddled together, freezing and hungry, in huts made of ice.

From the steward and cook, Tyson learned that the Germans were now thinking that any land where they could get something to eat would be good enough. Who knows? he thought. They may yet come to their senses.

It was as yet uncertain when they would have an opportunity of reaching land. Pushed on by strong, unrelenting currents and gale-force winds, they had been moving fast to the southward, but unfortunately they were not approaching either shore. Rather, they were heading down the middle of enormous Baffin Bay.

Notwithstanding the cracks in the old ice, Tyson thought the floe would not break up until later in the season. But there was no telling—the seasons varied much year to year. Still, he believed, and fervently hoped, that the floe would hold together for several weeks yet, allowing them to drift farther south and possibly closer to shore before a lack of food forced their hand.

As soon as the weather grew more moderate, Tyson intended to construct a false keel on the boat, in order to better protect her hull when pulling her across the ice. He had saved the keel of the other boat with this in mind. It was too cold as yet to work with tools, and they had little to work with, but they must get ready soon. Unless there was some change, they must move or starve. They would have to find open waters, for abundant seal would soon be their only source of nourishment.

Upon going into Hans' hut to check on the condition of the nine-year-old boy, Tobias, who had been sick for some time and was reportedly becoming worse, Tyson's heart sank at the sight of the misery the children were enduring. Their mother was trying to pick a few scraps of dried-out blubber from their lamp to feed to the crying children. Having turned thirteen, Augustina was almost as large as her heavy-built mother, but she looked peaked now. Tobias' head was resting on his sister's lap as she sat on the ground with a skin thrown over her. She seemed to be chewing on a little scrap of something, though he did not see her swallowing anything. Tobias was unable to eat pemmican or bread, and only wanted seal meat, of which there was none. He was sobbing softly, his eyes staring into nothingness.

The youngest girl, Succi, four years old, was crying, too—a kind of chronic hunger whine that seemed to have no beginning and no end, more like a loud whimper.

Tyson could just see the baby's head in his mother's hood, or *capote*. Eskimo babies wore no clothing whatever, and were carried about in this hood, which hung down the mother's back. Like kangaroo offspring, Eskimo babies stayed warm in the coldest weather by being close to their mother.

The sufferings of the children from hunger were painful to witness. Tyson was sorry he had nothing to give them—no chocolate or sugar, nothing. Looking at them, he had no idea how they could take these weakened children across ice-churned waters and an overland journey of hardship and peril. But then, what choice did they have?

On February 5, Tyson began work on the keel of the boat so it would be ready for traveling across ice as soon as possible. That day, as usual, the native hunters went out in search of game. They had been so long without seal that the Eskimos were afraid again of their families starving to death, and of what the men might do in desperation. Tyson could not tell which unthinkable scenario upset them the most.

Soon Hans came hurrying into camp, asking for help with the kayak. Tyson grabbed one end of the little boat, and off they went. Joe was standing at the far end on the floe. There was no open water in sight, but about sixty yards away, on a sheet of thin ice, lay the inert body of a medium-sized seal.

The seal, Tyson learned from the hunters, had stuck his head through the young ice, apparently to gaze at the sun. In its glare, it was dazed or charmed sufficiently that it was less on the alert for enemies than it should have been. Joe took advantage of the seal's rapt attention elsewhere to put a ball through its head.

Hans got in his kayak, and Tyson pushed him onto the young ice. By sticking his paddle in the ice and shimmying with back and forth movements of his body, Hans slowly slid the kayak toward the seal. The ice would not have borne him had he attempted to walk over it, but with his weight dispersed over a larger surface, it held.

He reached the seal and, making one end of a line fast to its head and the other to the kayak, he turned the latter with the same peculiar movements and got back safely to the floe. When Hans landed with the welcome prize, he was perspiring freely.

On the walk back to camp, Tyson told the hunters he would like to get enough seal in the next forty days to extend the bread and pemmican out until April. This could be done on a restricted allowance, he thought, if everyone stayed put and did not attempt to travel. The hunters nodded but said nothing. He knew that their natural inclination was to head for land anytime they saw it, whether it was the west coast of Baffin Island or Labrador, or the east coast of Greenland. If they were alone on the floe, that's what they would have done much earlier. And perhaps with only the Eskimos in the single boat, they and their families could have made it.

In their hut that night, Tyson joined Joe, Hannah, and Punny in eating their portion of the seal, only partly cooked.

"Anything is good that don't poison you," Joe commented.

"Yes," Tyson agreed. "Anything that will sustain life."

Down it went, everything, even the greasy water in which they had cooked the skin and added some seal's blood. It was amazing how this broth stimulated flagging energies. They saved the rest of the blood by letting it freeze in hollows made in the ice.

The next day, Hans returned with a seal and Joe empty-handed. That was unusual, since Joe was the more skilled hunter.

When he came into camp, Hans announced that it was his seal and would all go to his family.

Tyson would not hear of it. Hans and his family got their share of the provisions with all the rest. In fact, Tyson had been upset with Hans for some time. He found the Eskimo thoughtless, careless, even lazy. He was not very successful at hunting, although he went out most days. He hadn't even built his family's own igloo but had Joe do it. What sort of Eskimo wouldn't build a snow hut for his family? Tyson knew some of Hans' history, that Dr. Hayes' nearly disastrous Arctic expedition had relied on him as their Eskimo hunter and guide. It was no wonder to Tyson that people had died on the journey. Hans was not capable of taking care of himself, much less anyone else in a land so sparse of game. Thank God for Joe. Without his hunting and survival skills, they would be doomed.

Hans dug in. If he didn't get to keep the entire seal, he threatened to quit hunting.

"You were hired and will be paid, if we ever get home, for the very purpose of hunting for the expedition," Tyson said. "This is not a favor to us on your part."

Hans remained defiant.

Tyson knew he could not force the native to hunt. "Fine," he said. "Live off what you hunt, then. In that case, you will go hungry. You will not receive anything more from our stores."

The next day, Hans went hunting with Joe.

They saw a few seals but could not get any.

On February 12, a fierce gale blew through with such violence during the night that the huts were completely buried in a snowdrift. It was a frightful entrapment, like being buried alive by an avalanche. Long and exhaustive work with little wooden shovels was required to dig their way out to fresh air.

Deciding the Eskimos could use help hunting, Tyson patched up his old thin clothes as best he could, and tried to reclaim a rifle that had belonged to Captain Hall and had been passed to Hans. The Eskimo, who preferred his old Danish rifle, had given Hall's weapon to one of the seamen, who had broken it but refused to give it up when Tyson said he would like to try to fix it.

> They have taken possession of most everything from the first, and are very insolent and do as they please; I see no way to enforce obedience without shedding blood; and should I do that and live, it is easy to see my life would be sworn away should we ever get home. These wretched men will bring ruin on themselves and the whole party yet, I fear . . . Not a countryman of my own to talk to or counsel with; a load of responsibility, with an utterly undisciplined set of men; impossible to get an order obeyed or to have anything preserved which it is possible for them to destroy. They take and do what they please. If a man ever suffered on earth the torments of wretched souls condemned to the "ice-hell" of the great Italian poet, Dante, I think I have felt it here.

16

Abandoning the Floe

Feb. 14. We are entirely out of seal-meat. We have part of a skin left, which we will serve for lunch. Oh, the filth, the utter filth one is compelled to eat in order to appease the fierce hunger, and to secure a little life and warmth to the body! Tomorrow night it will be four months since we were set adrift on this ice. It is a long time to be starving and suffer as we do, and yet there is no prospect of escaping for a long time to come. There is only one month's provisions left at our present rate of consumption; but we could very easily eat it all in eight days, and not have too much—not have enough.

After several days of violent winds and snowdrifts, the weather cleared enough for hunting on the morning of February 17. Tyson, who had obtained from one of the men the loan of an old Springfield rifle, went out with Joe and Hans. They had the good fortune to kill a seal when it came up to its air hole. It was soon skinned and dressed, and though small, it was a welcome addition to the diet. They also brought in three dovekies, small Arctic pigeon-like birds—weighing about four ounces each—they brought down with a shotgun.

The next morning, the sun shone through the igloo's ice window made from freshwater ice. It was the first day that the sun had penetrated inside the little hut, but the blessing had its drawback. Though the sun was welcomed, it revealed too plainly the filthy conditions in which they were living. Tyson thought he had known the worst before, but the searching sun uncovered new revelations. He doubted the crusty pan that Hannah cooked with was ever washed. He had seen her rubbing it with her fingers, and he didn't doubt that sometimes she cleansed it in true Eskimo fashion, with her tongue.

That morning Punny, too, seemed to be enlightened by the sun. She hummed to herself, then looked searchingly at Tyson as he sat writing in a pocket memorandum with a pencil held in nearly frozen fingers.

"You are nothing but bone," she said gravely, as if seeing him for the first time.

Indeed, he did not feel like much else. He was glad there were no mirrors.

Tyson went out with the hunters midmorning. The wind cut through his thin clothes like a knife, and he was forced to return early. He had spent twelve winters in Arctic regions, and he considered himself tough, as did others who had sailed with him. But with his inadequate apparel he would have chosen to stay inside during such weather were they not in danger of starvation. Had he, that dark October night, known the long journey before him on the floe, he would have better prepared himself and taken with him a warm suit of clothes and a rifle he could call his own.

Upon arriving back at the hut, he was thankful to find that Hannah had a hot lunch ready: a piece of seal flipper and a pot of seal-blood soup. It was a heavy and ample lunch, and restored Tyson in every way.

In his ceaseless search for game, Joe got adrift on the young ice that afternoon, and was very near to spending a harsh night outside in the elements, but toward evening he succeeded in regaining the floe.

Feb. 19. The west coast in sight! I think it to be in the vicinity of Cape Seward, and distant thirty-eight or forty miles. If the ice were in condition today, I would try to reach the shore. In this latitude we could find Eskimo, and we could live as they do until June; then we could get to Pond Bay and find English whalemen. But these are castles in the air; the state of the ice forbids the attempt. We must bide our time.

That day Joe, Hans, and Tyson went off at sunrise to hunt. They saw only one seal, and Joe killed it. As they entered camp, several armed men approached Joe and took the seal from him. They did not ask for it or say, "Let us take it and divide it up," but just laid hands on the catch and took it away as if it were their own.

Joe by then was accustomed to cleaning his catch and dividing the rations under Tyson's supervision. He had always been willing for everyone to have an equal share in whatever he brought in, but he didn't like this menacing way the men had. Neither did Tyson, but short of having a violent confrontation then and there it seemed impossible to stop.

The men were seldom out of their igloo or off their beds before noontime. They took their rations and waited expectantly the rest of the day for the hunters to return. Then these idle men had the audacity to take a catch away from the men who had been up since dawn and exposed for many hours to wind and cold.

"I think they ought to be made to pay a hundred dollars apiece for each seal they have taken from me," Joe said sternly. "For their bad conduct."

"Joe, if seal were to be had for the buying," Tyson responded, "*I* would gladly give a hundred dollars apiece."

The seal was, at last, divided into eighteen pieces. Tyson

passed out rations of bread to go with it: one-tenth of a pound per person.

On February 21, the thermometer read 3 degrees—the first time it had gone above zero since they had been on the ice floe. The next day's high registered a balmy 20 degrees. Still, the ice in the bay showed no signs of breaking up. Everything was ready for a push to shore and all were anxious to start, but the wait continued. Seals remained scarce, though they could be seen under the ice—food so close, yet it escaped them.

> *Feb. 22. Prospects look dark and gloomy—eighteen to feed. The little allowance of pemmican and bread will not keep us going much longer, and we have not even a bit of seal skin or entrails to eat . . . The men are frightened; they seem to see Death staring them in the face and saying, "In a little while you are mine." Joe is frightened, too. He feels that if he and his family were alone on the shore, without this company of men to feed, he could catch game enough for his own use; but to catch a living for eighteen discourages him, and indeed it seems impossible without some great change occurring . . . There is a double game working around me. I must be on the watch. It is plain to me that the Eskimos are anxious to get on shore to preserve their own lives from dangers other than scarcity of game. I shall protect them to the utmost extent of my ability.*

Tyson went hunting with the Eskimos on March 1. They saw no seals that day, but returned with a total of sixty-six dovekies. Each bird contained but a few bites of flesh, and although it was not heat-giving like seal meat, it was a good deal better than nothing, allowing them to forgo their regular daily allowance, which, to preserve stores, had been cut in half to one meal of a few ounces, the barest minimum to sustain life.

The next day at five, Joe shot a monstrous *ugyuk*—a large bearded seal—he caught sunning on the ice. He cleanly put a ball into its brain at fifty feet. It was the biggest seal that Tyson had ever seen in his Arctic travels, and all hands were needed to drag it to camp, where several men broke out in dance and sang for joy at the great deliverance.

It came at a time when there was no seal meat left in camp. Hannah had but two small pieces of blubber left, enough for the lamp for two days, the men had but little, and Hans had only enough for one day. And now, on the verge of absolute destitution, along came this huge seal—the only one that had been spotted above ice in more than a week—that weighed six or seven hundred pounds. When dressed, it would furnish a week's worth of satisfying meals and some thirty gallons of oil for the lamps.

Truly we are rich indeed, Tyson wrote. *Praise the Lord for all his mercies!*

The warm blood of the seal was quickly scooped up in tin cans and relished by all like new milk. The huts soon looked like slaughterhouses, with meat, blood, entrails all over everything. Their hands and faces were smeared with meat and blood. Anyone coming among them at this moment would have taken them for a pack of carnivorous animals just let loose upon their prey. After such long fasting, they could not restrain their appetites, and some ate until they were sick to their stomachs.

Land to the west of them was still visible thirty miles off.

March 4. We are now approaching Cumberland Gulf—my old whaling ground. Should the weather prove favorable, I shall have no hesitancy about trying to get clear of the floe; for there, finding ships, we should end our misery. But should we drift past the gulf, then we can try Hudson Strait, and getting on Resolution Island, could safety wait there for Hudson Bay vessels or American whalers, who go there every year now . . . There is no more thought or talk of striking eastward for the coast of Greenland; that is seen to have been all a delusion, inspired by the desire to have it so. What some people wish they soon believe. Meyer, I believe, has given up taking observations, his countrymen having lost all confidence in him since finding how his prophecies have failed.

The next day, a gale struck with more ferocity than they had yet experienced on the floe. The igloos were completely buried in the snowdrift, and they could not even get into the outer passageway until the storm abated. If not for the supply of *ugyuk* stocked in every hut, they would have been in an even more deplorable condition because the supply hut was buried, too. No one ventured out in the storm but Joe, who cut his way out. Yet he was driven back after a few minutes with his face frozen. Everyone stayed inside, lamps burning in each igloo.

On the night of March 6, the ice began cracking and snapping underneath them, sounding like distant rolling thunder. The noise shook Tyson from his sleep. As he lay listening, several times he thought the ice was breaking in fragments. No two sounds appeared alike, except for the repetition of the grinding and explosive jolts.

The severe shaking augured the breaking up of the floe. The commotion suggested to Tyson that loose chunks of ice had gotten under the floe, and were rolling along until they came to an opening, where they came grinding up and rising to the surface. He began to have some idea of how people in earthquake regions must feel when the ground is trembling and shaking beneath their feet, especially on a dark night when one cannot see a foot before him, and knows not which way lies danger or safety—if there was safety to be had anywhere. But even a violent earthquake is usually over in a matter of seconds. Tyson listened to the overwhelming power of the pushing and grinding masses of ice throughout that night of misery. Their force, and the degree of human helplessness in comparison, brought home to him once again that there were elements in nature which man's ingenuity could never control.

By the light of morning the floe was still intact.

A few days of moderate weather arrived, then ended abruptly

on March 11 with another fierce gale that raged through the day. About 5:00 P.M. the ice began shifting and cracking, with a constant succession of dismal noises, mingled with sharp reports and resounding concussions that seemed to have their center immediately under the small encampment. These sounds commingled with the raging storm and the crushing and grinding from the pressure of the bergs and heavy ice all around them.

With a gale blowing and a thick swirl of snow everywhere, one could scarcely see his hand before him, or know with each moment whether or not the floe's foundation would split and their snow tenements come tumbling down atop their heads.

They got everything ready to grab and run—but to where?

At nine there was a heavy explosion, then a terrible grinding sound.

Joe and Tyson decided to take a look.

Through the snowstorm, they cautiously felt their way down in the darkness some twenty yards from the entrance to the hut, and there found that the floe had broken off. The severed pieces swayed back and forth, then rushed upon each other, grinding their sides together with all the combined force which the sea and the gale could give them.

The next morning, the wind abated and the snow ceased, enabling them to look around and see what had happened.

The large floe they had lived on all winter had shattered into hundreds of pieces. They were left on a piece of ice about seventy-five by a hundred yards.

When Tyson selected the place for erecting their igloos, he had picked out what seemed to be the thickest and most solid spot, not far from the center of the floe.

As he surveyed their new, precarious situation, he wondered if their island of ice was thick enough that it might yet endure for a time the shock of riding among the loosened bergs without being broken into still smaller fragments. But with a heavy sea running now, too, it seemed unlikely that the floe could hold together much longer after the tremendous shocks it had received.

He also saw a great change in the condition of the ice around them. The surrounding floes had formed a pack, and great blocks of ice—of all sizes and shapes—were piled and jammed together in every imaginable position. On his last extended walk before the storm, the floes had appeared to extend for many miles. They were now all broken up, the fractured pieces heaped over each other in utter disarray.

Fortunately, their boat—their one lifeline to shore—remained undamaged.

In a ship after such a storm, the first work, with returning light, would have been to clear the decks and set about repairing the damage. But how could they repair their shattered ice craft? They could look around and take account of loss and damage, but could do nothing toward making it more seaworthy.

Their reduced platform of ice was drifting along quietly, and they felt relatively safe for now, surrounded by icebergs that had drifted with them all winter and, oddly, seemed like old if unpredictable friends.

With the return of moderate weather, they were able to commence daily hunting again. As they moved farther south, they entered seal grounds and began to find their prey more plentiful. Also, they had open water all around them and could shoot any they saw, then use the kayak for retrieving the game.

That first day Joe shot two, Hans one, and Tyson one.

Notwithstanding the cataclysmic events of the previous twenty-four hours, all was relatively well, which Tyson considered astonishing. Their success in collecting food further raised the spirits of the party. Even Hans' little boy, Tobias, had rebounded from his illness with the addition of ample seal meat to his diet.

On March 14, Tyson shot an *ugyuk*, although not as large as the previous one, and Joe bagged two seals, keeping them in fresh meat and a good supply of blubber and oil.

With Meyer no longer interested in taking observations, he allowed Tyson use of his navigational instruments. Tyson determined on March 17 that they were 63 degrees, 47 minutes north, showing a drift of ten miles a day.

The next morning, Tyson was the first one up, and around five o'clock, he came across a polar bear close to camp. An exciting chase ensued, which Joe and Hans quickly joined. The bear appeared to be a young male in the five-hundred-pound range. They fired several shots but failed to bring him down, and the bear swam across a crack to make good his escape. They had seen tracks all around them and bears had been within twenty paces of the huts through the night, but this was the closest they had come in daylight. Polar bears were nearly as much water creatures as seals, and Arctic sailors would spot them swimming among the loose ice a hundred miles from land.

A few nights later, shortly after dark, Tyson had just settled into the igloo and taken off his boots, preparing to rest, when he heard a loud noise outside.

Joe, too, was about to retire, but on hearing the noise he thought the ice could be breaking up. He went out to see. He was not gone more than ten seconds before he came back, pale, exclaiming excitedly: "There is a bear close to the kayak!"

The kayak, Tyson knew, was within ten feet of the entrance to the igloo. As he quickly put on his boots, he remembered that his rifle, and also Joe's, were outside; his was lying close to the kayak, and Joe's inside it. They kept the guns outside because they soon would have been ruined inside the hut from the condensation. The exhalations from their lungs formed moisture that settled on everything, and would have rusted the firearms unless carefully cased, and they had no casings.

At least Joe's pistol was in the hut.

They crept out cautiously and, getting to the outer entrance, could distinctly hear the bear chewing. Several sealskins and a good deal of blubber were lying around in all directions. Some of the skins were drying for clothing; some were still uncured.

Once outside, they could plainly see a great white bear. He

could have been the granddaddy of the bear they had chased the other day because he was huge, in the thousand-pound range. He had hauled some of the skins and blubber about thirty feet from the kayak and was having a feast.

Joe, armed with the pistol, crept into the crew's igloo to warn them so no one would step outside to answer the call of nature and find himself interrupting a hungry bear in the midst of a meal.

While Joe was gone, Tyson crept stealthily to his rifle. In grabbing hold of it, he knocked down a shotgun leaning upright next to it.

The bear heard the noise, stood on his hind legs, stretching himself to eight feet, and growled. By then Tyson already had his rifle trained on him.

Tyson squeezed the trigger, but the gun did not go off. He pulled a second and third time. Still it did not go off.

In a surprisingly quick gait, the roaring bear lumbered directly for him. Tyson scrambled into the hut. He reloaded his weapon, replacing the bad cartridge with a new one, then put two reserves in his vest pocket.

He crept out again. The bear, back at his meal, looked up. Again, the creature stood defiantly to face Tyson, the role of hunter and prey, among two hungry and frightened living creatures, switching back and forth

This time the rifle ball hit its mark. The bear leapt backward, turned, and ran about ten yards before falling dead with a thunderous crash to the ground.

On skinning his kill in the morning, Tyson found that the ball had passed through the heart and out the other side—a very lucky shot in the dark.

The big bear provided a fine change of diet, tasting more like pork than anything they had eaten in a long time. He was a fine large animal, every part good to eat but the liver, which the Eskimos warned would make them sick. Hannah went to work preparing the bear hide for clothing.

On March 30, their latitude at noon was 59 degrees, 41 minutes north.

> *April 1. We have been the "fools of fortune" now for five months and a half. Our piece of ice is now entirely detached from the main pack, which is to the west of us, and which would be safer than this little bit we are on, and so we have determined to take to the boat and try and regain it. To do this we must abandon our store of meat, and we have sufficient now to last us a month, and many other things. Among the most valuable, much of the ammunition will have to be left, on account of its weight.*

In their single boat with nineteen persons and stores, they launched.

17

In God's Hands

Overloaded and riding very low in the water, the boat nearly swamped.

They hurriedly cast a hundred pounds of seal meat and their extra clothing overboard, but they still made little headway. Had a gale come up they would have capsized. They were towing the kayak and carrying, in a boat designed for no more than eight men, fourteen men and women, five children, a tent, heavy sleeping gear, and provisions.

They were so crowded in, Tyson could scarcely move his arms sufficiently to handle the yoke ropes for the sail without knocking into someone. The children were very frightened; the younger ones were beyond comforting, crying without cessation.

Tyson could not leave the tiller, even to eat, so Hannah fed him hunks of raw bear meat. It took them all day to go just twenty miles, and throughout the trip there was much complaining from the seamen, who feared the boat would sink in heavy seas, while Joe and Hans stayed busy bailing with old meat tins.

They were finally forced to overnight on the first piece of solid ice they could find. Spreading out the skins, they set up the tent and ate small portions of dry bread and pemmican. Hans and his family used the boat as sleeping quarters, and the rest stretched out in the tent or on the open ice.

The next morning, April 2, they started again, still trying to push to the west. The wind and snow squalls were against them, blowing from the quarter to which they were steering, and they made little progress, mostly in the direction of south-southwest.

They had several narrow escapes with loose ice before they found a piece on which to land safely. By this time the boat was fast making water. When emptied out on shore, a puncture was found in the hull. They patched her up as best they could the next morning. They also fitted up washboards of canvas to try to keep the water from dashing over the sides.

They started off again, heading west.

After two more days of struggling against unfavorable winds and currents, they at last regained the main ice pack. The piece of ice on which they landed was so heavy and appeared to be so compact that they considered themselves out of immediate danger, although Tyson knew no ice was to be trusted at that time of year. The struggle to reach the pack had been severe and fatiguing; everyone was happy to stop and rest.

Joe started building an igloo to provide shelter in the event of a sudden storm.

The following day, with a gale blowing from the northwest, two pieces broke off from their floe early in the morning. They hauled their things farther back to the center. Soon after, another piece of ice broke off, carrying Joe's igloo with it. The snapping and cracking of the ice had given warning so that those inside the hut had time to escape. Undeterred, Joe speedily went about building another.

There was no telling where or when the ice would split next.

April 6. Blowing a gale, very severe, from the northwest. We are still on the same piece of ice, for the reason that we can not get off—the sea is too rough. We are at the mercy of the elements. Joe lost another hut today. The ice, with a great roar, split across the floe, cutting Joe's latest hut right in two. We have such a small foothold. We have put our things in the boat, and are standing by.

April 7. Wind still blowing a gale, with a fearful sea running. At six o'clock this morning, while we were getting a morsel of food, the ice split right under our tent! We were just able to scramble out, but our breakfast went down into the sea. We very nearly lost our boat—and that would be equivalent to losing ourselves.

At midnight the next night, the ice broke between the tent and boat, which had been so close that there was not space to pass between them. The boat and tent separated; on the piece of ice with the boat also went the kayak and Frederick Meyer, who had been lying down nearby.

The main party stood helpless as the boats and a stricken Meyer drifted away.

The weather, as usual, was blowing, snowing, and very cold, with a heavy sea running. All around them the ice was breaking, crushing, and overlapping.

Meyer could manage neither the boat nor the kayak alone. The boat was too heavy for one man, and the kayak of no use to anyone unaccustomed to maneuvering it; he would have capsized in an instant. He cast the kayak adrift, hoping it would come to the others, and that Joe or Hans could get it and come for him.

Unfortunately, the kayak drifted to the leeward, away from the main party.

"Oh, my God, boys, we are all goners!" shouted one of the Germans.

The seamen openly cursed Tyson, blaming him for their predicament.

With minimal discussion, and fully understanding what must be done, Joe and Hans took their paddles and ice spears and set out, springing from one piece of ice to another. It was a brave act; the Eskimo hunters could easily become marooned on the drifting ice and never be seen again. Without a boat, however, the rest of the party would not be much better off.

After watching the hunters struggle for an hour, Tyson could make out in the growing darkness that they were close enough for Meyer to throw them a line, which he did. He then pulled them toward him.

When it became too dark to watch any longer, some in the main party lay down to rest and prepare for the next battle with ice and storm. The men were beside themselves with anger and frustration. Tyson, ignoring them, kept watch through the night.

When daylight arrived, they saw the boat and the three men were still about half a mile off. The Eskimos and Meyer together did not seem to possess the strength to get the boat into the water by themselves, although the hunters had corralled the kayak.

"Any volunteers to go with me to get the boat?" Tyson asked.

When no one stepped forward, he took an ice spear in hand to balance and support himself on the shifting ice cakes, and made his start. One man followed, and Tyson was surprised to see who it was: John Kruger, the sullen German seaman he had confronted more than once.

Together, they stepped and jumped from one slippery wave-washed piece of ice to the next. They would walk a few level steps, then face a piece higher or lower, so that they had to spring up or down. Sometimes the pieces were close together; then they would have a good jump to reach the next. So they continued their perilous ice dance, leaping from one patch to another until they made it to the boat.

Even the five men found their combined strength not enough to move the boat. Tyson called over for more men to help and two came, but that was still insufficient. Following more cries for help, at last all the men, except for two who were too afraid, joined them.

After a struggle they were able to get the boat and the kayak back safely to camp. En route Meyer and a seaman fell into the water and were pulled out, wet and nearly frozen. With no spare clothes to change into, they suffered mightily. Soon after arriving at camp, Meyer lost consciousness. When he came to, he announced that the toes on both his feet were frozen solid. Understanding the danger, the Eskimo women hurriedly wrapped his feet and kept his toes as warm as they could until the feeling began to come back in them.

Joe built his third igloo in as many days, and they pitched the tent alongside. They made a meal of a few bites of pemmican and bread. They set a watch to observe the movements of the ice, and everyone else lay down to rest.

April 9. During the night the wind was blowing a northeast gale. The sun shone for a few minutes—about long enough to take an observation: lat. 55 degrees, 51 mins. The sea is running very high again, and threatening to wash us off every moment. The ice is much slacker, and the water, like a hungry beast, creeps nearer. Things look very bad. We are in the hands of God; he alone knows how this night will end.

As the sun set in a golden light, an angry sea washed over the stranded party. Again, they piled everything into the boat, ready to shove off. Tyson feared they would never survive in such a sea, but if they were to be washed over or if the ice broke beneath them, they would have no choice but to launch. The women and children were moved to the boat as a precaution, for in an emergency there might not be time to collect them. The baby stayed in his mother's hood, but the rest of the children had to be physically moved whenever it was necessary to change the position of the boat on the shifting ice, as it often was.

As the heavy sea washed over them continuously, there was not a dry place to stand upon, nor a piece of freshwater ice to drink. The sea had swept over everything, filling all the little depressions where they could usually find freshwater ice. As a consequence, they all suffered badly from thirst.

By midnight, the storm had quieted down. With the ice well closed around them, they decided to set up the tent once more and try to get some rest.

The next day was calm and cloudy. Although they could not see land, they knew they could not be far from shore. They had seen a fox, some crows, and other land birds. The ice was closed around them—mostly solid ice in every direction, but they could neither travel over it nor use the boat. Their fate was not in their own hands. All they could do was wait for the ice pack to open up. They had two large bergs almost on top of them, but fortunately, there was no portion of the overhanging bergs that might fall and crush them. They saw some seals but could not get them. They were very hungry and likely to remain so.

Joe, who had been watching the men carefully, again confessed his fear to Tyson. The children would be eaten first, said Joe, who was convinced that the German seamen would not starve as long as there was an Eskimo child about.

Tyson, who was wearing the pistol at his side around the clock, impressed upon Joe and Hans the importance of keeping their rifles loaded and handy. He also took into his confidence the two non-German crew members: Herron, the English steward, and Jackson, the mulatto cook. Herron had already caught Kruger stealing food more than once. The two men, who were also armed, were equally horrified by the threat. Herron and Jackson, who had not always gotten along, assured Tyson they would together keep watch on the Germans and do what was necessary to protect the children.

April 13. Last night, as I sat solitary, thinking over our desperate situation, the northern lights appeared in great splendor. I watched while they lasted, and there seemed to be something like the promise accompanying the first rainbow in their brilliant flashes. The auroras seem to me always like a sudden flashing out of the Divinity; a sort of reminder that God has not left us . . . This has thrown a ray of hope over our otherwise desolate outlook.

April 14. Wind light, from the north. The pack still closed. No chance of shifting our position for a better one yet. See seals almost every day, but can not get them. We can neither go through the ice nor over it in its present condition. The weather is fine and the sea calm, or rather, I should say, the ice is calm, for I see no water anywhere. Our small piece of ice is wearing away very fast, and our provisions nearly finished. Things look very dark, starvation very near. Poor Meyer looks wretchedly; the loss of food tells on him worse than on the rest. He looks very weak. I have much sympathy for him, notwithstanding the trouble he has caused me. I trust in God to bring us all through. It does not seem possible that we should have been preserved through so many perils, and such long-continued suffering, only to perish at last.

April 15. Some of the men have dangerous looks; this hunger is disturbing their brains. I can not but fear that they contemplate crime. After what we have gone through, I hope this company may be preserved from any fatal wrong. We can and we must bear what God sends without crime. This party must not disgrace humanity by cannibalism.

April 16. One more day got over without a catastrophe. The ice is still the same. Some of the men's heads and faces are much swollen, but from what cause I can not discover. I know scurvy when I see it, and it is not that. We keep an hour-watch now through the night. The men are too weak to keep up long. Someone has been at the pemmican. This is not the first time. I know the men; there are three of them. They have been the three principal pilferers of the party. We have but a few days' provisions left. The *idea that cannibalism can be contemplated by any human being troubles me very much.*

At the break of day on April 18, the sight of land greeted them, on a bearing to the southwest. They saw it plainly in the early morning, then lost sight of it when a fog bank rolled in. It was as if God had raised the curtain of mist, Tyson thought, showing them the promised land to keep them from despair.

Later that morning Joe spied a small hole of water about half a mile off. He took his gun and ventured across the loose ice. Small, light, and nimble, he stepped cautiously but surely on surfaces that other men would have fallen through. He had no sooner reached the spot when everyone heard the welcome report of his rifle. He had bagged a nice-sized seal. *It will save us from starving,* Tyson wrote. *Perhaps worse.*

The cleaned carcass was carefully divided into eighteen parts in which nothing but the gall was rejected. Everyone was called in succession to step forward and receive his or her portion of meat, blubber, and skin. A general contribution was made of blubber and rags for a fire—they no longer had the oil lamps— over which soup was prepared, and then eaten with great relish.

Meyer, tall and very thin, wore on his hands a monstrous pair of deerskin gloves, much too large for him. He looked quite pitiable, though almost grotesquely amusing, trying to gather up some bones, already abandoned, to pick at again for a scrap of meat. The gloves were so large, and his hands so cold, he could not feel when he had got hold of anything, and as he would raise himself up, almost toppling over with weakness, he found time and again that he had grasped nothing.

Observing this from nearby, Tyson realized that had the French artist Gustave Doré, known for conveying dramatic action in mysterious, gloomy settings, wanted a model subject to stand for *Famine* in a suitable setting, he might have drawn the cadaverous Meyer hovering over the small pile of frozen bones.

At 9:00 P.M. on April 20, while some of the men were resting in the tent and the women and children in the boat, there was an alarming outcry from the watch. At the same instant a huge wave swept across the ice, carrying away everything that was loose.

Immediately, they began shipping one wave after another. Finally, a tremendous crashing wave swept away the tent, skins, and most of the bed clothing; only a few things were saved. Had the women and children not already been in the boat, the little ones would certainly have been swept off to watery graves.

All they could do now, with everything else lost, was to try to save the boat.

Tyson called all hands to man the boat in a new fashion—namely, to hold on to it to prevent it being washed away. Fortunately, they had preserved the boat warp, still attached to the bow, and had also another strong line made out of thick strips of *ugyuk* skin. With these they secured the boat as well as they could to projecting vertical points of ice. Having no grapnels or ice anchors, these fastenings were frequently unloosed and broken, and could not be trusted. All the men were needed to hold down the boat, and they had to brace themselves and hold on with all the strength they had.

As soon as it was possible, Tyson directed the men to drag the boat over to that edge of the ice where the seas were striking first, for he knew that if she remained toward the farther edge, the gathered momentum of the waves as they rushed over the ice would more than master them, and the boat would go. The precaution proved to be wise; as it was, they were nearly carried off—boat and all—many times during the dreadful night. The heaviest seas came at intervals of fifteen or twenty minutes, and between these, others struck that would have been thought very powerful if worse had not soon followed.

Every once in a while one of the tremendous waves would lift the boat up bodily and the entire party with it, and carry everything forward on the ice almost to the extreme opposite edge. Several times the boat got partly over, and was hauled back only by the superhuman strength of desperate men fighting for their lives. The sea was also full of loose ice, rolling about in blocks of all shapes and sizes. With almost every wave would come an avalanche of ice, striking legs and arms and knocking the men off their feet as if they were so many pins in a bowling alley. Some of these blocks were only a foot or two square; others were as large as a chest of drawers.

Oftentimes, after a wave had spent its strength, they would find themselves near the farthest edge, and sometimes precariously on the edge. They then had to push, pull, and drag the boat back to its former position, and stand ready, bracing themselves for the next assault and the battery of loose ice they knew would accompany it. And so the men fought, hour after hour, the sea as strong as ever, themselves weakening from fatigue. In the middle of the night, the two Eskimo women had to leave the children and get out of the boat to help hold it down.

From the first Meyer did not appear to have any strength to assist in holding back the boat, but by clinging desperately to it he at least kept himself from being washed away. This was a time, Tyson saw, when all did their best, for they knew their lives depended on the preservation of the boat.

This was their greatest fight for life they had yet faced.

For twelve hours there was scarcely a sound uttered, save for the crying of the children and Tyson's orders to "hold on," "bear down," "put on all your weight," and the responsive "aye, aye, sir," which for once came readily from the men, frightened to the depths of their souls and in need of strong leadership.

At last came daylight, which found the party exhausted and half-drowned.

Tyson spotted a piece of ice riding quite easy, near to them, and he made up his mind that they must reach it. The sea was fearfully rough, and a few of the men hesitated, voicing concern that the boat could not possibly make it in such a heavy sea.

"The ice we are on is even more unsafe!" Tyson yelled. "Launch away!"

And away they went, after the women and children were snugly stowed. The rest succeeded in getting into the boat safely except for the cook, who went overboard but managed to cling to the gunwale until Tyson pulled him back in.

They succeeded in reaching the piece of ice, where they hauled up the boat and distributed the last remaining morsels of food. Having no dry clothes, when the sun came out briefly they took off all they could spare and laid them out on the ice. Everyone was black and blue with bruises received during the night from all the blows and falls. While the sun showed itself, Tyson took an observation: latitude 53 degrees, 57 minutes.

The Germans, who settled some distance from the others, continued their angry complaints that Tyson was to blame for their hopeless situation.

Tyson divided the party into two watches, and one group slept in the boat as best they could, stowing themselves here and there in all sorts of positions. The ice pack around them was very thick. They could not force the boat through it, and so they once again had to wait for a change.

April 22. The weather was very bad again last night; snow-squalls, sleet, and rain. The ice is closing around us. What we want most now is food. We begin to feel more than at first the exhausting effect of our overstrained efforts. As I recall the details, it seems as if we were through the whole of that night the sport and jest of the elements. They played with us and our boat as if we were shuttlecocks. Man can never believe, nor pen describe, the scene we passed through, nor can I myself believe that any other party has weathered such a night and lived . . . The more I think of it, the more I wonder that we were not all washed into the sea together, and ground up in the raging and crushing ice. Yet here we are, children and all, even the baby, sound and well—except for the bruises. Half-drowned we are, and cold enough in our wet clothes, without shelter, and not sun enough to dry us even on the outside. We have nothing to eat; everything is finished and gone. The prospect looks bad enough; but we can not have been saved through such a night to be starved now. God will send us some food.

Afternoon. If something does not come along soon, I do not know what will become of us. Fearful thoughts careen through my brain as I look at these eighteen souls with not a mouthful to eat. Meyer is actually starving. He can not last long in this state. Joe has been off on the soft ice a little way, but can not see anything. We ate some dried skin this morning that was tanned and saved for clothing, and which we had thrown into the boat when the storm first came on—tough, and difficult to sever with the teeth.

Joe ventured onto the ice again to see if he could spot water where seals might be found, and after looking a while from the top of a hummock, he was surprised to see a big bear, its nose in the air on a scent, lumbering toward them. He hadn't expected to see a bear in this latitude, as it was farther south than Arctic bears usually wandered.

The hunter returned as fast as possible, anxious lest the creature be frightened off and turn another way. All the party was ordered to lie down, in imitation of seals on the ice, and keep perfectly still. Joe climbed to the top of the hummock and Hans secreted himself behind it, both with rifles ready. Food seemed within their reach, but it might yet escape.

The bear came on slowly, having seen their forms on the ice, no doubt thinking that they were seals and he would soon be making a good dinner of them.

After a few more steps, he was within range of the rifles.

Both fired, killing him instantly.

Everyone arose from the ice with a shout, the dreaded uncertainty over. They all rushed to the spot of the kill—the polar bear who had come for supper but who would instead provide supper. Lines were tied above the bear's paws, and with a dozen men pulling, the body was dragged over the ice to camp, where it was cleaned and skinned.

Everyone agreed that the blood of the bear was exceedingly

refreshing, as they were very thirsty from a lack of fresh water. As he was far south of his hunting grounds, the bear's stomach was empty, and he was quite thin. His flesh, eaten raw, was the better for that, for when permeated with fat, bear meat can be very strong to the taste.

After spotting land off and on the day before, they launched the boat at 5:00 A.M. on April 25, determined to get to shore even though there were no favorable winds. Once in the water, the light, overladen, scratched, and patched-up little boat looked as if she would founder in the next big wave, but she made it through a fearful running sea, filled with small shards of ice as sharp as knives. After eight hours of fruitless labor at the oars—for they made it no closer to land—they hauled up on a floe, completely spent.

All night and the next morning it snowed, which brought them ample fresh drinking water. They saw plenty of open water some distance off, but knew they could not get to it through the ice pack. With the sun hidden behind the overcast, they could not take an observation. How far had they drifted? The coast, shrouded in heavy weather, was not recognizable to anyone.

That night, a gale sprang up from the westward, and with a heavy sea running, water again washed over the small floe they called home. They had to stand at the ready by the boat again all night, although the waves were not as bad as the other night.

The next morning, with the ice left in an unsafe condition from the storm, they again launched the boat, but could get no-where for the jagged ice, a heavy sea, and a head wind blowing a gale right in their teeth. They had to haul up after an hour's exhausting but useless effort.

By early afternoon, their position grew worse. Heavy icebergs threatened to smash their floe to pieces. The bergs were having a loud battle amongst themselves, all the time bearing right for them. The gale had set everything that could float in motion—a grand and at the same time awful sight. Accompanying the frightening collisions was the ceaseless roar of powerful waves.

Tyson called the watch in and ordered another move. They launched at one o'clock, this time for the purpose of getting out of the way of the approaching icebergs. Shortly after they left, the ice seemed very slack, and they saw more open water than they had seen in a long time.

"As far south as we must be," Tyson said, "we could see whalers soon. Everyone keep a sharp lookout."

Joe shot three young seals as they were under way, and they were brought aboard.

At 4:30 P.M., they spied a distant column of smoke. A steamer right ahead and bearing north of them! She was a commercial sealer, going southwest, and apparently working through the ice.

Tyson hoisted their colors atop the mast, and the men with oars pulled toward her.

For a few moments joy filled their breasts—the sight of relief so near.

But the ship did not see them, and they could not get to her.

When evening descended around them, she was lost to sight.

18

Hope of Rescue

The night was calm and clear. A new moon showed, and stars—the first they had seen for a week—shone brilliantly overhead like a monarch's bejeweled cape. The sea, as if acting in concert with the rest of the elements to provide a brief respite, was quiet and still.

They took the remaining seal blubber and built fires on the floe so that if a vessel approached in the night, they might be spotted. There was much hopeful talk—most of the party felt not discouraged that the steamer had passed them, but rather took it as a sign that more ships would soon be seen and that help could not be far off.

To see the prospect of rescue so near, Tyson scrawled with a nub of a pencil so small he could barely grip it, *though it was quickly withdrawn, has set every nerve thrilling with hope.*

The men were divided into two watch sections—four hours on, scanning the horizon for ships, and four hours off. The anticipation of relief kept everyone extremely wakeful.

Morning dawned fine and calm. All were on the lookout for ships, and soon one was sighted about eight miles off. They quickly launched the boat and made for her. After an hour's pulling, they gained on her a good deal, but still the ship did not see them. In another hour, they were beset with ice and could row no farther.

They landed on a floe and hoisted their colors. Climbing onto the highest part of the ice, they mustered their rifles and pistols and all fired together, hoping to attract the ship's attention. The combined effort made a considerable report.

The steamer began to head in their direction. They were certain that the time of their deliverance had come. They shouted, involuntarily almost, but the ship was too far off yet to hear their voices.

Before long, the steamer changed course: first to the south, then north again, then west. They did not know what to think. They watched, but she did not get any nearer. She kept on all day, back and forth, as though trying to work through the ice, but unable to force her way in. Tyson thought it strange; any large sailing ship, especially a steamer, should have been able to break through the ice in its present state to reach them.

They fired several more rounds, but she came no closer, staying four or five miles off. All day they watched, making every effort within their means to attract attention. Whether the ship saw them or not they did not know, but late in the afternoon she steamed away, heading southwest.

Reluctantly, they abandoned the hope that had carried them through the day.

For a while she was lost from sight, but in the evening they saw her again farther off. While they were looking at her, though no longer with the expectation that she had seen or heard them, another steamer hove into sight. They now had two sealers near—one on each side of them—although as yet neither had made any signal. They began to count the hours before help arrived. One sealer would surely come closer, or they might be able to launch first thing in the morning and work their way toward a ship.

At five o'clock the next morning, Tyson was reclining in the boat, resting after coming off watch, when one of his reliefs suddenly let out an excited cry.

"There's a steamer! A steamer!"

Tyson sprang up and saw a boat coming through a fog bank not more than a quarter of a mile away. He ordered the guns to be fired, after which everyone simultaneously sent up a loud shout. Quickly running the colors up the boat's mast, Tyson held them in place, fearful that the ship might not see or hear them, though she was much nearer than the others had been.

Hans spoke up excitedly. He wanted to take the kayak out to them.

"Yes, Hans!" Tyson yelled, waving him forth. "Go!"

Hans started off, paddling through the thin ice and around the thicker pieces.

Since it was very foggy, Tyson feared that they would lose sight of the ship any moment, but to his great joy and relief the steamer's bow turned toward them.

They had been spotted!

Hans kept on and paddled right up to the vessel. Singing out in his fractured English, "A-merry-con-stem-ar!" meaning to get across that they were survivors from an American steamer. He also tried to tell them where the stranded party had come from, but they did not seem to understand him.

In a few minutes, the steamer was alongside their piece of ice.

As the vessel slowed on her approach, Tyson took off his old Russian sailor's cap, which he had worn all winter, and waved it over his head. He gave them three cheers, which all of the castaways heartily joined. It was instantly returned by a hundred men who had congregated on the steamer's deck and aloft in her rigging.

She was the sealer *Tigress*, a three-masted barkentine out of Conception Bay, Newfoundland. Two of her small seal boats were lowered.

When the *Tigress'* crews stepped onto the ice, they peered curiously at the dirty pans that had been used all winter over the oil lamps. They also saw the thick soup that Hannah had been brewing out of the blood and entrails of a small seal Hans had shot the day before. They saw enough to convince them that everyone on the ice floe was sorely in need of a proper meal, soap and water, and clean clothes. No words were required to make that plain.

They took the women and children in the seal boats, and the men tumbled into their own boat, leaving everything behind save their guns. What they left behind amounted to just a few battered, smoky tin pans and the suddenly unappealing debris of their last seal.

Soon they were alongside *Tigress*.

On stepping aboard, Tyson was at once surrounded by a horde of curious sailors. He explained who they were, and from what ship.

"How long have you been on the ice?" someone asked.

"Since the fifteenth of October," Tyson replied.

They were so astonished that they looked blank with wonder, even disbelief.

One of *Tigress'* mates, looking at him with open-eyed surprise, asked: "And was you on it night and day, sir?"

The peculiar expression and tone, along with the absurdity of the question, was too much for Tyson. He laughed from deep in his belly, filling him with an unfamiliar but glorious sensation. He laughed until his stomach ached and he could not catch his breath, at which point he saw the man who had asked the question looking at him with grave concern, as if seeking evidence of madness.

Tigress was commanded by Captain Isaac Bartlett, who approached the party on deck and introduced himself. He invited Tyson to his cabin.

"Sir, there's another officer in our party," Tyson said respectfully. "Mr. Meyer of the scientific department."

Before food was served to the two hungry *Polaris* officers, the captain had questions about their party's "miraculous escape," as he kept calling it. As for Tyson's question about the fate of *Polaris*, the captain had heard no reports.

They politely answered all their host's questions, but Tyson and Meyer were very hungry, having not eaten anything since a few bites of raw seal the previous afternoon.

Tyson saw no signs of food or tobacco, and finally asked the captain if he would give him a pipe and some tobacco.

"I don't smoke," the captain replied.

Tyson's great disappointment showed, and the captain quickly procured both pipe and a pouch of tobacco from one of his officers.

When breakfast arrived, Tyson and Meyer stopped everything else and ate.

Codfish, potatoes, bread, butter, and hot coffee.

Never in my life did I enjoy a meal like that; plain as it was, I shall never forget that codfish and potatoes. No one, unless they have been deprived of civilized food and cooking as long as I have, can begin to imagine how good a cup of coffee with bread and butter tastes. No subsequent meal can ever eclipse this to my taste, so long habituated to raw meat, with all its uncleanly accessories. How strange it seems to lie down at night in these snug quarters, and feel that I have no more care, no responsibility. To be once more clean—what a comfort!

Two days later, the heaviest and coldest gale of the season hit, with violent winds and monstrous seas; lasting for three days. As the steamer thumped hard against the ice, turning to the westward to escape a huge swell coming from the Atlantic, Tyson and the others realized how close they had come to facing perhaps their final storm.

Could we have outlived it had we remained exposed? How we would have fared on the ice throughout this long, cold gale, I know not. It is the general opinion on board that we should have perished, being so near the ocean. But He that guided us so far was still all-powerful to save.

Tigress rescued the nineteen *Polaris* survivors at latitude 53 degrees, 35 minutes north, off Grady Harbor, Labrador, on April 30, 1873.

Their journey on the drifting ice floe had lasted 197 days and taken them fifteen hundred miles.

IV

Inquiry and the Search

19

The Board Convenes

St. Johns, Newfoundland, May 9, 1873
The English whaling ship Walrus has just arrived, and re-ports that the steamer Tigress picked up on the ice at Grady Harbor, Labrador, on the 30th of April last, ten of the crew and eight of the Eskimo of the steamer Polaris, of the Arctic expedition. Captain Hall died last summer.
Tigress is hourly expected at St. Johns.
—Telegram sent by U.S. Consul
at St. John's, Newfoundland

When the first news of *Polaris* and her crew in nearly two years flashed to the world over the telegraph wires from Newfoundland, it made headlines nationwide.

Vying for space in the newspapers of the day were the indictment and upcoming trial in the criminal case of the *United States* v. *Susan B. Anthony* for "illegally voting" in the November general election, and the government's efforts to convince two hundred Kickapoo Indian warriors to give up their raiding ways and live on a reservation. There was other breaking news—in New York, the Brooklyn Bridge was under construction, and

Boss Tweed was lining his pockets with the widening of Broadway from Thirty-fourth to Fifty-ninth streets; the Ku Klux Klan was being fought down South; and the Boston Red Stockings were playing Washington in an exhibition of a new sport called baseball.

In Washington, D.C., however, the biggest story was the *Polaris* castaways, and the failure of America's grandiose design to plant her flag at the North Pole. This had been, after all, an expedition of historic proportions funded by Congress and made a priority by influential U.S. senators and representatives of the Navy Department, and even the White House.

Navy Secretary George Robeson wired the United States consul at St. Johns to "instruct Captain George Tyson to keep his party together and remain in command" of the survivors. The consul was to ensure that they were amply provided for and did not want for food, clothing, or other necessities. Robeson promised to dispatch a Navy ship to bring the rescued party directly to Washington, D.C., where a full inquiry into the matter of the Tyson party's separation from *Polaris*, and the shocking report of Captain Hall's death, was to be held without delay.

The *New York Times* reported on May 11:

> *The news which appeared in THE TIMES yesterday of the death of Captain Hall, the probable loss of the Polaris, and the breaking up of the American Polar expedition, add another to the long list of Arctic failures, The story of the little band rescued by the Tigress is a strange one, and needs further explanation before its statements can be fully understood. We have, however, the consolation of knowing that whatever may be the fate of Capt. Buddington and his thirteen men, who were last seen on board the leaky and drifting Polaris, eighteen people at least are alive.*

Even as additional details were received daily, sufficient to convince reasonable people that the rescue could not be a fabrication, Arctic experts were found who pronounced the story of the ice-floe survivors as "impossible" and "ridiculous." Six months on the drifting ice pack? So ghastly were the perceived difficulties that would have had to be overcome to survive such an ordeal, some of those who knew the region best were the last to be convinced of the truth.

Prominent captains and navigators expressed their opinion that there must have been disaffection, insubordination, and even mutiny on board *Polaris* for such a large number of its crew to be left behind. Publicly, Robeson said he attached no importance to such speculation, pointing out that the ship and crew had been carefully chosen, the vessel strengthened and equipped for polar service, and furthermore, he would not have been surprised if Captain Buddington had remained with her in Arctic waters and, if the vessel was in seagoing condition, attempted with his remaining crew to return northward.

In a surprisingly callous statement, Robeson, who had been a strong supporter of Charles Francis Hall and his expedition, also told the press that "as soon as the sad news of Captain Hall's death is confirmed," Hall's government pay of nine hundred dollars per annum, paid in monthly increments of seventy-five-dollars to his wife, Mary, would cease immediately. Robeson added that the government would "probably not" attempt to seek a return from the widow of any overpayment.

On May 15, USS *Frolic*, a side-wheel steamer of 880 tons built during the Civil War and armed with five howitzers, was dispatched from New York. After skirting more than a hundred icebergs and three ice floes the previous night, *Frolic* had arrived at St. John's on the morning of May 22. Unavoidably detained in port until May 27, *Frolic* sailed that afternoon with the Tyson party on board, arriving at the Washington Navy Yard shortly after one o'clock on June 5.

The Washington Navy Yard, the U.S. Navy's oldest shore establishment, had been in operation since 1799. Its original boundaries along 9th and M streets southeast were still marked by a white brick wall that surrounded the yard on the north and east sides. The yard had been completely rebuilt since it was burned, on orders of its commandant, during the War of 1812, rather than letting it fall into enemy hands during the British march on Washington. Following that war, the yard never regained its prominence as a shipbuilding center, since the waters of the Anacostia River were too shallow to accommodate larger vessels and the yard was deemed too inaccessible to the open sea. Its mission shifted to ordnance and technology, and workers presently were busy building the very latest in steam engines for American vessels of war. During the Civil War, the yard had become an integral part of the defense of Washington, and President Abraham Lincoln was a frequent visitor. The famous ironclad *Monitor* was repaired at the yard after her historic battle with CSS *Virginia*. The Lincoln assassination conspirators were brought to the yard following their capture, and the body of John Wilkes Booth had been examined and identified on the monitor *Saugus*, which had been moored there at the time.

Now another bit of history was about to be made at the yard. Assembling at four that day aboard USS *Tallapoosa*, a 974-ton, 205-foot steamer with a complement of 190 officers and men, was an official board of inquiry composed of Commodore William Reynolds, the senior officer of the Navy Department, Professor Spencer F. Baird of the National Academy of Sciences, Captain H. W. Howgate of the Signal Service Corps, and its presiding member, Navy Secretary George M. Robeson.

Tallapoosa was a ship with a colorful past even before the historic inquiry about to take place aboard her. After the Civil War, she had served in the Gulf Squadron, cruising the West Indies and the Gulf of Mexico, until assigned as a dispatch vessel that brought her one of her more interesting missions. In January 1870 she carried Admiral David Farragut, a naval hero of the Battle of Mobile Bay during the Civil War who rallied his men with the famous cry "Damn the torpedoes, full speed ahead!" as he sailed into torpedo-mined waters near a Confederate stronghold, to meet with HMS *Monarch* at the end of that British turreted battleship's voyage across the Atlantic. Early the following summer, *Tallapoosa* carried Farragut from New York City to Portsmouth, New Hampshire. It was hoped that the cool sea breezes of New England would improve the aged and ailing admiral's health. As *Tallapoosa* neared Portsmouth on July 4, she fired an Independence Day salute with her two one-hundred-pound howitzers and four twenty-pounders to her famous passenger, the Navy's highest-ranking and most respected officer. Upon hearing the warship's guns, Farragut left his sickbed, donned his dress uniform, and walked to the man-of-war's quarterdeck. There he commented, "It would be well if I died now, in harness." A month later, Farragut passed away while still at Portsmouth.

In a spacious, well-appointed cabin, the board members sat lined up on one side of a polished mahogany table. Situated directly in front of the board was a single chair. A male stenographer sat close by. There was no gallery, press, or public section.

Before anyone in the Tyson party was called, Commander C. M. Schoonmaker, the captain of *Frolic*, reported to the board. A dapper officer with a distinguished naval record in peace and wartime, he described the journey from St. John's as a "pleasant voyage, except that we encountered a gale after leaving St. John's, and had to slow down, as the ship is not suited to combat ice."

Schoonmaker said he had found the ice-floe survivors in the charge of the consulate at St. John's, and he took them aboard *Frolic* on May 27. "I had no trouble with any of them. They are all well-behaved, orderly people, and all seem to be good men. Captain Tyson seems to be very intelligent. I have seen him more than any of the rest, as I have had him with me in the cabin. He has made a very favorable impression on me."

The board heard from George Tyson first. Seated in the chair facing the high-ranking officials, Tyson, after a month of shipboard meals and plenty of rest, appeared well on his way to regaining full strength after his long ordeal. He had a recent haircut—his slicked-back brown hair was parted on the side—and a shave that left longish sideburns and a mustache. A healthy color had returned to his complexion, and he had put a few pounds back on his lanky frame, which had begun to resemble Ichabod Crane's.

"Captain Tyson, I desire your statement about this voyage," began Secretary Robeson, whose unruly hair, bushy side whiskers, and large mustache had grayed considerably in the two years *Polaris* had been gone. Robeson was Grant's second Secretary of Navy following a disastrous, short-lived appointment—all of three months—of an old friend, Adolf Borie, who had won Grant's undying gratitude when he bought a house for the general at the close of the Civil War. Like most members of Grant's beleaguered cabinet, Robeson had been the subject of a congressional investigation. The previous year, allegations had surfaced that Robeson, a Camden lawyer who had served as New Jersey's attorney general, had received kickbacks from contractors awarded shipyard work for the Navy. While as yet unsubstantiated, persistent rumors of skulduggery continued to shadow Robeson into the first year of Grant's second term.

"All that you know about it," Robeson went on, "and all that happened to you on the ice. Your own statement, made in your own way, not mixed up or colored with any outside suggestions. For that reason I have sent for you first, as the chief person of the expedition, among those who are here. You are aware, perhaps, that this subject has attracted a great deal of attention, and that there is a good deal of interest in the expedition, and in the persons who composed it, on the part of the government and the public. It is proper, therefore, that an investigation should be had, which will develop all the facts as they occurred and that the government may be rightly informed. I will ask you a few questions by way of opening your statement, but I prefer to have you give a regular detailed account in your own way."

Tyson nodded.

"Your name?"

"George E. Tyson."

"Your home?"

"Brooklyn, New York."

"Your age, and business?"

"Forty-four, last December. I have been a whale man, and have been a master on several cruises: of the brig *Georgiana*, of the bark *Orra Taft*, the bark *Antelope*, and schooner *Erie*, for two voyages. I have made five whaling voyages as master. I have been in the whaling business since I was twenty-one."

Tyson told of meeting Charles Francis Hall in 1860, and ten years later Hall offering him the sailing-master position aboard *Polaris* but his turning it down due to a prior commitment to serve as master of a commercial whaler. After that whaling voyage fell through, he had called on Hall at the Washington Navy Yard in the summer of 1871, while *Polaris* was being outfitted. By then, he explained, Sidney Buddington had been appointed sailing master; nonetheless, Hall had made it clear he wanted Tyson along in some capacity.

"You knew Captain Buddington?" Robeson interjected.

"I was acquainted with him slightly."

Tyson continued with his narrative, describing the departure of *Polaris* for the Arctic, their arrival at St. John's and various ports of call up the coast of Greenland. Sans questions from the board, he told of their passage north and achieving a northernmost latitude of 82 degrees, 16 minutes, before being stopped by heavy ice.

"Did you force your way any farther?" Robeson asked.

"No, sir. There was no forcing of the way. It was pretty foggy, and when we got pretty well through, I could see open water beyond, and the land lying as far to the north as I could see. I was at the masthead a great deal of the time. The working of the ice through the winter, too, led me to think there was a large and extensive bay beyond."

Tyson told of Hall landing provisions on the ice one day in case the ship was crushed by the floe. "We took the supplies aboard again the next day. Captain Hall steamed in under the land, and came to anchor behind some bergs. The next morning, he called the mate, Mr. Chester, and myself to join a consultation to see whether we should proceed north or not. Our decision was to go north, but it was overruled by Buddington."

"How?"

"By his influence over Captain Hall."

"What reason did he give?"

"He said we would never get back again, and we had no business to go. Buddington, with an oath, said he would be damned if we should move from there. He walked off, and Captain Hall followed him, and they had some conversation together."

"Then you considered that that conversation decided the fact that the ship should then and there be laid up for the winter?"

"Yes, sir."

Tyson's narrative turned to the conditions of their winter quarters, then to Hall's last sledge journey of October 10 and his return two weeks later. "I exchanged a few words with him on shore. He said he was never better in his life. He enjoyed his sledge journey amazingly, and was going right off on another journey, and wished me to go with him. As soon as he went on board, I resumed my work. It soon came on dark, and I went on board. I heard he was sick; I cannot remember who told me. I went into the cabin, and he was lying in his berth. He said he felt sick at his stomach. I asked if he did not think an emetic would do him good. I said, if he was bilious, I thought an emetic would do good. He said he thought he was bilious. He grew rapidly worse. I do not think it was twenty-four hours before he became delirious. He was under medical treatment; Dr. Bessels was attending him. The doctor said that it was 'apoplexy'—that was what he called it. He said Captain Hall was paralyzed on one side. He said he ran a needle into his leg, and that there was no feeling in it. Captain Hall took medicine, but at times he strongly objected to taking it, and to having anything done for him. At other times, he would be quite docile."

Robeson wanted to know if Hall ever talked rationally after he was taken ill.

"After he had been sick seven or eight days, he got better, around the second or third day of November. He talked rationally and went around tending to his business and writing in his journal. He got around, and appeared to have the use of his side and leg. He appeared rather strong. He again proposed another sledge journey and said he wished me to go with him. But he still appeared to be thinking that someone was going to injure him. He was very suspicious. He thought somebody was going to poison him. He was very careful as to what he ate and drank. While Captain Hall was sick I saw him every day."

"Did he accuse anyone when you were with him?"

"Yes, sir. He accused Buddington and the doctor of trying to do him injury. After not more than twenty-four hours, he became very sick again."

"Was he taken again with the same symptoms as at first?"

"He retired in the evening. Mr. Chester was with him, and Mr. Chester said that Captain Hall was recovering rapidly and felt first-rate, and would be around in a few days. During the night he grew worse. I got the information first from Buddington, who came to my room and told me the captain was dying. I got up and went to the cabin and looked at him. He was insensible—knew nothing. He lay upon his face in his berth, breathing very heavy. I could not see his face. His face appeared to be buried in his pillow, and he was breathing heavy. He died that night."

Without waiting for a question, Tyson continued: "Before his death there had been some difficulty between Buddington and himself." He told of Hall twice being close to suspending Buddington from duty—once early in the trip, and again just before his last sledge journey. In the first instance, "the difficulty was Buddington taking anything he could lay his hands on—the provisions about the ship," Tyson explained. "Captain Hall said he was going to put him off duty, and asked me what I thought of it. I objected to it. I thought it would be breaking up the ship's company at that early stage. I told him to give him a good talking to, and perhaps the man would do better. On the strength of that he passed it over."

"How did Captain Hall and the doctor get along?" Robeson asked.

"Not very well. Captain Hall was sometimes a little stern with the doctor. He did not think the doctor was qualified for his position; he said so, but the doctor did not have any words with him, at least, I never knew of any."

Tyson described Hall's burial, then the change of command.

"Captain Buddington assumed command in his way, and the winter we passed was wretched indeed. The spring came on, and there was nothing done. He swore that nobody should do anything, and he kept his word."

"How came he to do it?"

"We lay inactive until June, when he allowed Mr. Chester and I to attempt an expedition with the boats. Before leaving, I told Captain Buddington that he knew very well those boats could not do anything, and he agreed."

Tyson explained the fiasco of the boat expeditions, and the loss of the two boats.

"We returned to the ship by land," Tyson went on, "and found the ship was leaking from the stem forward, at the six-foot mark, but not very seriously. We could pump out in four minutes one hour's leakage, and we pumped her every hour."

Robeson asked Tyson if he had been privy to any consultations between Buddington and Bessels as to whether *Polaris* should sail for home.

"I do not know. Buddington asked me if I wished to stay another winter. I told him no. If a man swears that nobody shall do anything, I want to get home as soon as possible. I thought that, under the circumstances, with him in command, I would rather get home. We started for home on the twelfth day of August. The ship was leaking still the same. The leak did not increase any at the time. On the fifteenth day of August we were beset in the ice, just north of Cape Frazier, in latitude 80 degrees, 2 minutes north. The cause of that, I think, was that Captain Buddington got intoxicated, and ran the vessel off in the middle of the sound."

The board members exchanged glances, but waited for Robeson.

"Was Captain Buddington *drunk* at the time you were beset?" asked the Navy Secretary, sounding somewhat offended.

"Yes, sir, he was drunk. Not on rum or whisky, but alcohol reduced to preserve specimens."

"How do you know that?"

"It was all there was to get drunk on. He got it from the scientific stores."

Curiously, Robeson seemed to be losing patience with his own line of questioning.

"How do you *know* that?"

"The doctor caught him at it. I was not present. I was on deck."

"Tell all you know about that."

"Captain Buddington was drunk, and the doctor decided he was going to catch him and he did. There was no liquor on board, except a couple jars of this alcohol, at that time."

From there, Tyson segued to the drama of October 15. He told of the engineer's report that *Polaris* had sprung a new leak, and Buddington's order to throw provisions overboard. Tyson described the panic that night, and his dropping down onto the ice with other volunteers to save what provisions they could.

He told of later going back aboard ship and finding out that the engineer had issued a false alarm, and that *Polaris* was not taking on more water than usual. A short time after returning to the ice, he told the board, the ship broke away in the darkness "when the piece of ice on the starboard drifted away and she righted from her beam ends."

"How did you happen to have all the Eskimos on the ice?"

"They said that Captain Buddington told them the ship was going to be lost and they must get out."

At that point, the board adjourned for the day. Tyson was told to return in the morning at nine o'clock, and to refrain from discussing his testimony with anyone.

The next morning, Tyson picked up where he left off, telling of the first "terrible night" on the ice: "The wind was blowing strong, it was snowing, and fearfully dark."

He described their efforts the following morning to launch the boats and try to make their way toward land, but held back criticizing the crew for their slowness. "They were very tired, and very hungry, and very wet. They had had nothing to eat since three o'clock the day before."

He told of their being stopped by ice and having to haul the boat onto a floe, then seeing *Polaris* come around a point about eight or ten miles distant, under sail and steam, but their hope for rescue were soon dashed when the ship anchored behind a nearby island.

"I did not feel right about the vessel not coming for us," Tyson admitted.

He told about the other abortive efforts to make for land and eventually, giving up hope of immediate rescue, how they settled in on the ice floe for the winter.

"How did you live on the ice?"

"We built our snow huts," he began, delving into details of their hardscrabble life on the ice during the Arctic winter. He told of the men burning one of the boats for firewood, and the difficulty he had trying to control them. "I endeavored to maintain the discipline of the party as well as I could, but there was little or nothing that could be called discipline. All the men were armed with pistols but myself. I was on the ice without anything, and they did as they pleased. I could merely advise them. They had been under no discipline on the ship, and the ice was no place to establish discipline without assistance. If I had attempted to do it by force, I could have made an example of one of them, but why should I? They were all leagued together. I endeavored to preserve discipline, but I could only do it by advice, and doing the best I could for all of us."

"Did they get better afterward?" asked a board member.

Tyson considered the question. "They got really no worse. They had many plans of their own, concocted during the winter, but they did not know how to carry them out, and it all ended right. They all had to come eventually to me. I thought they were going to make disturbances, but it was through fright. They were afraid of starvation."

That was as close as Tyson would get to the overt threat of cannibalism, a word that would not be uttered by anyone at the inquiry.

He described the near-starvation rations they ate during the winter, and how, come March, the natives were able to start catching more seals, which saved all their lives.

After Tyson provided details of their rescue, Robeson backtracked, wanting to know more about any difficulties Hall had with the officers aboard ship.

"Well, the conduct of Sailing Master Buddington—I don't like much to speak of it, sir, but if I must tell all I know and thought, I must say that he was a disorganizer from the very commencement."

"How do you mean? How did he disorganize?"

"By associating himself with the crew, and slandering his commander, and in other ways that I might mention."

"Let us have the whole of it."

"He cursed his commander and blamed him. On the most frivolous things he would be among the crew and complaining of Captain Hall. His ground of complaint was that the captain was not a seaman."

"Was he insubordinate to the captain in any way?"

"Oh, he was very subordinate to the captain in his presence."

"Anything else?"

"He was inclined to take provisions, sir, and privately consume them."

"When did Captain Hall become aware that he was acting in this way?"

"Just as we were leaving St. John's, Captain Hall first had difficulty with Buddington, and he threatened to send him home at Disco. It was about taking provisions from the ship's stores for himself. I don't mean liquor. It was something to eat."

Robeson probed some more about Buddington's drinking habits, then asked, "When you left *Polaris*, Captain Buddington was in command?"

"Yes, sir. Nobody disputed his command from the time that Captain Hall died until our separation. We were all law-abiding people on board. There was no violence whatever at any time. I believe about everybody thought the command was not a good one, but we still all submitted."

"Did you know of any difficulty between anybody who was left on board and Captain Buddington?"

"Nothing more than that feeling that will always be between an incompetent man and a subordinate who thinks him so."

"The criticism you have to make of Captain Buddington is that he would get drunk when he had a chance?"

"The criticism I have to make is that the man had neither heart nor soul in the expedition. It was not his intention to go north if he could help it. His idea was to go to Port Foulke, and spend his time, while the others tried to get to the Pole; while he was taking care of himself the others should go on. And then he would return home with the rest. That was the headquarters he had fixed on; he did not want to go above that. He wanted the ship to lie there, and the rest to go on. That was his whole ambition."

If Robeson was starting to be sorry for the public comments he had made in support of Buddington, he did not show it. "How did you gather that?"

"I gathered it from his own conversations. He tried to keep the ship from going farther north, and succeeded in stopping her for the winter. As soon as Captain Hall died, he tried to have the ship return farther south. He swore nobody should do anything."

"Didn't he let you go off with the boats?"

The question seemed to have been put forth in Buddington's defense.

"Yes, sir, but I told him we should lose them. He would not advise with the doctor about a sledge journey, and between the two of them there was a mess made of it. If we had started an expedition overland, there would have been a high latitude reached. I told them so."

"How do you account for the ship's not coming to you to help you off the ice?" asked the Navy's most senior officer.

Tyson lowered his eyes and shook his head. Throughout the winter he had asked himself that same question countless times. It was still a mystery, and a sore point. He had been quoted in the press as saying that he and his party had been turned adrift due to Buddington's "anger or incompetence"—both possibilities galled him equally.

"That I do not know how to account for. I was surprised that it did not come. It might have been that it was in a sinking condition, but I think not. The vessel that I saw under steam and sail at sea could not be in a sinking condition. He went in there and tied up. She was upright, and appeared to be all right when I looked at her with the eyeglass."

"Have you any reason to think they saw you?"

"I cannot see how they could avoid it, if they were looking for us. It was daylight, and they were within four miles. I could have seen on board the ship. I could have seen a man if one had been walking on deck. The moment I saw her in safety, I knew we were about to be abandoned for some cause or other."

"Would not he naturally think that he should save the ship and let you come to him in the boat?"

"That may have been his idea, but at that time I thought the first thought should have been to save the people off the ice. When the wind changed so suddenly, it was his duty to come and save us."

"Still, the possibility may remain," Robeson said, "that in

securing the ship in the harbor, he may have supposed that you and the Eskimos could reach him?"

Tyson was getting the secretary's drift; *"Abandonment on the Ice"* was a scandalous headline.

How difficult it was to sit in a clean, pressed suit on a Navy ship in the safety of a harbor, after a good night's sleep and a hot meal, and describe desperate times during life-and-death situations. Everything had been so simple to see then, but now events could be obscured and made more complicated by important men asking lawyer-like questions.

Perhaps that is why Tyson held back and did not tell the board of inquiry the story that he had already told several people since his rescue—including Captain Bartlett of *Tigress* as well as one of that ship's owners—of Buddington's "astonishing proposition" to scuttle *Polaris* in waters frequented by whalers, go ashore in boats, and wait for rescue in the spring; collecting full pay while taking few risks. In any case, the board did not hear of it from Tyson this day, nor did they question him about it, even though the *Tigress* owner had promptly passed word of Tyson's charges on to the American consulate, which in turn advised the owner to keep secret what he had heard.

"Sir, I cannot imagine he would abandon us," Tyson said, "but that it was a matter of bad judgment and perhaps some indifference. The other people on board would not have been content to abandon us if they had known it was his intention to do so. They might not have known that it was possible to save us, and if they did, they would not have known what to do."

The questioning turned to the survival prospects for the remainder of the *Polaris* crew last been seen aboard her nine months earlier.

"They had enough provisions to last them two years, if they lived with economy," Tyson said. "Should they stay with the vessel, this should be enough. I think that under almost any other commander the vessel would be all right, but under his command, I don't know."

"Was the vessel left in a place where they could get any food?"

"Yes, sir, there was game in plenty—walrus, seals, bears, and in the summer, ducks and eggs. I believe there are salmon there at times. There is an abundance of birds. I think about July they will break out if they have stayed with the vessel. It is about three hundred miles to the nearest permanent Danish settlement. If he had a clear way, he could make it in two days, and in about three days under sail if he doesn't have sufficient coal. She sails well with good winds. She gets off five or six knots under sail, which is well for the amount of canvas she carries. But she is not easily handled under sail in rough water."

The commodore wanted to know the latest that a steamer, bent on rendezvousing with *Polaris* and bringing back her crew, should start from New York.

"It would be well to start by the first of July."

Someone asked what had become of Hall's journal and papers after he died.

"I do not know."

"Was there no examination of his papers in the presence of the officers?" asked the commodore.

"No, sir. His journal was taken around and scanned by one and another."

"Did Captain Hall keep a regular journal?"

"Yes, sir. It was one of the bound books, one that could not be put in a pocket."

"Were they not certified and sealed up?"

"No, sir. I saw some of them. I know many remarks were made about them. I understood some were burned. Buddington told me he was glad the papers were burned because they were much against him."

"When did you see Captain Hall's journal last?"

"After Captain Hall's death. Captain Buddington was reading it."

Robeson removed his rimless spectacles and pressed thumb and forefinger to the bridge of his long, patrician nose. "Have you any opinion of your own," the secretary finally asked, "as to the cause of Captain Hall's death?"

"I thought at the time that the man came to his death naturally. It has been talked on board ship that it was foul, but I have no proof of it, and I could not say much about it. There were those that rejoiced in his death."

Robeson blinked. "Who rejoiced in his death?"

"Captain Buddington."

"Did anyone else?"

"I thought it relieved some of the scientific party of some anxiety. They did not mourn him, at least. I know Captain Buddington so expressed himself, that he was relieved of a great load by the death of Captain Hall."

"Why?"

"He was too strict for him, I suppose."

"Did Captain Hall do anything to interfere with the work of the scientific men?" asked the professor from the National Academy of the Sciences.

"I believe Captain Hall was not allowing them to take all the advantages they thought he should."

"In what way?" came the follow-up question.

"He wanted them to do as he said, and they wanted to do as they pleased. He wanted them to do their work in his way, and they wanted to do it in their own way. I do not think Mr. Bryan, the astronomer, was included in this. I do not believe he had any difficulty with Captain Hall whatever. I know that Mr. Meyer had some trouble on that score. He wished to do his work in his own way, and Captain Hall wished to have him do it in his. It was settled, I believe, so that Meyer did it in his own way."

"Did you know of any difficulty in this regard between Captain Hall and Dr. Bessels?"

"Nothing serious."

Asked whom aboard ship he was closest to, Tyson named Chester and Bryan.

"Chester is a peaceable, good man. Bryan was a very fine

young man. He was a general favorite, at least I thought so. He was my favorite."

Robeson was back to asking most of the questions.

"You did not think there was any difficulty between Captain Hall and any of the scientific party that would be an inducement for them to do anything toward injuring him?"

"I did not think so then, and unless a man were a monster, he could not do any such thing as that. He had not sufficient provocation, and no provocation should induce a man to do such a thing."

"When Captain Buddington told you that he was very much relieved by Captain Hall's death, what did you understand to be the reason?"

"That Captain Hall was too strict for him, and if Captain Hall had lived he would have continued on northward, and Captain Buddington knew it. He did not wish to go any farther north, and so Captain Hall's death was a relief on the part of Captain Buddington."

"Did Captain Buddington make these remarks to you alone?"

"He made them publicly, on board the ship. He is a carelessly spoken man, and he certainly should not have made any such remarks. Perhaps he did not mean all he said. I hope he did not."

With that, the board had no more questions of Tyson and dismissed him.

Frederick Meyer was summoned next.

One by one, over the course of the next four days, every adult member of the ice-floe party testified, but none for the length of time that Tyson had. In all, six persons, including Tyson and Meyer, testified to the inappropriate drinking habits of Buddington, and several to the fact of his having expressed himself "relieved," and "a stone taken off his heart" by the event of Captain Hall's death. Others, quoting Hall's own vociferous charges of foul play, threw serious doubt over the cause of the commander's death. Some testified that Hall had become suddenly ill upon drinking the coffee upon his return from the sledge journey, and others saw Dr. Bessels administering daily medicine and injections to the weakened commander.

After departing *Talapoosa*, Tyson walked down the pier to *Frolic*, where he would continue to berth during the inquiry, and climbed the gangplank. As he crossed the main deck, he passed Meyer, in a Signal Corps sergeant's uniform, who was heading off.

The two former shipmates, who had survived together on the ice for six months, walked by each other without speaking a word.

20

Return to the Arctic

George Tyson, newly appointed acting lieutenant in the U.S. Navy and ice master of *Tigress*, was headed back.

Upon completion of the testimony before the board of inquiry, Navy Secretary George Robeson met with President Grant. Both men came to the same conclusion: a search for *Polaris* and her fourteen missing crewmen must be organized immediately.

Tigress was a 350-ton steamer that had been built in Canada two years earlier expressly for the sealing trade. Due to her hull strength and peculiar adaptation to the Arctic regions—her "flared" hull allowed the vessel to rise upon floe ice and break through it with her sheer weight—*Tigress* was considered the best ship for the search. In an unusual move, Grant authorized the purchase of *Tigress* for sixty thousand dollars from her owners, who were granted the right to repurchase the ship from the U.S. government after the rescue mission for forty thousand dollars.

The vessel was brought to the Brooklyn Navy Yard, where a few alterations were made to her boiler and cabin, while an all-volunteer, experienced crew was put together. While she lay at the Navy Yard, crowds of visitors, anxious to see the now famous sealer that had rescued Captain Tyson and his company from the ice floe, was constantly streaming through the gates and overrunning the vessel, to the consternation of the workmen, who had been given little time to fit out the ship.

Commander James A. Greer, a professor of seamanship at the U.S. Naval Academy and a renowned sea captain, was given command of *Tigress*. Few line officers in the Navy stood in higher estimation among their peers for their courage and skill than Greer. His orders were explicit: *Tigress* was to "find *Polaris* and relieve her remaining company" if at all possible. Everything else, whether scientific observations or geographical discoveries, was subservient to that mission.

A naval vessel, USS *Juniata*, was also assigned to the search, and on June 24 *Juniata* set sail for Greenland, followed on July 14 by *Tigress*, amidst the cheers of thousands assembled to witness her departure.

Tigress steamed away through the East River and toward the Narrows, saluted on all sides by the shrill whistles of passing steamers, who recognized her and knew the assignment she had been given. Ironically, her departure for the Arctic rescue mission created far greater interest and attention than had the sailing of *Polaris* two years earlier.

Tigress, carrying provisions for two years, had a complement of eleven officers and forty-two men, including one Frank Y. Commagere, an energetic correspondent of the *New York Herald*, who by reputation was ever ready to dive into any story where reportorial honors were to be won. Finding no other way to secure passage, he shipped as an ordinary seaman, but soon thereafter was appointed, considerately so, to the far less strenuous position of yeoman by Commander Greer.

Joining Tyson in volunteering for the search was the indefatigable Joe, who signed on as interpreter after sending Hannah and Punny to stay with friends in Groton, Massachusetts. (Mary Hall, who had requested that her husband's body be brought back by *Tigress* if at all possible, had come to Washington to see

Joe and Hannah and learn more about her husband's death, but missed them both.) Joe, who had testified briefly at the inquiry, would prove invaluable in the likely contingency of seeking information about *Polaris* from natives. Several *Polaris* crewmen agreed to go but failed to show up at the dock. Three of the German seamen, however, did make the trip: William Nindemann, Gustavus Lindquist, and John Kruger. Also on board were Hans Hendrik and family, who were catching a ride back to Greenland, which they preferred to remaining in the United States, a clime they found uncomfortably warm.

On the afternoon of July 22, *Tigress* had a narrow escape off Newfoundland, nearly running afoul of a large iceberg, which was fortunately revealed in time off their starboard bow by a sudden lifting of the fog. For many aboard ship, it was the first iceberg they had ever seen, and it attracted great attention as they slipped silently past it.

"Is it as large as the one you drifted on so far?" Tyson was asked in awe.

Like the old Arctic hand he was, Tyson explained the difference between a floe—"comparatively flat"—and an iceberg, with "an elevated structure like a mountaintop."

Some pronounced the giant berg "beautiful," and others thought it "looked cold."

"You'll see many a beautiful, cold berg before we get back," Tyson laughed.

At Disco, Hans and family—the children outfitted in colorful dresses, sacques, and shawls given them by Washington donors—disembarked amid many good-byes. Hans had in cash his back pay for two years: six hundred dollars, a veritable Eskimo fortune.

On the way up the coast of Greenland in a light rain, *Tigress* found herself surrounded by whales of various types—the fin, the humpback, the bottle-nose, and the huge sulphur-bottom—large numbers of them. It reminded Tyson of his old whaling days, which seemed so long ago. Another officer with a similar history forgot the moment, too, and exclaimed the whaler's call as he caught sight of the first spout: "Thar she blows!"

Fostering the momentary illusion, Tyson gave the answering response: "Where away?" and could almost hear men clambering into whalers with harpoons.

Tigress rendezvoused with *Juniata* on August 11 at Upernavik, three hundred miles up the Greenland coast from Disco. From there—after *Tigress* shipped a supply of coal—the two vessels parted company. The eight-hundred-ton *Juniata*, not built to contend with ice packs, remained at her anchorage and sent out a coastal exploring party in a small steam launch, and *Tigress* boldly struck north for the last-known position of *Polaris*.

Near Cape York, *Tigress* encountered heavy pack ice, which prevented them from getting close to shore, but she went in close enough to observe any flag or signals. Several lookouts were kept aloft at all times.

Clearing the pack, they skirted the western shore of Greenland, and, on August 14 approached Northumberland Island, which Frederick Meyer had confidently testified before the board of inquiry as the location of *Polaris* at the time of her separation from the ice floe party. Captain Greer had been ordered to search here first, even though Tyson had always suspected they were separated farther north, near Littleton Island.

With the handful of *Polaris* crewmen on deck watching for familiar landmarks, *Tigress* came within range of Northumberland Island in full daylight—being midsummer, it was light twenty-four hours a day at this latitude. The scene was unfamiliar, though. Evidently, it was not the place. Since they were quite certain they had not passed it, they sailed farther north. They passed Capes Parry and Alexander, looking sharply around not only for signs of *Polaris* and her crewmen, who they knew might now be living on shore, but also for the location of the October 15 separation.

At last Littleton Island came in sight. Simultaneously, a shout of recognition rose from all the *Polaris* members on board, declaring *this* was the spot. Everyone was excited as one and another pointed out familiar rocks and other objects that had been indelibly impressed upon their memories.

Tigress stopped about a mile and a half offshore. A small boat was lowered, carrying Tyson and other officers, but before it had gone far, some on the ship heard a distant sound appearing to come from shore.

"Silence!" Commander Greer bellowed from the bridge.

In the stillness that followed, the sounds were recognized as human voices.

From his elevated spot, Greer exclaimed: "I see their house—two tents, and human figures on the mainland near Littleton Island!"

No one doubted that they had found the missing *Polaris* crew, but those in the boat discovered otherwise when they landed. The human figures turned out to be Eskimos, whose language was unintelligible to all the officers except Tyson, who obtained some facts from them and looked around the camp while the launch returned to *Tigress* to bring back Joe to act as interpreter for more complete information.

It turned out that *Polaris* had been abandoned soon after she broke away from the floe, and the crew had built a house on the mainland, where they wintered. It had been fitted up with berths from the ship; Tyson counted fourteen in number, indicating that the entire party had made it ashore. They had furnished it with a stove, table, chairs, and other articles taken from the ship.

With Joe's help, they learned further that during the winter the crewmen had built and rigged two sailboats with wood and canvas taken from the ship and that "about the time when the ducks begin to hatch"—approximately two months earlier—the whole party had sailed southward in these boats, taking along with them ample provisions.

Upon hearing this, Tyson knew that there was an excellent chance that the *Polaris* survivors had already been picked up by a whaler in Davis Strait or even farther south.

The winter camp was a scene of complete disorder and willful destruction, although it was not possible to tell how much of this was the work of the retreating party and how much of the Eskimos. But its condition showed that no pains had been taken to seal up or preserve in any way the records, books, or scientific instruments. Also, a careful search failed to reveal any written record of *Polaris* being abandoned. Violating one of the oldest rules of Arctic exploring, there had been nothing left in writing about which route the men intended to go looking for rescue.

Tyson uncovered a log book, out of which was torn, he noted, all reference to the death of Captain Hall. Also strangely missing from the chronology, much to Tyson's discontent, was any account of the October 15 separation of eighteen souls left on the ice. He did find this disturbing undated note: "Captain Hall's papers thrown overboard today."

The old Eskimo chief had a final surprise. He claimed that Captain Buddington had made him a present of *Polaris*. Soon after the white men left, the chief explained, the vessel broke loose from the ice she was tied to in a gale and, after drifting about a mile and a half toward the passage between Littleton Island and the mainland, had foundered. The chief spoke sadly of how he witnessed his prized possession sink.

Polaris lay at the bottom of the arctic waters she had sought to conquer.

Aboard *Tigress*, making a run for home after receiving word at St. John's that the *Polaris* party had been picked up by a whaler, Tyson stood at the rail.

It was a particularly clear, starry night, and he was enjoying a smoke on his pipe, which filled the air around him with a rich hickory aroma.

Next to him was the newspaperman, Frank Commagere, much esteemed by all on board, for his intelligence and good humor had enlivened the voyage considerably. Tyson was relaxed, and at that moment the reporter asked his questions.

"How did this story about Captain Hall being poisoned start? Was there any talk of it on the ship?"

"Well, there was a good deal said on board, one way or another," Tyson said. "When it was suggested, of course, it set all hands wondering whether there was anything in it or not."

"When was it first said?" asked Commagere. The reporter was keeping the conversation casual. "Who started it?"

"The first I heard was within an hour after the old man died, when I was in the cabin. Before the body was cold. Buddington came and called me out of the cabin into the little alleyway between the cabin and the rail, and said, 'Don't you say anything about it to anybody, but that bastard little German doctor poisoned the old man.' I said I didn't believe it. He said again, 'Yes, he did it. I know it. But don't you say anything.' "

Commagere began writing in a small notebook he kept handy.

Two days after *Tigress* arrived in New York, while Tyson was home in Brooklyn with his wife and children, an article ran on the front page of the *New York Herald* that contained everything he had told the newspaper correspondent that night.

Reporter Frank Commagere had done it again; he had his scoop.

That night at the rail, he'd heard more about poison than had the board of inquiry.

21

Unanswered Questions

All fourteen members of the *Polaris* party were picked up at sea by *Ravenscraig*, a Scottish whaler, on June 23, 1873—twenty days after they had left their winter camp, and a full three weeks before *Tigress* put to sea for the rescue mission. They were found sailing south in two small boats, twenty-five miles southeast of Cape York.

After the rescue *Ravenscraig* continued whaling for nearly three months until her holds were filled with valuable whale oil and bone. She returned to her home port of Dundee, Scotland, in mid-September, with Captain Sidney Buddington and his thirteen officers and crewmen, who had enjoyed the warm hospitality of their genial hosts.

Word of the rescue reached the U.S. via the Trans-Atlantic telegraph cable. The Buddington party arrived in New York aboard a commercial steamer, *City of Antwerp*—their passage paid by the U.S. government—on October 7, and were transferred to USS *Talapoosa*, awaiting them at the Brooklyn Navy Yard. *Talapoosa* sailed immediately for Washington, D.C., where the board of inquiry was gathering to interview the final group of *Polaris* survivors. *Talapoosa* pulled into the Washington Navy Yard the evening of October 8.

Shortly after noon the following day, Navy Secretary George Robeson arrived at the yard in his carriage, and was received with the customary thirteen-gun salute reserved for cabinet members. He proceeded at once to the headquarters of the commandant of the yard, and after a brief conference was escorted down to the wharf where *Talapoosa* was tied up. He was met on the quarterdeck by Captain D. G. McRitchie, commander of the vessel, and shown into a cabin on the upper deck where Captain Buddington and his party were assembled.

After determining all were present and in good health, the Secretary addressed the group. "You must be exceedingly careful as to any statement you make," he warned. "You must say nothing but what you are willing to swear to."

The interrogation of the Tyson party had raised many questions that remained unanswered. The return of the Buddington party offered hope that some of those questions would yet be answered, perhaps enough to stifle the rumors and innuendos circulating in the halls of Congress and in newspaper articles that suggested criminal prosecution might be necessary in the case.

A national expedition had failed, and an expensive Navy ship had been lost amid charges of command negligence. Its hero-like commander had died under mysterious circumstances. His death had been compared with that of another famous explorer, Dr. David Livingston, in Africa five months earlier, whose demise had turned British attention once more on the dark continent. Hall was America's Livingston, and his voice had been dramatically heard from beyond the grave through the words of those who had served under him: Charles Francis Hall had died with the charge on his lips that he was being poisoned to death on his own ship. It had all the makings for a high-visibility scandal.

Two weeks earlier, on Friday, September 23, the New York Stock Exchange had suffered a major financial crash that would usher in what became known as the Panic of 1873—this, nearly four years to the day after Black Friday, early in Grant's first term, when speculators James Fisk and Jay Gould attempted to corner the U.S. gold market and threw the stock exchange into confusion, with prices of commodities fluctuating wildly.

As Grant was entering his second term, a series of new scandals in government had begun to be unearthed. Although the President was not implicated in any of them, the improprieties committed by officials in his government and by members of his party in Congress reflected badly on his ability to govern, as did his continued loyalty to friends whose abuse of public office was well known. The very last thing the beleaguered Grant Administration needed was another scandal, especially one emerging from a glorious expedition—backed solidly by Grant—that was meant to restore national pride.

Secretary Robeson left the yard not long after, leaving instructions that all in the *Polaris* party who so desired were free to go ashore, but that they were expected to return "clean and sober" by eight o'clock the following morning for the start of the inquiry.

Soon after, Dr. Emil Bessels came down the gangplank with a long, leather-covered map case slung over his shoulder. He left the yard, but not before catching the eye of a reporter for the *Washington Evening-Star*:

> *Dr. Bessels is a brisk, natty looking little fellow, apparently about thirty years of age, with a thin, straggling beard, and a sharp, restless gray eye. He wore a black frock coat and gray pants with a black stripe down the side. When accosted by a reporter of THE STAR, he . . . hurried away, as if desirous of avoiding all questions.*

Bessels had also drawn the attention of the press during his stay in Dundee, where he had kept himself apart from the rest of the Buddington party, even residing at a different hotel. Several reporters, including one from the *New York Herald*, went to great length to draw him out on the subject of Hall's death. They found him, according to the *Herald* reporter, "always ready to receive one with the utmost frankness and politeness" and "ready to enter upon all subjects of conversation save that of the death of Captain Hall."

The doctor did state at all times, however, that Hall had died a natural death.

Beyond that, "we shall be placed under arrest on our arrival," a somber Bessels told the *Herald*, "and I prefer, therefore, to reserve what I have to say until I meet the authorities in Washington."

The first witness called before the board the next morning was Sidney Buddington.

"Captain, you are aware that when the party from *Polaris* who were on the ice floe arrived," Secretary Robeson began, "we thought it proper to examine them and obtain their full statements with a view to preserving everything, not only that the government may be informed of what has been done and what has been omitted, but that whatever there was of value to history or science might be secured at once."

Robeson had opened the proceedings sounding more like the consummate politician he had become than the state prosecutor he had once been.

Buddington watched the Navy Secretary with sleepy eyes and parted lips, giving the impression he would rather be anywhere but here. His thin brown beard was tinged with gray around the chin, and his gray eyes were plainly marked with crows' feet. That day's edition of the *Evening-Star* had pointedly suggested "his ruddy face and ruby nose indicate that he is a man who would never throw his grog over his shoulder."

"It seems also proper," Robeson went on, "that we should go on with your party in the same way, so that we may have the statements of everybody freely and fully made from their own recollection of what occurred. We have sent for you first as the commander of the expedition after the death of Captain Hall, and we desire you to give a statement, so far as you can, of everything which seems to have any reference to the subject matter. What is your name?"

"Sidney O. Buddington. I live in Groton, Connecticut. My profession is whaling."

"How long have you been engaged in that business?"

"Since the summer of 1840."

Buddington listed the ships he had sailed on, and those he had commanded.

"You cruised in what waters?" Robeson asked.

"Baffin Bay and Davis Strait. Several times during the season in sight of Cape York, but couldn't get through."

"Had you ever spent a winter north in those waters?"

"Ten before this voyage."

"You had been higher than Cape York before?"

"No, sir."

Buddington told of shipping aboard *Polaris* as sailing master and, once they departed New York, making their way up the coast of Greenland.

"Did anything of interest happen after you left New York up to the time you reached Greenland?"

"Nothing, except that there was some little difficulty at Disco."

It had not taken long for Buddington to go on the defensive. He had to have known there was every likelihood that the board had heard about his getting caught by Hall helping himself to extra provisions.

"Captain Hall had a very slight difficulty with me about some of my—well, it was a very careless trick in me, and he gave me a reprimand. I apologized about it in the best way I could, and there was nothing more thought about it by either him or myself."

Setting the tone for the second round of the inquiry in which a number of logical questions would simply not be asked, the board did not inquire of Buddington the exact nature of his "careless trick."

Buddington told of the voyage north, and the council of officers held to decide whether to proceed farther. He said he had recommended they turn around and head south eight or ten miles where there was "less risk of getting beset in the ice."

He then told about Hall leaving on his last sledge journey and returning two weeks later, "appearing lively." Buddington said he went to Hall's cabin about an hour later and found him sick in his bunk with several other people standing around him. "He said he thought he was having a bilious attack, and the question came up as to whether he should be given an emetic. Dr. Bessels was present, and he said he didn't think it would do for him to take an emetic."

During the course of his illness, Hall would "at times be perfectly rational and then he would be out of his head," Buddington explained. He told of Hall getting better for a couple of days a week or so later, then suddenly taking a turn for the worse one evening.

"Do you know whether he took any medicine that day?"

"Nothing but injections, as I understood. I never saw them. I understood the doctor used an injection, as he said, of quinine. He told me so. The doctor, I mean, told me so."

"Did Captain Hall seem to have an idea that people were poisoning him or murdering him or something of that kind?"

"Yes, sir. He insisted upon it."

Buddington told of the night Hall had asked him how to spell murder.

"Did he accuse anybody in particular?" asked Robeson.

"Yes, sir."

"Who?"

"Dr. Bessels. At times he thought everybody was at it. But he appeared to spit out his whole venom on him—he appeared to think that the doctor was the proper one."

"Did anything occur at that time which induced you to believe that anybody was trying to poison him or trying to injure him in any way?" asked the Navy Secretary.

Buddington shifted noisily in his seat. His bulk was enormous, much too big for the chair creaking under his weight.

"Well, sir, only the doctor came to me one night and said, 'Captain Hall is quite unwell and won't take any medicine.' I said, 'Mix up a dose more than you want him to take, and if he sees me take some of it, he will take it then without any difficulty.' The doctor said, 'It will not do for you to take the first drop of quinine.' That's all the remark I heard. The doctor spoke once about Captain Hall having a very strong constitution."

"Have you any reason to believe that Captain Hall died of anything but a natural death?"

"I really have not."

"Did you ever think that he died of anything but a natural death?"

Members of the inquiry board had obviously seen the front-page newspaper story in which Tyson quoted Buddington as accusing Bessels of poisoning the commander.

"I thought there was something very strange about it. I could not believe but what he did die a natural death, but once in a while, in thinking it over, I thought there was something that appeared rather singular to me. But I have told before what I thought."

"Did you ever have any real reason for suspicion? If so, state it."

"No, sir."

"Did you ever hear him accuse anybody of poisoning him except when he was delirious?"

"No, sir, I think not, and then he accused almost everybody, though he appeared to speak more against the doctor than anyone else. We had a very good crew. The mate, the second mate, the seamen, engineers, firemen, cook, and steward did their duty faithfully. I never want to see any better men. I had no occasion to complain of them in any shape whatever after Captain Hall's death or before."

"Did you have occasion to complain of anybody else?"

"Yes, sir. Somewhat."

Robeson had given Buddington the opportunity to jab back at Tyson.

"Let us hear all about it," said the Navy Secretary.

"Captain Tyson. He was a man that was rather useless aboard, and complained bitterly about the management, generally. He did not appear to be satisfied with anything that was done."

The Buddington group greatly resented the public comments made by Tyson and his party—particularly about their suspicions concerning Hall's death and the circumstances of the October 15 separation. Although the proceedings before the board of inquiry would be kept secret until all the interviews were finished—at year's end a complete transcript, some three hundred fifty pages, of the testimony would be made public—Tyson had not been alone in speaking to reporters and others about events aboard *Polaris*.

"And"—Buddington was not finished—"Dr. Bessels and I did not agree very well. However, we got along peacefully, and had no trouble to speak of. We had no outbreaks of any kind."

Buddington told of passing the first winter aboard *Polaris* locked in the pack ice. Typical of his often bitter testimony, he attempted to counter charges by Tyson and others that he had not had the heart for the expedition or for getting farther north. "I have seen that report printed in the papers, but it is not correct. I did my very best to get the ship north. I never said anything about never going any farther north."

One of the more serious charges that came out during Tyson's testimony was that Buddington had been a "disorganizer" and openly subverted the authority of Captain Hall, his commanding officer. In the shipboard U.S. Navy there were few allegations as serious. However, even though *Polaris* sailed under the auspices of the Department of Navy during the expedition, Buddington was still a civilian whaling captain on a ship with other civilians. Whereas a Navy officer could be court-martialed for such a breach of conduct, punishing a civilian would have been sticky business. Such a prosecution, too, would have kept the entire sordid matter in front of the public that much longer. The board of inquiry stayed quiet on this issue, asking no relevant questions.

Buddington told of the ice pack opening enough for *Polaris* to start steaming for home August 12 only to be beset by ice a few days later. When he came to the October 15 separation, Robeson interrupted Buddington for a question: After the party had been stranded on the ice in the middle of the night, had Buddington kept a lookout aloft the next day?

"Yes, sir. I had the best lookouts at the mast-head—Mr. Chester and Henry Hobby—at daylight looking for the men, and they could not see them even with the best glasses on the ship. They were aloft nearly the whole time."

"You did not see these men or any signs of them?"

"No, sir."

"How was the weather?"

"Quite clear that day."

"How do you account for not seeing the people on the ice?"

"I cannot say, sir. The lookouts, I am sure, did the best they could to see them, and how it was I do not know unless they were behind some hummock or some berg. If they saw us, however, we ought surely to have seen them."

The next day, Buddington said, he ran the ship aground two miles north of Littleton Island with the intention of spending the winter ashore. He claimed that the badly damaged *Polaris* had at the time only five to six tons of coal, barely enough to light the main boiler. They moved provisions ashore and began to set up camp. Within twenty-four hours of landing, Buddington said, they made contact with the friendly Eskimos living in the area. "There we lived very comfortably through the winter, and nothing notable happened."

Buddington told of leaving on June 3 in the two sailboats they had built and meeting up with the Scottish whaler off Cape York about three weeks later.

Without waiting to be questioned about Hall's journal and

private papers, Buddington said they had come up missing. "Captain Hall's journal unfortunately has been lost." He volunteered that Hall had actually kept three different journals, and together with all his private papers he kept them in a locked box set in one of the cupboards in the cabin. "It was there until we were putting the things out on the ice. I never knew it was gone until we were adrift and it could not be found. I never troubled them in any shape or form."

"Were any of his papers burned?" Robeson asked pointedly.

"At one time during his sickness we were having a talk together about one thing and another. He said he had written a letter to me, and he thought I had better not see it, but if I insisted, he would show it to me. I told him it didn't matter. He then said he thought it ought to be burned, as he did not approve of it, and he held it to the candle and burned it. I never knew what was in it."

Although Tyson had testified to seeing Buddington reading Hall's journals after Hall's death, and Frederick Meyer had testified that he had seen the box containing Hall's paper sitting on a table in Buddington's cabin, the board did not press Buddington any further on the issue of Hall's missing journals.

Buddington did, however, present a journal to the board: his own. "This journal was commenced after Captain Hall's death. Some of the first part of it was copied from another one that was kept during his sickness. It was written day by day as the events happened." He had dictated it, he explained, to seaman Joseph Mauch, whom Hall had appointed ship's clerk after Frederick Meyer refused to help with the captain's journal.

The board of inquiry would receive, in all, nine journals kept by *Polaris* crewmen. These included journals by George Tyson, which he had pointed out to the board he began after separation from the ship, and meteorologist Frederick Meyer and steward John Herron from among the ice-floe party. Among those crewmen who had remained with *Polaris*, the board was presented journals kept by Dr. Emil Bessels, second mate William Morton,

American seaman Noah Hayes, seaman Herman Sieman (translated from German), and seaman/clerk Mauch. In addition, first mate Hubbard Chester kept the official log of *Polaris*, which survived the trip as well.

Given Hall's penchant for laborious note taking, his own journals certainly would have assisted in reconstructing events leading up to his illness, if not beyond, such as entries he had been observed making in his journal when he had felt better for a couple days—entries that might have contained specifics about his worst suspicions. (Hall's papers, which he had left in Greenland for safekeeping, were subsequently recovered. However, they covered previous Arctic adventures of his, and made no mention of the *Polaris* expedition.)

Buddington turned to another sensitive topic, again without waiting for a question, and again with the tone of a man wrongly accused. "I never expressed myself as being relieved when Captain Hall died. I never made use of such an expression. I thought quite the reverse, and I think so still, that I got into more trouble through his death and had a great deal more to contend with twice over than if he had lived. I did make one remark after his death. I was aggravated about something, and I said, while speaking about Captain Hall's death, that he got me into a fine scrape and has left me in it. That is all the remark I have any recollection of making after his death regarding his decease. It was very careless of me to make such a remark, but I was a little irritated about something that was going on at the time."

The board did not query Buddington as to what was going on that had irritated him. Instead, they asked him several questions based on testimony they had heard from the Tyson party.

"Did you ever say concerning Captain Hall's death, 'That's a stone off my heart?' "

"I do not recollect ever saying such a thing. I do not think I did."

"Did you ever say, regarding Captain Hall's missing journals, or any part of them, that you were glad they were burned or destroyed, as part of it would have been unfavorable to you?"

"Never," Buddington said, puffing up with great offense. "I never said anything of that kind. All that I ever spoke about was that letter that he burned, and what Captain Hall said when he burned it."

Robeson wanted to know if Buddington ever had any difficulty with Dr. Bessels.

"Only once. I had a few words with him upon one occasion. I had been taking something to drink, and he said something to me regarding it. I just took him by the collar and told him to mind his own business. That is the only difficulty I had with him. I do not remember what he said, exactly. It was alcohol reduced that I was drinking; alcohol and water, I suppose."

Buddington had himself opened the door to his drinking habits.

"Was not that alcohol put on board for scientific purposes?"

"Yes, sir."

"Why did you drink that?"

"I was sick and downhearted and had a bad cold, and I wanted some stimulant—that is, I thought I did. I do not suppose I really did."

"Are you in the habit of drinking?"

"I make it a practice to drink but very little. I did take too much twice during this voyage, that I remember: once the latter part of April, and on the occasion I have just referred to. When I so indulged in the latter part of April, it was when we were in winter quarters. The ship was not moving then. The other time was the night that I had the difficulty with the doctor; we were tied fast to the floe. I did not consider, however, that I was not in a condition to do my duty. I merely felt the liquor. I do not think a stranger would have seen it on me at all. I had drank occasionally before, but not to any excess."

First mate Chester Hubbard testified next, telling the board of his extensive sailing experience and being hired by Hall for the expedition.

Chester told of traveling with Hall on his last sledge journey, and finding his health and stamina "first-rate" during the two-week trip. Chester said he had been busy cleaning up their gear upon their return, and did not hear about Hall's sudden illness until more than an hour later. "I went to see him somewhere about half past six o'clock that evening. He was lying in his berth. I asked him how he was, and he said he felt pretty sick. I stayed only a few moments with him. I do not know whether it was that evening or the next morning that the doctor told me that his left arm and side were paralyzed."

The first mate told of staying up nights with Hall; taking turns with second mate William Morton caring for their sick commander.

"The doctor attended to him pretty closely. He seemed to do everything he could. I do not know what medicine he gave; nothing more than injections of quinine, I think, into his arm. I saw him do it several times. He did not give him any other medicine that I saw; nothing more than a foot bath and mustard plasters. The doctor wanted to give him medicine, but he would not take it. I don't know what he wanted to give. The captain appeared suspicious and absolutely refused to take it. Then all the doctor could do was to inject quinine in the skin of his arm or leg."

"Have you any reason to believe that Captain Hall died anything but a natural death?"

"No, sir."

"Do you believe anything else?"

"No, sir."

"Did anybody else express to you any other opinion?"

"No, sir. I did not even talk with anybody about it. All this suspicion of his, and all this talk about his being afraid of being poisoned, were matters of delirium, when he was out of his head. And that was understood so at the time."

Robeson wanted to know if Chester had seen Hall's journals after his death.

"I think I saw them in Captain Buddington's room once or twice."

"Did you hear anybody after Captain Hall's death say that he felt relieved or anything of that kind?"

"No, sir."

Chester told of the ill-fated boat journeys in the spring, and then of the October 15 separation. He had his own perspective about being left on the damaged ship. Those who had gathered their things and gone onto the ice that night, he said, "were very glad to get there. They considered themselves in the safest place; everybody thought that was the safest place. I know at the time it was very difficult to keep men enough on the main deck to get the provisions and stores off the ship."

When the ship broke adrift of the floe, Chester saw "the piece of ice upon which some of the provisions were, broke adrift at the same time, and I saw one or two men on that piece of ice. But we could not render them any assistance."

Contradicting Buddington, the first mate said that the only way he could account for the men on the floe not being seen the next morning was that no one was at the masthead looking for them. "I was on deck. We supposed there was no possibility of seeing our party anywhere, and the only hope we gave them was that they were near land somewhere, and they could reach it by boat."

Chester went on. "I will state that, as regards personal safety, I think I should have preferred being on the floe to being on the ship because we did not know the condition the ship was in at the time of the separation. The snap and crackle of the timbers of the vessel when she was nipped and thrown onto the ice of course led everyone to feel uneasy. There was no one on board but who thought that she was more or less injured, and when she settled back into the water, that she would likely fall to pieces and sink. That was the general impression of all hands at the time. The other party had the boats and the kayaks, the natives, and many provisions had been landed on the ice."

As for the condition of *Polaris* after she suddenly broke free, Chester said, "I did not know how the vessel could float when I looked at her broken stem. She was in such a condition that she could not possibly have been repaired and brought out."

Hence the decision, he said, to run her aground near shore.

Without being asked, Chester gave his opinion of Buddington.

"As a whaling commander, Captain Buddington, I think, does very well, but not so good for a North Pole expedition. He has not that enthusiasm for the North Pole that Captain Hall had. I could not say that Captain Buddington was opposed to going farther north, but I think it likely if there had been someone else there as sailing master, the ship would have gone farther north. He drank a little, and I have seen him once or twice in a condition that we would call 'boozy.' Captain Hall appeared to have a kindly feeling for Captain Buddington—more than Captain Buddington seemed to have for Captain Hall. I got that impression from what I saw on the vessel of the actions of the two men. [Buddington] at times rather depreciated Captain Hall, in using language around the main deck that should not have been used by a man in his capacity. When I say 'main deck,' I mean among the seamen. He did this when he was sober, too. He did not speak very respectfully of the commander or of the expedition."

When Chester stepped down, the board adjourned for the day.

The first witness the next morning was second mate William Morton, who introduced himself by saying, "I am a seaman—I follow the sea for my living." He told of the *Polaris* expedition being his third to the Arctic, and of having spent most of his adult years in the United States Navy serving as a petty officer.

The first thing of interest that happened on the *Polaris* expedition, he said, were the "words of misunderstanding" between Captain Hall and "the scientific officers—Mr. Meyer and Dr. Bessels. It was, however, all arranged amicably before we left."

Morton's testimony about Hall's illness and death was noteworthy, as the second mate had been present shortly before and after Hall took ill, and subsequently spent much time at his sickbed. The second mate explained that he had been ashore when Hall returned from his sledge journey.

"I met him on the ice between the ship and the shore. I shook hands with him; asked him how he was. He said he was right well. I went on board with him to the upper cabin, and stayed with him at that time, except when he ordered the steward to get him a cup of coffee. The steward went to the galley to get the coffee. While he was gone, I went to get Captain Hall a shift of fresh clothing."

In his testimony before the board months earlier, steward John Herron had said that Hall asked him if there was any coffee ready. "I told him there was always [some] in the galley. I asked him if he would have anything else. He said that was all he wanted. I went down the stairs and got a cup of coffee. I did not make the coffee. I told the cook it was for Captain Hall. He drank white lump sugar in his coffee. Never cared for milk." The English steward said he did not see Captain Hall get sick that evening; he had departed Hall's cabin soon after delivering the coffee. (Two members of the Buddington party, including fireman Walter Campbell, who sometimes served as assistant steward, would testify that the coffee *had* been specially prepared for Captain Hall and his returning party. Joe, in his earlier testimony, told of having a cup of coffee from the galley shortly after returning from the sledge journey, and feeling no ill effects.)

Conflicting testimony about the coffee had been given earlier by the cook, William Jackson, who had been confronted at least once by an angry Hall over the quality of the meals he prepared. Jackson, testifying a short time after the steward, brought up the coffee right away, telling the board that it was "taken from the galley the same as everybody else had. It was directly after dinner, and he got the same coffee we had for dinner." However, the cook's memory was flawed: dinner had not yet been served when Hall had arrived aboard *Polaris* at three o'clock and wouldn't be for several more hours. In his brief appearance before the board, Jackson was asked only three questions. Not one pertained to the coffee that Hall drank.

"Did the steward bring the coffee while you were there?" Robeson asked Morton.

"I don't recollect. I went to Captain Hall's private store-room to get him some clothing, and when I came back he was sick. I was alarmed and asked him what was the matter. He said, 'Nothing at all—a foul stomach.' I was not gone more than twenty minutes."

"Who was with him when you went after the clothing?"

"Hannah was there, and I don't know whether Captain Buddington was there or not. He came on board also with Captain Hall. There was also Joe, the Eskimo, and the steward. I don't know of anybody else, except perhaps Dr. Bessels."

"Who was with him when you came back?"

"The doctor was there at the time he was sick, and I believe while he was taking the coffee. He asked the doctor for an emetic and, as far as I could understand, the doctor said no, that he was not strong enough or it would weaken him too much or something to that effect. Captain Hall got delirious very soon after the second day. He got suspicious of some people, and said they wished to harm him, and he said to me, 'They are poisoning me.' I thought he was out of his head. He continued that way for six or seven days, and he then got right smart, and got up. He spoke about his journey, and went about his ordinary business for a day or two, then relapsed.

"The doctor told me, I think the second day, that Captain Hall's illness was very serious, and that he would not recover. I cannot rightly recollect what the doctor said was the matter with him; apoplexy, I think. Captain Hall was not smart in his move-ment. He was feeble-like—prostrated. He showed that feeble-ness very soon, not immediately, but I noticed it the next day, when I put on his clothing."

"Had he taken any medicine or anything before the vomiting?"

"No, sir. Nothing but the coffee from the galley."

"Who gave him his medicine?"

"Dr. Bessels, although Captain Hall was opposed to taking medicine from the doctor when he was delirious."

Morton explained that Hall was also suspicious of taking food or drink from anyone, and asked others—usually himself, Hannah, or Joe—to taste everything first.

The second mate told of being at Hall's side when "he breathed his last."

He went on, "After Captain Hall's death, it appeared that there was divided authority. I heard that Dr. Bessels had authority, and Buddington went among the men and made very free with them, and of course, told them he was captain."

Robeson asked Morton if he had any reason to suppose that there was foul play toward Captain Hall.

"I have not, indeed."

"Did you think so at the time?"

"I did not. It never struck me."

"Do you think so now?"

"I do not."

"Then you consider these expressions of suspicion by Captain Hall the ravings or hallucinations of a man out of his head?"

"I do, sir, and I hope so."

22

Cause of Death

By special invitation from Secretary Robeson, Surgeon-General W. K. Barnes of the United States Army and Surgeon-General Joseph Beale of the United States Navy were present at the hearing on October 16 for the testimony of Dr. Emil Bessels.

"I was born at Heidelberg, in 1844," Bessels began in accented English. "Graduated at Heidelberg. Joined the *Polaris* expedition as chief of the scientific department." Bessels told of *Polaris* arriving at Disco, and the "little difference" between Hall, Meyer, and himself.

"Some kind friends wanted to make out that we had a mutiny on the ship," Bessels said, his tone scoffing. "But the whole amount of it was that Captain Hall wanted Mr. Meyer to write his journal, and Meyer did not want to do it. Captain Hall intended to discharge him, and spoke to me about it. I told him that I did not think Mr. Bryan and myself would be able to perform the whole of the scientific work to be done on the expedition. I told him I preferred to go on shore myself if Mr. Meyer was dismissed. Finally, Mr. Meyer agreed to conform to the orders and instructions of Captain Hall, and the matter was settled. Happily, I am able to produce the original copy of the original instructions belonging to Captain Hall. I found it when the vessel broke adrift, and here you will find a statement on this page in Captain Hall's own handwriting. I think it explains the matter."

Bessels handed the board the memorandum in Hall's handwriting signed by Meyer on August 16, 1871, stating that Meyer did "solemnly promise and agree to conform to all the orders and instructions as herein set forth by the Secretary of the United States Navy to the commander."

Notwithstanding his explanation that he found it on the ice, the fact that Bessels was able to produce this single sheet that had certainly been part of Captain Hall's collection of personal papers—since missing—was curious, yet the board did not probe.

Bessels rushed on, reading from the log kept by the three scientists aboard *Polaris*. It presented a dizzying array of geographical references, locations, and times that he recited in a heavily accented monotone for nearly an hour. Finally, he came to something considerably more interesting: Hall's return from his last sledge journey.

"I was at the observatory, about a quarter of a mile from the ship, at the time he returned," Bessels said. But even then he found a tangent to veer off onto. "I had fixed the Observatory, and got the instruments ready to take our observations. Up to that time, meteorological observations had been taken every three hours. We noted hourly the height of the barometer, the temperature of the air, and the amount and kinds of clouds." He finally came back on track. "As I say, I was at the observatory when I heard the sledges approaching, and went out to meet Captain Hall and his party. He shook hands with me, and I accompanied him about halfway to the ship; then I returned to the observatory."

Contradicting the testimony of Morton and others that placed the doctor in Hall's cabin when he took ill, Bessels told the board that after returning to the observatory, he stayed there about an hour and a half before coming aboard and finding Hall already sick in bed.

Bessels summarized his medical care of Hall over the two weeks of his illness.

He said he had found Hall's cabin "rather warm" upon entering it. The doctor said Hall complained of pain in his stomach and weakness in his legs. "While I was speaking to him he all at once became comatose. I tried to raise him up, but it was of little use. His pulse was irregular—from sixty to eighty. Sometimes it was full, and sometimes it was weak. He remained in this condition for twenty-five minutes without showing signs of any convulsions. While he was in this comatose state I applied a mustard poultice to his legs and breast."

The nation's two top military doctors, who were listening to Bessels' testimony and taking notes, knew mustard was used in a poultice as a counterirritant, and as a method of providing localized heat for relief of pain.

"Besides that," Bessels continued, "I made cold-water applications to his head and on his neck. In about twenty-five minutes he recovered consciousness. I found that he was taken by hemiplegia. His left arm and left side were paralyzed, including the face and tongue, and each respiration produced a puffing of the left cheek. The muscles of the tongue were also affected. The hypoglossus nerve was paralyzed, so that when the patient was requested to show his tongue and he did so, the point would be deflected toward the left side. I made him take purgatives. I gave him a cathartic consisting of castor oil and three or four drops of croton oil. This operated upon him three times, not to any great extent, however."

The board failed to ask Bessels about testimony that he had been vehemently opposed to giving Hall anything to induce vomiting. An emetic would cause poison to be vomited out before further absorption, while a purgative, or strong laxative, would draw that same poison through the system—at least to the lower intestinal tract—before expelling it from the body. It was a vital medical point that was never addressed.

Hall slept that first night, Bessels said, with second mate Morton watching over him.

"The next morning, he experienced some difficulty swallowing. He complained of numbness of the tongue. Sometimes he was entirely incapable of speaking distinctly. Again I gave him a dose of castor oil and croton oil, and he recovered from his paralysis pretty well. He complained of chilliness, and indeed he had some rapid changes of temperature like you find in cases of intermittent fever. His temperature was higher in the evening."

"What was the state of his mind at that time?" asked a board member.

"The state of his mind was as well as ever before—quite clear. After having experienced these sudden changes of temperature, and having recovered from his attack of apoplexy, I gave him a hypodermic injection of about a grain and a half of quinine to see what the effect would be. He felt better in the evening."

He had administered quinine as a kind of *experimentation?*

When no one questioned the quinine injection, Bessels continued. The next day, Hall "showed the first symptoms of a wandering mind," he said. "He accused everyone. He was apparently well, but he did not take anything except canned food, and he opened these cans himself so as to be sure not to be poisoned."

Bessels told of not being able to see Hall between October 29 and November 4—"he would not allow me to go and see him. On the fourth, he grew more reasonable, but on the fifth, when I tried to give him a foot bath, he said I was going to poison him with the bath. At one A.M. on the seventh I examined him, and found that the pupil of his left eye was dilated and the right contracted. After taking some water, he went to bed. He became comatose, and I could hear gurgling in his throat. He died the next night."

The two surgeon-generals were given an opportunity to question Bessels.

First came Surgeon-General Barnes of the U.S. Army.

"Give us your opinion as to the cause of his first attack."

"My idea of the cause of the first attack is that he had been exposed to very low temperatures during the time that he was on the sledge journey," Bessels said. "He came back and entered a warm cabin without taking off his heavy fur clothing, and then took a cup of warm coffee, and anybody knows what the consequences of that would be."

Bessels seemed to be suggesting the implausible: that someone who came in from the cold and became overly heated would be inclined to have a stroke.

"What had been his physical condition before he went on the journey?" asked a board member.

"He appeared to be in his usual health. When I first came to him, after his first attack, I asked him how he had been during the last days of his sledge journey, and he said that he had not felt quite well; that he felt a weakness in his legs, and sometimes suffered with a headache."

If Hall had not felt well on his journey, Bessels was the only person he told. Even those who accompanied Hall on his last sledge journey knew nothing about his suffering any "weakness" or headaches. In fact, according to their accumulated testimony, quite the opposite seemed to be the case: Captain Hall never seem stronger or more energetic.

"What medicine did you administer to him during the course of his sickness?"

"Some castor oil and croton oil, and some citrate of magnesia. During such intermittents I gave him injections of sulphate of quinine. That is all the medicine I gave him."

Injections of quinine were commonly given in the nineteenth century for relief of fever. The surgeon-generals would have known that quinine was most often given in oral form as a liquid. It was rare to administer it by injection unless the patient was comatose or unable to take an oral medication. However, neither surgeon-general asked a single question of Bessels about the quinine injections. Curiously, Bessels had testified that Hall's fever broke the second day and did not return. That being the case, why had the doctor continued to intermittently give Hall injections of quinine for two weeks?

That question was never asked.

Surgeon-General Beale of the U.S. Navy came next.

"How did you know that his first attack was a comatose condition and not a case of his having fainted?"

"Oh, he was paralyzed."

"He was lying in his berth?"

"Yes, sir."

"How did you ascertain he was paralyzed? Was it paralysis both of motion and sensation?"

"It was only paralysis of motion after the recovery. His paralysis did not leave him until the next day."

"Motion and sensation both?"

"Yes, sir."

"Did you try the sensation in the first attack?"

"Yes, sir. I tried it with a needle."

"How did you try the paralysis of motion?"

"I lifted his hand, and as soon as his hand was lifted it would fall. He was not able to support it."

"You have mentioned that there was an interval of four days during which you did not attend him professionally. Did you see him during that time?"

"I saw him in the morning before I went to the observatory, and in the evening before I went to bed."

"Was there any medicine administered to him?"

"Nobody gave him any. He had some in his drawer. I examined it after his death. I found some cathartic pills and some patent medicines. I found no narcotics, no opium."

Neither surgeon-general had further questions.

The remainder of Bessels' testimony that day, and into the next morning, concerned scientific observations, many of which he documented with original logs.

"How does it happen," asked a curious Secretary Robeson at one point, "that these records of yours were not put on the ice?"

In other words, why hadn't they been lost like Captain Hall's logs and records?

"I wanted to keep them with me," Bessels said. "I really saved them."

"But you know that the box with Captain Hall's papers was put on the ice?"

"I am quite confident of that."

Bessels claimed that "the records of Captain Hall . . . there were several diaries," as well as some astronomical and magnetic records, were thrown over the side of the ship on the night that everyone thought *Polaris* might sink—on October 15.

"I know they were put overboard because I helped myself to take some of the boxes out of the cabin. I saw a large box belonging to Captain Hall, and containing his papers, which was put overboard. I do not remember exactly who did it, but it was done. It was put on the ice."

"Did you ever have any difficulty with Captain Hall?" asked Robeson.

"None whatever."

"Did you have any difficulty with Buddington about liquor?"

"Yes, sir, a slight difficulty. I knew that he had been getting some of the alcohol. I thought it would be to the interest of the expedition to take it away from him. Captain Buddington was in the habit of drinking at times. He did not refuse a drink when he could get it."

After providing summaries of the scientific findings on the expedition, ranging from astronomy, magnetism, ocean physics, meteorology, zoology and botany, and geology, Bessels was dismissed.

The inquiry in the cabin aboard *Talapoosa* was not a court of law, and its members had as much latitude as to the procedures they wished to follow. Still, there was no recalling of witnesses or cross-examination or much attempt at all to sort out conflicting testimony and contradictory stories. Indeed, the most troubling aspect of the inquiry was the questions they did not ask.

Why, for instance, had they not attempted to pin down the

exact whereabouts of Bessels when Hall drank the coffee that made him deathly ill? Bessels took pains to place himself at the observatory, a quarter mile away, while others testified that he was present in the cabin when Hall first took ill. Why had the discrepancies not been cleared up?

Why had the board, or the surgeon-generals who were attending specifically for the medical testimony, not asked Bessels to address whether Hall, when he first took ill, might have benefitted from an emetic, medicine used to cause vomiting. Given the voluminous testimony concerning fears and rumors of poisoning, why wasn't the issue squarely faced? Vomiting, in cases of acute poisoning, purposeful or accidental, would be desirable to purge the toxin from the patient's system. Testimony from witnesses indicated that Bessels was most insistent in not wanting Hall to receive an emetic.

Why hadn't Bessels wanted Hall to vomit?

"There were a couple of officers who were greatly relieved by Captain Hall's death," said German seaman Henry Hobby, who told the board about Buddington's remark on deck, shortly after Hall's death, that the party "shan't be starved to death now."

In addition to Buddington and Meyer, Hobby said, "The doctor was greatly relieved. He did not know what to do when Captain Hall was alive. When Captain Hall would call one of the scientific men, all three of them would jump up, and each one would suppose he was called on. Some of them did not want to behave very well. Captain Hall said he would court-martial the doctor if he kept on in the way he was doing."

After *Polaris* had been abandoned, Hobby said that Bessels had concocted a plan that, if successful, would have brought him great personal glory. Bessels' scheme revealed a kind of chasm of ambition and envy that must have opened between himself and Hall, who certainly had his own plans for glory, both national and personal.

"In the spring [after Hall's death] the doctor wanted me to

go to the North Pole with him on a sledge journey," said Hobby. "I thought it was a very foolish idea, with fifty pounds of canned meat and sixty pounds of bread on one sled, to go to the Pole from there. As this time we were two hundred miles farther south than we had been the year before, and yet we did not try it then when we were farther up. I was told to go, however, and I said I would go. The doctor promised me one hundred dollars to go to Thank God Harbor with him—what he was going to do there I couldn't say—and two hundred dollars if I would go with him so that he could reach a higher latitude than Parry had reached. Dr. Bessels was constantly speaking to me about going with him, but before we were able to start, the ice broke and the journey was abandoned."

Hobby's testimony, brief as it was, was potentially explosive.

"Joe Mauch, the captain's clerk, came into the cabin one morning about a week after Captain Hall had been taken sick. He said there had been some poisoning around there. He did not say any more about it. He did not mean to say that Captain Hall had taken this, but that the smell was in his cabin—used there for some purpose or other."

Hobby was asked only a single question by the board having to do with events after the October 15 separation: "How often did you go to the masthead to look after your companions on the ice?"

"Twice. I stayed there for ten minutes to a quarter of an hour."

American seaman Noah Hayes came next, and told the board about the shocking statement of a "very lighthearted" Bessels at the observatory, shortly after Hall's death, that Hall's death had been the "best thing that could happen for the expedition."

Astronomer and ship's chaplain Richard W. D. Bryan, a clean-cut young man who obviously made a good impression on the board, said that during Hall's illness, "he accused nearly all the officers, at one time or another, of trying to murder him." But Bryan made a distinction; the emphasis was his and was subsequently preserved by a careful stenographer in the transcript of his testimony: "the doctor was the only one, however, who Captain Hall ever accused of *poisoning* him."

"Do you know what medicine Captain Hall took?"

"I do not know all the medicine he took. I know that the doctor at one time wanted to administer a dose of quinine and that the captain would not take it. The doctor came to me and wanted me to persuade Captain Hall to take it. I did so, and I saw him prepare the medicine. He had little white crystals, and he heated them in a little glass bowl; heated the water, apparently to dissolve the crystals. That is all I know about any medicine. I only knew that because I had persuaded Captain Hall to take the injections. It was given in the form of an injection under the skin in his leg. I believe he gave him the medicine at other times, but that was the only time I had any knowledge of it."

"Did you have any difficulty in persuading the captain to take it?"

"Not very much."

"Why did he object?"

"He did not like the doctor very much at that time, and he was a little delirious, I think. He thought the doctor was trying to poison him."

Byran testified he was in Hall's cabin when the steward returned with the coffee.

"Was this within half an hour of his coming into the cabin or coming on board the vessel?" he was asked.

"Yes. I think it would be safe to say it was within that time."

"Did he then take the coffee?"

"Yes. I think I saw him then take the coffee, and almost immediately afterward—"

"Within five minutes afterward?"

"I do not know about that because he might have given the cup back, and he might have spoken a little while. But I associated the two facts in my mind, that just as soon as he took the coffee he complained of feeling sick and went to bed."

The board did not ask him to clarify who else was in the cabin at the time, and Bryan did not volunteer the information.

One of the last witnesses was Joseph Mauch, who served as the captain's clerk and became a favorite of Hall's.

Mauch weighed in on the whereabouts of Bessels. The clerk remembered going in to see Hall shortly after he had taken ill. "Dr. Bessels was there and Mr. Morton was undressing Captain Hall for bed." Mauch also had something to say about the cup of coffee; it had been specially prepared "for Captain Hall, or rather, for his party that returned."

Mauch had an interesting background for a twenty-four-year-old seaman.

"Have you been brought up as a seaman?" he was asked at one point.

"No. I have been a druggist. I passed my examination in New York, in the College of Pharmacy. I did not have seaman experience until this expedition."

Even with that information, the board did not ask him about Henry Hobby's claim. They did not ask the former druggist about the smell of poison in Hall's cabin.

The inquiry into Charles Francis Hall's death and his ill-fated expedition was over.

WASHINGTON, D.C., DECEMBER 26, 1873

President of the United States

Sir: We, the undersigned, were present by request of the honorable Secretary of the Navy, at the examination of Dr. Emil Bessels, in regard to the cruise of Polaris and the circumstances connected with the illness and death of Captain Hall. We listened to his testimony with great care and put to him such questions as we deemed necessary.

From the circumstances and symptoms detailed by him, and comparing them with the medical testimony of all the witnesses, we are conclusively of the opinion that Captain Hall died from natural causes, viz, apoplexy; and that the treatment of the case by Doctor Bessels was the best practicable under the circumstances.

Respectfully, your obedient servants,

> W. K. Barnes
> *Surgeon-General United States Army.*
>
> J. Beale
> *Surgeon-General United States Navy.*

The board of inquiry added nothing to the surgeon-generals' statement, accepting their medical finding that Charles Francis Hall died from natural causes. Navy Secretary George Robeson and the board recommended no actions to be taken against anyone among the *Polaris* crew. No further investigations would be conducted, official or otherwise.

As far as the United States government was concerned, the matter was ended.

EPILOGUE

OCTOBER 1968
TORONTO, ONTARIO, CANADA

The carefully preserved bodily tissues arrived at Toronto's Centre for Forensic Sciences, one of the leading pathology laboratories in the world, two months after they had been removed from the remains of Charles Francis Hall.

Dartmouth professor Chauncey Loomis and Dr. Frank Paddock, the internist who had conducted the autopsy of Hall in his ice-bound coffin, submitted the samples to the renowned forensic laboratory for a more detailed analysis after the Massachusetts Department of Public Safety Laboratory conducted tests on a piece of frontal bone removed from Hall's skull and found an increased level of arsenic, once used extensively as a "criminal poison" because it is odorless and nearly tasteless.

Dr. Auseklis Perkons, a leading researcher at the Centre, sliced the hair and nail samples into numerous sections, and subjected them to neutron activation in the McMaster University nuclear reactor—a highly sensitive test for analyzing tiny amounts of material—together with two chips of bone, two samples of soil from the grave site, and a weighed amount of pure arsenic standard. The gamma activities subsequently produced were measured, and the amounts of arsenic in the samples were calculated by comparison with the standard reference arsenic photopeak.

Assuming the average daily growth rates of 0.4 mm for hair and 0.1 mm for fingernail, the results showed that elevated amounts of arsenic had been deposited in the hair and nails grown during the last two to five weeks of Hall's life, with the highest amounts being incorporated in the hair and nails within one week of his death.

"These results are fully consistent with the theory of arsenic poisoning being the immediate cause of Hall's demise almost a century ago," wrote Dr. Perkons in his report.

In reviewing descriptions of Hall's symptoms from the eyewitnesses interviewed by the board of inquiry nearly a century earlier, Dr. Perkons and Douglas Lucas, director of the Centre, were in agreement that Hall's symptoms, during the final two weeks of his life, were "quite in keeping with acute arsenic poisoning."

The presenting symptoms that could be expected from acute arsenic poisoning, according to references such as *Clinical Toxicology of Commercial Products* and *Gradwohl's Legal Medicine*, include:

- sweetish metallic taste
- within thirty minutes to one hour after ingestion, constriction in the throat and difficulty in swallowing; burning and colicky pains in esophagus and stomach
- feeble pulse and cold extremities
- vertigo, frontal headache; in some cases, stupor, delirium and even mania
- numbness and tingling of the hands and feet
- coma, occasionally convulsions, general paralysis, and death

The Centre's director, Lucas, an amateur history buff, found the old case enthralling and spent many hours on his own time reviewing the evidence and trying to piece together what had happened from both a medical and legal standpoint.

It seemed likely to Lucas that the first dose of arsenic was contained in the cup of coffee Hall received on boarding the vessel from his sledge journey—coffee Hall described as "too sweet." Beyond that, the lab results clearly indicated that Hall continued to ingest lethal amounts of arsenic during the last two weeks of his life, proving, first, that Hall had a strong constitution to be able to last that long while being slowly poisoned, and second, that someone was very determined to finish him off.

After he became familiar with the makeup of the expedition party, Lucas had to include sailing master Sidney Buddington as a suspect in Hall's death. But no one was as tempting to accuse as Dr. Emil Bessels, who had motive, knowledge, material, and access.

Arsenic would have been available aboard *Polaris*, Lucas knew. It was a commonly administered medicine in the nineteenth century in the form of arsenious acid, which was prescribed for a great variety of diseases, such as headaches, ulcers, gout, chorea, syphilis, even cancer. Used in a popular patent medicine called "Fowler's Solution," it was a well-known remedy for fever and various skin diseases. It would have been a standard part of any sizable medical kit, and the North Polar expedition, records showed, had a large medical store assembled by Dr. Emil Bessels for the long journey.

Lucas knew that arsenic could have been administered in the nineteenth century in one of two ways: liquid—probably used in the cup of coffee and perhaps later mixed in medicines given orally—and in the form of a white powder. There had been ample testimony of witnesses observing Bessels melting down a white powdery substance to inject into Hall by hypodermic needle; that could certainly have been an efficient delivery system for the poison.

As for Loomis, when he received the lab reports, he finally had the evidence that he had sought in disinterring Hall's remains. Toxic amounts of deadly poison *had* been administered to the expedition commander, but the question remained: by whom and for what reason? The professor was a careful, studious man, and he resisted the temptation to call it murder. He allowed himself to consider the possibility that Hall had dosed himself, although he knew suicide was inconceivable for a man of such ambition and strength. Hall did have his personal medical kit, however, which Bessels testified had contained, among other things, "patent medicines" that may well have included Fowler's Solution. And Hall certainly could have gained access to the ship's medical supplies. Had he overdosed himself, resulting in fatal arsenic poisoning? That scenario did not, Loomis knew, account for Hall's condition markedly improving for the several days that he refused the ship doctor access to him. He had gotten better *without* Bessels' medicines and services.

Loomis knew if it was murder that Bessels was a prime suspect. Buddington was a sad, pathetic figure; a coward who was probably too much of a desperate drunk and incompetent to pull off such a venal plan without bungling it or bragging about it later. While other members of the crew, including Frederick Meyer, had their own documented gripes with Hall, Bessels was a trained scientist with the necessary knowledge, and as the ship's doctor, he had at hand the material he needed to administer arsenic. Also, he had access to Hall much of the time.

There were other "straws in the wind," as Loomis came to call them: Bessels' refusal to administer an emetic, which would have emptied Hall's stomach, when the captain first took ill; the unexplained persistence of his quinine injection treatment after Hall's fever broke the second day of his illness, and Bessels not allowing Buddington to take Hall medicine's first as an inducement to the then-suspicious captain.

If Bessels had the opportunity and skill to poison his commander, what was his motive? Unlike Buddington, who had come under Hall's scrutiny and was close to being suspended from duty upon Hall's return from his last sledge journey, Bessels gained nothing as concrete from Hall's demise. Also,

Buddington was frightened that Hall would take them farther north and wanted to retreat south at first opportunity. Bessels was an ambitious man, and he certainly had his sights set on future glory for himself through major scientific and geographical discoveries. Testimony revealed he had even, after Hall's death, tried to bribe crewmen to accompany him north so *he* could be the discoverer of the North Pole. Had he thought ridding the expedition of its ambitious commander would allow such glory to fall on him? Had he simply wanted full credit? Was outsized ambition motive enough for murder?

No careful person could rule out the possibility that Hall suffered a stroke upon returning from his sledge journey, as Bessels claimed he had and as the board of inquiry had "conclusively" accepted as the cause of death from "natural causes." But the modern-day lab results proved another cause of death; a most unnatural one.

As Charles Francis Hall had feared those last two frightening weeks of life, he *was* being poisoned to death aboard his own vessel and by someone from among his small, handpicked crew. It hadn't been done with one massive dose of poison in the cup of coffee, administered perhaps in a fit of anger, bitterness, or envy. Rather, it was done systematically. Hall had been killed a little bit at a time over the course of two weeks. The nature of the act strongly suggested cold-blooded, calculating, premeditated murder by a diabolical killer who had gotten away with his crime.

Doug Lucas would never forget the case. Some twenty years later and by then retired from his position as head of the Centre for Forensic Sciences, he made a presentation called "Arsenic and Old Ice" to the American Academy of Forensic Sciences' Last Word Society, a group of professional scientific sleuths.

"The story I am about to tell you," Lucas began, "has a little bit of science, a bit of mystery, a dash of history, but in the end—there is no real last word."

AFTERMATH

Ulysses S. Grant's two terms as president of the United States are regarded by many historians to be the most corrupt in the country's history due to his picking of numerous old friends for cabinet-level positions who would provide the nation with neither competent service nor stature. The former Civil War hero who wished to see the U.S. flag planted at the North Pole during his presidency died near Saratoga, New York, in 1885, shortly after finishing work on his acclaimed memoirs, *Personal Memories of U. S. Grant*, which highlighted his military, not political, service.

George M. Robeson, Grant's second Secretary of the Navy and a strong supporter of the North Polar Expedition, was fond of good living and true to his friends, but he did not have much aptitude for the reins of administration or the details of naval business. A second investigation into his stewardship of the Navy Department in 1876 revealed that he had personally profited by nearly half a million dollars from payments received from shipyard contractors awarded naval work. As Secretary of the Navy, Robeson spent millions of government dollars in repairing and rebuilding ships, but at the end of his reign the Navy had nothing to show for his work but an obsolete fleet in poor condition. Following his cabinet-level service, Robeson was twice elected to the House of Representatives, then returned to the practice of law in Camden, New Jersey, until his death in 1897.

Tigress and **USS** *Tallapoosa*. The civilian steamer *Tigress*, whose name passed into polar history for rescuing the ice-floe party and her subsequent trip to the coast of Greenland in search of the remaining *Polaris* crew, was repurchased from the government by her original Canadian owners and put back into service as a commercial sealer. On April 2, 1874, *Tigress* was working through the ice pack near St. John's, Newfoundland, when a fiery explosion occurred, badly damaging the vessel and instantly killing ten of her crew. Eleven others were so badly injured that they died the next day. The Navy gun ship *Tallapoosa*, upon whose deck the official board of inquiry met, was patrolling off the coast of Rhode Island shortly before midnight on August 24, 1884, when she collided with a schooner and sank.

Sidney O. Buddington, who had been regarded as one of the most experienced whaling captains of his time, never returned to sea. His career was over following his testimony before the board of inquiry, which revealed his lack of discipline and uninspired leadership. "In my judgement Buddington merited the condemnation of the public in this world and the damnation in the world to come, for I believe him to be an unmitigated scoundrel," wrote, in 1874, another experienced New England whaling captain by the name of James M. Buddington, who was Sidney Buddington's uncle.

Dr. Emil Bessels for several years held a position with the Smithsonian in Washington, D.C., at least part of that time compiling the scientific records of the *Polaris* expedition. Not much is known about his later life and career, but at some point he fell out of favor at the Smithsonian and was evicted from his office following numerous attempts, after being informed that occupancy of his office was needed so as "to make improved toilet arrangements for visitors." Bessels returned to Germany and authored a book about the North Pole expedition: *Die Amerikanische Nordpol-Expedition* (Leipzig, W. Engelmann, 1879), published only in his native language.

Bessels presented himself in his book as a scientific observer given to accurate and detailed observations, and had virtually nothing to say about the colorful personalities and dramatic conflicts aboard *Polaris*. About Hall's final illness, Bessels wrote of Hall returning from his last sledge journey:

> *"Hall appearing fully fit, immediately went to his cabin without taking the time to take off his heavy furs and quickly drank a cup of coffee. A few minutes later he had a severe attack of dizziness and headache. Unfortunately, this indisposition was not temporary, as he first thought, but heralded a stroke which paralyzed his left side that same evening. In the next few days he started to recover slowly, hot foot baths with mustard and cold compresses placed against his head and neck gave him some relief. For a while, Hall had mental disturbances that occasionally deteriorated into a light frenzy. He believed somebody wanted to kill him by knifing, poisoning or shooting. On Nov. 4 he seemed a little better, but his mind was still obscured. Against every advice he ate a lot of boiled seal and drank more red wine than was good for him. On the 6th he could not be prevented from leaving his bed, walking around the cabin, and trying to dictate the results of his sledge trip. The following day he had another stroke, which carried him off in the early morning of the 8th. So had this impetuous heart stopped beating before the great plans had been brought to a conclusion, the brazen dice of fate had fallen before the first success had been attained."*

Oddly, his book quotes verbatim three times from Captain Hall's private journals from the trip—the very same journals that he testified had been left on the ice and lost. One direct quote comes from Hall's journal, October 19, near Cape Brevoort, during his last sledge journey. "Now and then," Hall writes in his diary, "I left the hut to look for plants and coal. I am infinitely anxious to find coal here, for that would undoubtedly be significant for our success and enable us to reach a higher latitude with the ship next year." The quote continues for more than a hundred words, and Bessels goes on to write many small details of the sledge journey that he did not go on. Subsequent to the publication of his book, Bessels' house burned to the ground, and all his papers and personal possessions were lost. Bessels died in Stuttgart on March 30, 1888, at age forty-two. Ironically, the cause of his death was apoplexy.

Joe "Ebierbing" and **Hannah "Tookoolito"** returned to New England, where Joe worked as a farmer, carpenter, and fisherman, and Hannah made fur clothing for fishermen in Groton and New London, Connecticut. Punny, who was christened Sylvia, attended school at Groton and proved herself to be a very intelligent student. Joe, unable to adapt, joined another Arctic expedition. While he was gone, Sylvia died in 1875, at age nine. A year later, Hannah, mourning the loss of her child and the long absence of her husband, and weakened further by tuberculosis, died at age thirty-nine. Joe returned to visit the graves of his wife and daughter, and weeded the tall grass. In 1878 he joined another Arctic expedition. Years after the *Polaris* expedition, Joe was asked why he hadn't packed up his family and left the ice floe when they had the opportunity to do so. "Cap'n Hall a good man. *Good* man. If Cap'n Hall alive, *he* not run away. I not run away either."

George Tyson returned to the Arctic in 1877 as commander of the schooner *Florence*. The primary object of the Howgate Expedition was the collection of material and personnel for the establishment of a future colony on the shores of Lady Franklin

Handbill publicizing an Arctic lecture by George Tyson, 1881.
(The Tyson Collection, National Archives)

Bay. Weather and luck went against them, and *Florence* returned to civilization the following year, badly leaking, and the crew starving, for they had eaten the last morsel of food on board. Terrific gales were encountered their last days of the voyage, threatening them with destruction at almost every moment. Following that trip, Tyson never returned to sea. He occasionally lectured about his Arctic experiences. His book *Arctic Experiences: A History of the Polaris Expedition* (1874, New York, Harper & Brothers), did not sell well, and he fell on hard times. At the personal intervention of President Rutherford B. Hayes, Tyson was hired at the War Department, first as a laborer, then as a messenger, clerk, and lieutenant of the watch. He divorced his first wife, Emmaline, and married a Washington widow, Mrs. Myers, who had three children. He died in 1906 at seventy-six. His death was the subject of a long article in the *Washington Post*: *"Hero of the Arctic, George E. Tyson's Career of Adventure Ended."* Three weeks after his passing, his son, George E. Tyson Jr. of Port Hill, Idaho, who had been estranged from his father for many years, wrote to his mother, Emmaline:

> *Dear Mother: The article that you sent giving the account of father's death I did not open until I reached home. In the solitude of my cabin, I read the news of father's death. And when I saw his picture, I noted his face wrinkled with age through the lapse of all these weary years. Then I thought of all the suffering he must have endured during the long Arctic night, starving and freezing. He caused us many a pang, Mother, he caused us many a pang, but he was my father, and the news of his death saddened my heart. I often think that the awful hardships he endured affected his mind and caused his heart to wither. The love I bore him when a baby boy, awoke again to life. And I wondered if he ever thought of his boy through the last 20 years or did he go down to his grave and never a word of me? Poor father, for you I shed tears both of pity and of love. Seek his grave, Mother dear, and place some flowers there for me. And let your loving radiance glow around the place. It was noble of you to forgive him. You are a good mother and I love you, and am proud of you. He is gone now, gone forever. He is forgiven. Let us remember him as he was when his*

smile was long and his voice was soft and tender. Let us ever
cherish loving in our hearts his sweet memory. Peace to his
ashes. He bore an honored name. May it never perish.
Your loving son, George

The North Pole. On April 6, 1909, nearly four decades after the death of Charles Francis Hall and two years after Ernest Shackleton's first quest for the South Magnetic Pole, American Robert Peary, his assistant Matthew Henson, and four Eskimos completed their final sprint by dog-driven sledge across 153 miles of shifting ice, pressure ridges, and open leads to conquer one of the last great frontiers of human exploration: the North Pole. Hall and George Tyson were proven wrong. There was no open Polar Sea or land or natives to be found at the Pole—only ice and more ice. Reaching the Pole had been Peary's obsession since 1886, when he took leave from the U.S. Navy to spend several months exploring the Greenland ice pack. After his initial trip to the Far North, he crossed northern Greenland twice and mounted two unsuccessful polar expeditions, losing all but two of his toes and, on at least one occasion, nearly his life. *"My life work is accomplished,"* Peary wrote in his diary soon after planting the U.S. flag at the earth's northernmost point. *"The thing which it was intended from the beginning that I should do, the thing which I believed could be done, and that I could do, I have done. I have got the North Pole out of my system."* In 2000, ninety-one years after Peary reached the Pole, polar visitors were shocked to find the North Pole melting. The thick ice that for ages had covered the Pole has turned to water, leaving an ice-free patch of ocean about a mile wide at the very top of the world. "I don't know if anybody in history ever got to 90 degrees north to be greeted by water, not ice," said Dr. James McCarthy, an oceanographer, and director of the Museum of Comparative Zoology at Harvard University and co-leader of the expedition that made the discovery. "There was a sense of alarm," he reported. "Global warming is real, and we were seeing its effects for the first time that far north."

Aftermath   **293**

Many think that I am of an adventurous spirit and of bold heart to attempt to go to the North Pole. Not so. It does not require that heart which they suppose I have. For the Arctic region is my home. I love it dearly—its storms, its winds, its glaciers, its icebergs. When I am among them, it seems as if I were in an earthly heaven. Or perhaps a heavenly earth.

—Charles Francis Hall

ACKNOWLEDGMENTS

The National Archives, at its two facilities in Washington, D.C., and College Park, Maryland, has met the challenge of its goal to acquire, preserve, and make available to the public records of enduring value. I realized just how much so when, one rainy winter day, I sat in a reading room with the log of *Polaris* and the nine surviving original journals kept by her crewmen on the North Polar Expedition a hundred and twenty-eight years earlier. I was awed, first, that they had survived the perilous Arctic trip even though the ship had not, and then that they were still around after all these years for an inquiring writer to delve into. It was that day I began to get a feel for the vessel, her crew, and their mission.

My research at the Archives was made much easier (and more fun) with the guidance and friendship of Neil Persinger, who has lived a life there researching his own upcoming book about the service of U.S. patrol frigates in World War II and Korea. Neil not only introduced me to key archivists and the ins and outs of a system for finding archival material, he also ably served as my naval authority on matters small and large. Even in the face of questions such as, "How would a circa-1870 steam boiler work aboard ship?" Neil always seemed to have the answers or be able to tell me where to go to find the information.

In my research on Charles Francis Hall, I was aided by the Hall Collection at the National Museum of American History, Washington, D.C., but mostly by the collegial guidance, hard facts, and keen observations provided by Hall's biographer, Chauncey Loomis, author of *Weird and Tragic Shores: The Story of Charles Francis Hall, Explorer* (Knopf, New York, 1971). Chauncey, in between fishing trips to Peru, Canada, and China, also shared with me his own adventures in trying to solve the mystery of Hall's death, and his visit to that desolate grave in the Far North.

I realized early on that George Tyson was the hero of the ice floe, and a character I wanted to follow from beginning to end of the story. Somewhere along the line his heirs realized the importance of his contribution, and donated all his personal papers to the U.S. government. The Captain George E. Tyson Papers, consisting of eight boxes, are available to the public today at National Archives, College Park. This collection was an enormous help in my getting to the core of the man—especially the discovery of a never-published 133-page letter, dated April 4, 1874, which Tyson sent to a former shipmate. That said, this book would not have been possible without Tyson's own journal of the *Polaris* expedition, originally written in pencil on scraps of paper as he lived the most exciting adventure of his life, and published, in 1874, as his memoirs, *Arctic Experiences: Capt. George E. Tyson's Wonderful Drift on the Ice-Floe, A History of the Polaris Expedition* (Harper & Brothers, New York).

Much valuable information was acquired, via the Internet, from individuals I have never met but whose books I had read or who were recommended to me as experts in their fields. These "e-mail buddies" include Kenn Harper, author of the poignant *Give Me My Father's Body* (Steerforth Press, South Royalton, Vermont, 1986.) Kenn has lived in the Arctic for over thirty years in Inuit communities in the Baffin region and in Qaanaasw, Greenland, and speaks Inuktitut, the Eskimo language of the eastern Canadian Arctic. Douglas Foster, retired director of Toronto's Centre for Forensic Sciences, spent a day going back to his old office and retrieving the original forensic report I so desperately needed and had not been able to find, and then more hours interpreting the results, recalling his own observations, and answering my queries. In Germany, Lars Bergland, a professional translator, provided invaluable assistance in locating the memoirs of Emil Bessels in the closed-stacks section of the Stuttgart library, then spending many afternoons translating key sections for me, and also researching what became of Bessels upon his return to Germany.

Among the books I read while researching the *Polaris* story, in particular, and the Arctic, in general, several stand out: Pierre Berton's *The Arctic Grail* (McClelland and Stewart, Toronto, Canada, 1988); Leonard Guttridge's *Ghosts of Cape Sabine* (Putnam, New York, 2000); Ann Savours' *The Search for the Northwest Passage* (St. Martin's Press, New York, 1999), and *Memoirs of Hans Hendrik, The Arctic Traveller*, published in London in 1878 (Trübner & Co., Ludgate Hill).

I thank the publisher of NAL, Louise Burke, for her enthusiasm from the get-go, my editor, Doug Grad, who shared his brilliant idea and trusted me to carry it out, and his associate, Ron Martirano, for his able work poring over microfilmed, century-old newspaper clips at the New York Public Library. Also, my literary agent, Mike Hamilburg, for his sage advice and brotherly friendship over the years, and his assistant, Joanie Kern, for her attentiveness and devotion.

My Washington, D.C., research efforts, including dealing with the Library of Congress, were assisted greatly by two special individuals who were my "secret weapons" when it came to dealing with the federal bureaucracy: my daughter, Chelsea Henderson Maxwell, a U.S. Senate staffer, and her husband, Carl Maxwell, who works on "the other side of the hill" for a U.S. congressman.

Closer to home, I thank my sons Grant, fourteen, and Evan, twelve, for putting up with me during the writing of this book, and for lowering their music when asked.

INDEX